THE HISTORY OF MEDIEVAL VAISHNAVISM IN ORISSA

Prabhat Mukherjee, M.A. Dip. Ed.
Maharaja's College,
Pralakimedi (Orissa)

GYAN

Published by

GYAN

Gyan Publishing House
5, Ansari Road
Daryaganj, New Delhi-110002
Phone: 011-47034999, 9811692060
E-mail: books@gyanbooks.com

Distribution Network
gyanbooks.com
India, USA, Canada, UK, Australia, France

ISBN : 978-81-212-4523-4 (HB)
First Published, 1940

2nd Impression 2020

Printed at: Gyan Press, Delhi.

The History of Medieval Vaishnavism in Orissa
Author: Prabhat Mukherjee

FOREWORD

SIR JADUNATH SARKAR, C. I. E.,
HONY. M. R. A. S., D. LITT., F. R. A. S. B.

Professor Prabhat Mukherji's *History of Medieval Vaishnavism in Orissa* carries our knowledge of a very interesting aspect of India's religious history a long step forward. In this collection of studies he has not only brought the fruits of former research together in a compact form but also directed a critical and detached mind to a fresh valuation of the evidence, and supplied a wealth of information from hitherto unknown or neglected Oriya manuscript sources of very great value and relevancy to this subject.

Many Indian religions and even small cults have been driven out by the political pressure from the North and the South to seek refuge in the sparsely inhabited but hospitable land of Orissa, tucked away in a corner of India hard to traverse and off the beaten track of armies. Here, during centuries of tolerated but stagnant life, they have shed their angularities and gradually come to assimilate to a common type, finally gathering themselves under the shadow of Jagannath and thus gaining mass sympathy in this new home. It is next to impossible, however interesting the problem might be,—to reduce this chequered mosaic of faiths and fables to any systematic or regular pattern, or even to trace with absolute precision their mutual relations. Only a few outstanding features can be recovered from the extant books nearly all of which are in manuscript and some now known by name only.

One part of this laborious task has been undertaken by Prof. Mukherji with adequate linguistic equipment, patient industry, and what is rarer still, the spirit of scientific inquiry untinctured by dogmatism or love of airy theorising. He occupies a position of distinct—probably unique, advantage by reason of his mastery of the Vaishnav literature of Bengal (without being a sectarian propagandist), which is here combined with his thorough exploration of Oriya manuscript sources and printed fugitive periodical literature.

Professor Mukherji has been able to establish two propositions by a chain of evidence which can be shaken only by the marshalling of original Oriya documents of a contrary import. The first is that the diverse religions of Orissa in all ages have tended to gravitate towards and finally merge into the Jagannath-worship, at least in theory.

The second is that the medieval or indigenous Vaishnavism of Orissa is not the creed of Chaitanya as developed by Nityānanda and the "Seven Goswamis," which our author marks out by calling it "Gauḍiya Vaishnavism" though it has now completely swept over Orissa and submerged the indigenous Vaishnavism developed in that province. The result is that the people there—75 per cent. of them being Vaishnavs, —have all but forgotten the Oriya disciples of the Great Master (Chaitanya) and the cult (radically different from Bengal Vaishnavism) which they taught in their works. The differences between the two have been brought out in detail in Chapters VIII and IX, which will help to open our eyes to a now forgotten world of thought.

One chapter of striking originality and profound interest to us is the Tenth, in which Professor Mukherji studies Chaitanyas as the *incarnation of Buddha-Jagannath* and suggests a novel solution of the veil of mystery with which all early Vaishnav writers have shrouded the passing away of their Great Master. He takes his stand on Achyutananda Das's Oriya *Sunya Samhita*. Briefly put, it is this:—Krishṇa in order to cleanse the world of sin incarnated himself as Jagannath, known in early Orissa religious history as *Adi Buddha* or *Jagannath Buddha*,—not to be confounded with the Shakya prince of Kapilāvastu. After a cycle things became as bad again, and therefore a new incarnation became necessary and appeared in the person of *Gautam* Buddha. Then, ages afterwards, came another repetition of Jagannath-Buddha, namely, our Chaitanya. (P. 155).

Hence it logically follows that Chaitanya's earthly end was bound to be absorption into the image of Jagannath-Buddha in the great temple at Puri,—however unpalatable such a view might be to the Bengal school of Vaishnavism, to whom the very name of Buddha is anathema. A wealth of quotations from old Oriya works supports this view.

A chapter marked by great historical acumen is the Eleventh, where Professor Mukherji successfully combats the popular theory that "the Chaitanya movement was responsible for the fall of the empire of Orissa" and that king Prataprudra Gajapati was enervated by his excessive devotion to Chaitanya and after his initiation by the Master let his kingdom go to the dogs. This explanation is cheap and has exactly the value of cheap things.

A new world of study has been opened to us by the young author of this book and I hope that others will take up the thread of his inquiries and carry it further with the same linguistic equipment, zeal and impartiality. What I admire equally well in this book is its concise writing and carefully avoidance of that prolixity and love of irrelevant digression which so often drives the examiners of our doctorate theses mad.

J. Sarkar

PREFACE

The name of the book requires some explanation. I have divided the history of Vaishnavism in Orissa into three periods, early. medieval, and modern. The history of early Vaishnavism in Orissa is obscure, and can not be systematically traced. The medieval period in the history of Orissan Vaishnavism begins from the eleventh century A. D., with the accession of Chodaganga on the throne of Kalinga. Vaishnavism not only predominated during this period, but it also absorbed certain ideas from the existing schools of faith in Orissa. This catholicity of spirit was the distinguishing feature of the Medieval Vaishnavism. In the sixteenth century A. D., the Chaitanya Movement spread in Orissa and the Medieval Vaishnavism decayed. The Modern Vaishnavism in Orissa is an offshoot of the Chaitanya Movement.

After the first four chapters were printed, I found out some valuable references. I have taken advantage of them by adding supplementary notes at the end of the book. Pains have been taken to free the book from errors, but I cannot expect that a first edition will be perfect in this respect. I shall thankfully recieve notifications of errors and suggestions for the improvement of the book.

I wish to express my grateful thanks to Sir Jadunath Sarkar for kindly consenting to write the Foreword of the book, and for securing financial help from Rao Bahadur G. S. Sardesai research publication fund. I also owe a deep debt of gratitude to Sri Nityananda Kanungo, ex-minister of the Government of Orissa, for a grant from his discretionary fund. I am also grateful to the Raja and Ruling Chief of Baramba State, to Professors A. B. Mohanty and G. S. Das of the Ravenshaw College for valuable suggestions. I have to thank Professors T. Krishnamurti and T. E. Jayraman of the Maharaja's College, Parlakimedi, who read a portion of the MS., and gave me the benefit of their comments. Lastly, I thank the Manager, Prabasi Press, and his Staff, for their prompt work.

PRABHAT MUKHERJEE
P.O. Chandni Chouk, Cuttack

LIST OF CORRECTIONS

Line	11	Page 37	Read	*Koṇarka*	in place of Koārka
Line	6	„ 39	„	*names*	in place of namas
Foot-note	785	„ 58	„	पशा	in place of पथा
„	209	„ 27	„	महापुण्यां द्रष्टुं	
Line	11	„ 74	„	after Bhīmā Dhivara, *the author of Kapaṭa Pāśā,*	
Line	27	„ 82	„	*where*	in place of whither
Foot-note	340	„ 105	Add	at the end	*Brahmsankuli, III.*
Line	8	„ 112	„	*it*	after understand
Line	15	„ 113	„	*The*	before Chaitanya Age
Foot-note	372	„ 121	Read	*LVI*	in place of *IVL*
Line	17	„ 123	Add	*him*	after advised
Line	25	„ 135	Read	*opines*	in place of explained
Line	20	„ 155	„	*would*	in place of will
Line	11	„ 174	„	*state*	in place of states

Add *the* before Radha-idea and Gopi-idea, where it is left out.

Read *jña* in place of jñya

CONTENTS

GLOSSARY

Āchārya—A family name of the Brahmins.

Agastya—The name of an ancient sage.

Akrura—The name of an uncle of Krishṇa.

Ananta—The name of a serpent ; also of Balarām.

Arjuna—One of the five Pāṇḍava brothers.

Āshārh—The third solar month (June-July) of the Hindu calendar.

Balarām—The elder brother of Krishṇa.

Bhairava—The *Tāntric* conception of Siva.

Bhairavi—The *Tāntric* conception of Durgā.

Bhārati—The title of an order of monks.

Braja—The district consisting of Vrindāvana and the adjoining places, famous for the exploits of Krishṇa.

Dāsa—The customary Vaishṇava surname.

Devaki—The mother of Krishṇa.

Draupadi—The consort of the five Pāṇḍavas.

Dvāpara Age—The name of the third Yuga or Age of the world.

Garuḍa—The Sun-Bird. He is the vehicle of Krishṇa.

Gauḍiya—A native of Bengal.

Gauḍiya Vaishṇavism—The Chaitanya Movement.

Goloka—The paradise of Krishṇa.

Gopi—The milk-maids of Vrindāvana.

Goswāmi—A title of respect, given to the spiritual leaders among the Vaishṇavas.

Guru—Spiritual preceptor.

Hari—A name of Vishṇu.

Kaṁsa—The maternal uncle of Krishṇa, who killed him.

Karaṇa—The Kāyastha caste of Orissa.

Khuntiā—One of the servitors in the temple of Jagannāth. See Foot-notes Nos. 255 & 407.

Kshetrapāla—An attendant deity in the temple of Jagannāth.

Kūrma—The second *Avatāra* or incarnation of Vishṇu, in the shape of a Tortoise.

Lakshmaṇa—The name of a younger brother of Rāma.

Lakshmī—The consort of Vishnu.

Mantra—A sacred verse ; any mystical formula.

Māgh—The tenth solar month (Jan.-Feb.) of the Hindu calendar.

Maṭh—A Hindu monastery.

Mohunt—The abbot of a Hindu monastery.

Nakula—One of the five Pāṇḍava brothers.

Nanda—The foster-father of Krishṇa.

Nārada—An ancient sage, devoted to Krishṇa.

Nilāchala—Puri, lit., the Blue Mountain or Abode of Jagannāth.

Nrisiṁha—The fourth incarnation of Vishṇu, in the shape of a lion-headed man.

Parichhā—Formerly, the Superintendent of the temple of Jagannāth.

Pārvatī—A name of Durgā, the consort of Śiva.

Parśurāma—The sixth incarnation of Vishṇu.

Phālguna—The eleventh month (Feb.-March) of the Hindu calendar.

Pothi—Manuscript.

Pradyumnya—A son of Krishṇa.

Prahara—The eighth part of a day.

Purushottam Kshetra—Purī, the place of Purushottam or Jagannāth.

Rārha—The portion of Bengal, west of the Ganges.

Rāma—An incarnation of Vishṇu, and the hero of the Rāmāyaṇa.

Rāsa Arena—The *maṇḍapa* of the Rāsa dance of Krishṇa and Gopīs.

Rāvaṇa—The *Rākshasa* chief of Laṅkā (See the Rāmāyaṇa).

Rukmiṇī—A consort of Krishṇa.

Sahasra Rāvaṇa—A son of Rāvaṇa.

Sakhi—Female associate of Rādhā and Krishṇa.

Śakuni—The notorious dice-player in the Mahābhārata.

Śāmba—A son of Krishṇa.

Saṅkarshaṇa—A name of Balarām.

Sankīrtana—The chanting of Hari's name to the accompaniment of music.

Sannyāsi—Ascetic ; religious mendicant.

Śāstra—Any holy text of the Hindus.

Satyabhāmā—A consort of Krishṇa.

Sitā—The consort of Rāma.

Subhadrā—The sister of Krishṇa and Balarām.

Sudām—One of the associates of Krishṇa at Vrindāvana.

Śūdra—The lowest caste in the Hindu society.

Tantra—Esoteric science.

Tirtha—A sacred place.

The Master—Lit., *Mahā-Prabhu.* Chaitanya is generally called *Mahā-Prabhu.*

Toṭā-(Ṭoṭā in Bengali) A garden.

Vaikunṭha—Vishṇu's heaven.

Vaiśākh—The first solar month (April-May) of the Hindu calendar.

Vaivasvata Manu—The seventh Manu. An ancient king in the Hindu mythology.

Varāha—The third incarnation of Vishṇu in the shape of a Boar.

Varuṇa—The lord of the Sea in the Hindu mythology.

Vāsudeva—Krishṇa, the son of Vasudeva.

Yantra—Mystical diagram.

Yaśodā—The foster-mother of Krishṇa.

THE HISTORY OF MEDIEVAL VAISHNAVISM IN ORISSA

CHAPTER I.

THE EARLY HISTORY OF JAGANNATH

"There, then, is a great phenomenon in the inner history of a nation, over which those who would study the workings of the religious instinct in man's heart will do well to pause. In order to understand what Jagannath is now to the Hindus, it is necessary to learn what *He has for Ages Been.*" —*Hunter—'Orissa" Vol. I. p 88.*

For a long period, the history of religion in Orissa identified itself with the history of Jagannāth. All other deities were subordinated to and associated with Jagannāth. He was the presiding deity—the embodiment of the nation's adoration and belief. The result was that every religious movement, which flooded Orissa at a certain period of history, established its sway in the temple-precincts of Jagannāth ; and when the flood subsided, it had left water-marks within the temple-precincts. Thus traces of Buddhist, Śaivite and Tāntric forms of worship are to be discerned in the worship of Jagannāth.

To quote Hunter again ; "Of this religious syncretism, Jagannāth forms the ultimate result. He has assimilated to himself a wider range of attributes, than any of the gods of Rome or Greece."[1]

This gradual absorption of heterogeneous attributes by Jagannāth had a great effect on the Medieval Vaishṇavism of Orissa, which centred round the conception of Jagannāth. Thus many non-Vishṇuite elements were accommodated within the fold of Vaishṇavism.

1. Orissa, Vol. I, p. 300.

Early Vaishṇavism in Orissa led a precarious existence. Though Jagannāth was a Vishṇuite deity, the form of his worship was materially affected as a result of Buddhist, Śaivite and Tāntric influence. He was conceived as Buddha, Śiva and even as the Bhairava. The preaching of Rāmānuja and the zeal displayed by Choḍagaṅga and his sons marked a turning point in the history of Vaishṇavism. Jagannāth was rehabilitated as a Vishṇuite deity but the non-Vishṇuite elements in his worship were not rejected. Thus even now "the worship of Jagannāth is carried on according to the Tantras."[2] This heterogeneity was the distinguishing feature of Medieval Vaishṇavism.

In the first-half of the 16th century, Vaishṇavism in Orissa had again undergone a change. Chaitanya came from Bengal and settled in Orissa. His superhuman personality and religious fervour arrested popular imagination. The triumphant Chaitanya Movement made no compromise with the old school of Vaishṇavism in Orissa—which it denounced as heterodox.

Jagannāth has its allotted place in the structure of the neo-Vaishṇavism. But he is no more the fountain-head of inspiration as he was in the past. The history of Jagannāth is marked by such vicissitudes. It gives us an excellent opportunity of systematically studying Orissan Vaishṇavism, with which Jagannāth was and still is indissolubly connected. So we agree with Hunter that it is necessary to learn what Jagannāth has for ages been.

It is difficult to determine when Jagannāth was first worshipped. The Purāṇas love to dwell upon the extreme remoteness of the advent of Jagannāth. The Utkal Khaṇḍa section oi Skanda Purāṇa elaborates this theme. According to Utkal Khaṇḍa, Raja Indradumnya of the Satya Yuga installed the sacred Log within a sky-scraping temple reared by him. The temple of Purusottam at

Reference to Jagannath in the Puranas

2. "The Early Temples in Orissa"—S. N. Rai Mahasaya. The Prachi. Vol. II. Pt. 2.

Nilāchala was visited by Raja Ratnagrīva who lived in the Treta Yuga.[3] Clearly, such evidences are useless for our purpose. Thus it is unsafe to rely on the Purāṇas for the early history of Jagannāth.

There is consensus of opinion that Jagannāth is identical with Krishṇa-Vāsudeva. The Utkal Khaṇḍa also refers to this fact.[4] Balarām-Saṅkarshaṇa and Subhadrā are the brother and sister respectively of Krishṇa-Vāsudeva. Thus the history of the Bhāgavata cult (the cult of Bhagavat Krishṇa-Vāsudeva) will help us to trace the beginning of the worship of Jagannāth.

Bhagavatism and the Puri Triad

Bhagavat Vāsudeva-Krishṇa was the son of Devakī and disciple of Ghora Āṅgirasa (Chhāndogya Upanishad. III. 17. 6.). He was a scion of the royal family of Mathurā (Ghata Jātaka). It will be useful to trace the development of the Bhāgavata cult chronologically.

1. Chhāndogya Upanishad.

It cannot be later than the 6th century B. C.[5]

2. Ashṭādhāyī of Pāṇini.

Dr. H. C. Raychaudhuri places the book in the fifth century B. C.[6] Pāṇini refers to "Vāsudevaka", as a person whose object of devotion is Vāsudeva (IV. 3. 98). Traditions are unanimous that Krishṇa's father was Vāsudeva. The word Vāsudevaka shows that Krishṇa had been already exalted in status.

3. The Indika of Megasthenes.

The accepted date is the fourth century B. C. Herakles or Krishṇa was worshipped as a demigod in Kleisobora (Krishṇapura) and Methorā (Mathurā).

4. The Taittirīya Āraṇyaka (X. 1. 6).

According to Dr. H. C. Raychaudhuri, it belongs to the third

3. Padma Purana, XII, 71.

4. Chapters, XIX-37, 40 ; XXX-46, 92, etc.

5. See Macdonell—History of Sanskrit Literature, p. 226. See also. Cambridge History of India. Vol. I, p. 147.

6. Early History of the Vaishnava Sect, p. 30.

century B. C.[7] Vāsudeva has been identified with Vishṇu. This is the first sign of contact of Bhāgavatism and Vishṇuism, though the complete identification of the two cults took time.

5. Ghasundī Stone Inscription.

We now come to the second century B. C. Saṅkarshaṇa appears along with his brother in this inscription and jointly are addressed as "Bhagavat" (the Supreme Lord).

6. The Besnagar Pillar Inscription.

A Garuḍa-dhvaja (Standard) was erected in honour of Vāsudeva, the god of gods (Devadeva). The association of Garuḍa, the Vehicle of Vishṇu, with Vāsudeva proves that the identification of Krishṇa with Vāsudeva was now a *fait accompli*.

7. The Mahābhāshya of Patañjali.

Patañjali was the contemporary of Pushyamitra and so, he flourished in the second century B. C. While commenting on Pāṇini (IV. 3. 98) he mentions Vāsudeva "as a specially honoured and perhaps divine, being". The reference in the Great Commentary of Patañjali, shows that Bhāgavatism spread to Magadha not later than the second century B. C.

8. The Nānāghat Cave Inscription of Nāganikā.

The names of Saṅkarshaṇa and Vāsudeva appear along with other deities. This inscription of the second or first century B.C. shows that the Bhāgavata religion "had spread to the South".

Gradually the cult found its way into South-Eastern India. "The China stone inscription of the time of Yajña Śrī Śātakarṇi shows that the faith flourished in the Kistna district in the second century A. D."[8]

A Tentative Time Limit for the Advent of Bhagavatism in Orissa

This retrospective survey of the history of Bhāgavatism enables us to fix up a tentative time-limit for the commencement of the worship of Jagannāth. The Nānāghat inscription shows that, by the first century B. C., Bhāgavatism had crossed the boundary of Northern India.

7. Early History of the Vaishnava Sect, p. 87.

8. Early History of the Vaishnava Sect, p. 180. For the history of the development of the Bhagavata cult, we have mainly depended on this book.

Within four hundred years, it had reached as far as the Kistna district in the South ; and there is no reason to assume that Orissa remained unaffected.

Bhāgavatism, in all probability, found its way into ancient Orissa, between the second century B. C. and the first century A. D.

This surmise has been corroborated by the hypothesis of Sten Konow.

"Sten Konow finds a reference to the youthful deeds of Krishṇa (Sirikaḍāra) in the Hāthi-Gumphā Inscription".[9] The words in question are as follows : "Siri kaḍāra sarira -vatā kiḍitā kumāra kiḍikā". Banerjee & Jayaswal translate the line as follows :—"Having played princely games with a body majestic with fair-brown (Complexion)". [10]

Allusion to Krishna in the Hathigumpha Inscription

Though a Jaina, Khāravela associated himself with Brāhmanical religious customs. He performed the Rājasūya sacrifice. "Further, he gave lands to Vedic Brahmins and built houses for them with sacrificial pits, which are pointedly mentioned in line 9." [11]

Thus there can be no valid objection to Sten Konow's hypothesis that Khāravela, though a Jaina, compared himself to Krishṇa in his Hāthi-Gumphā inscription.

"Epigraphical considerations", writes Rapson, "show that the Hāthi-Gumphā inscription of Khāravela and the Nānāghat inscription of Nāganikā, the queen of Śātakarṇi belong to the same period."[12]

The Time of Hathi-Gumpha Inscription

But a fresh objection might be raised at this stage. Granted that Khāravela did allude to the exploits of Krishṇa—the allusion, it may be argued, does not presuppose the existence of Vaishṇavism in Orissa. The sculpture of Anantagumphā comes heie to our rescue.

9. Quoted in Early History of the Vaishnava Sect.

10. J. B. O. R. S. Vol. III. Pt. IV.

11. *Ibid.*

12. Cambridge History of India. Vol. I, p. 535.

In the opinion of Sir John Marshall, Anantagumphā belongs to a date not much earlier than the middle of the first century B. C. "Over the doorways of this cave are ornamental arches enclosing various reliefs ; in one is a standing figure of Lakshmī, supported by the usual elephants on lotus-flowers. In another is the four-horse chariot of the Sun-god (?)".[13]

The Sculpture of Ananta Gumpha

Taking all these indications together one can hardly escape from the conclusion that Vaishṇavism, in some form, existed in Orissa in the century immediately preceding the Christian era.

"In the early centuries of the Christian era, Time's horses gallop forward with an impetuous speed. An outburst of rain washes out their foot-prints." A pall of dense darkness descends upon the religious history of Orissa. Even after the Gupta Age the darkness continues, though there are occasional rifts in the mist. It appears most likely that Orissa came under Gupta influence as a result of the famous invasion of Samudragupta (reign 330-375 A. D.).

M. M. Ganguly has referred to the Gupta influence on the Orissan Sculpture.[14] Gupta Samvat was adopted in Orissa.[15]

The Gupta Influence in Orissa

"Some of the Gupta sovereigns," remarks Dr. H. C. Raychaudhuri, "were unquestionably great champions of the religion of Vāsudeva. With the rise of their power Bhāgavatism, which was now synonymous with Vaishṇavism, naturally came to the forefront and spread to the remotest corners of India."[16]

Vishṇu cum Vāsudeva were now worshipped under new nomenclatures, *e. g.*, Sārṇgin, Chakrabhrit, Ananta-Svāmin, etc.

13. Cambridge History of India. Vol. I, p. 640.
14. Orissa and Her Remains, p. 272.
15. The Inscriptions of Madhavaraja II & Sivaraja. Epigraphica Indica Vol. VI. & IX.
16. Early History of the Vaishnava Sect, p. 168.

One wishes that the veiled history of the rise of Vaishṇavism in Orissa might be traced back with some amount of certainty. Till then we are to be content with the conclusions, deduced from the history of development of Bhāgavatism in India.

We are of opinion that Bhāgavatism flourished in Orissa in the 5th century A. D. as it did everywhere under the imperial patronage. There can be little doubt about the fact that Saṅkarshaṇa and Vāsudeva came to be known as Jagannāth and Balarām in Orissa—just as they elsewhere appeared under new nomenclatures.[17]

The Worship of Jagannath And Balaram in Orissa

More difficult is the attempt to determine the origin of Subhadrā worship. Subhadrā is not mentioned in the early inscriptions, or Purāṇas like Mātsya, Brahmāṇḍa, Vishṇu or Vāyu. There is reference to a queen Subhadrā in white Y. V. XXIII., but she seems to be altogether a different person.

The Origin of Subhadra

Later Purāṇas, like Agni Purāṇa (116.19.) and Garuḍa Purāṇa, (in the chapter on the sanctity of Gayā) mention Subhadrā along with her brothers. These Purāṇas were composed long after the fourth century A. D. Varāhamihira's reference to the image of "Ekānaṁsā",[18] standing between the images of Baladeva and Krishṇa, seems to indicate the conception of Subhadrā in making. Curiously, in the later Sanskrit texts Ekānaṁsā has been identified with Pārvati. Subhadrā seems to have been introduced as the "Śakti" (Energy) of Vāsudeva-Krishṇa. Śakti conception was an important feature of Guptan Vaishṇavism and received impetus from the Sānkhya doctrine of 'Purusha' and 'Prakriti'.

Early References to Subhadra Worship

Probably Subhadrā's close relation with both the brothers, accounted for her elevation on the dais. Subhadrā thus becomes the Śakti of Jagannāth. She is both his sister and wife.

Reason for the Inclusion of Subhadra

17. Such as Rama and Kesava, in the Nasik Cave Inscription, Epigraphica Indica, Vol. VIII, p. 60.

18. Brihat Samhita. LVIII. 36, 37.

"तस्य शक्ति स्वरूपेयं भगिनी श्री प्रवर्त्तिका"[19]

She is but another embodiment of Lakshmī.[20]

But Subhadrā as the Śakti of Vāsudeva-Jagannāth could not gain popular support. Such a sister-consort conception naturally proved repugnant and Subhadrā as the Śakti of Vāsudeva gave way to the conception of Rādhā. Rādhā and Krishṇa are depicted in the reliefs of Pāhāḍpur Stūpa, which are approximately assigned to the fifth century A. D. This is the earliest representation of Rādhā.

Origin of the Conception of Radha

Rādhā is not mentioned in the early Purāṇas. Krishṇa's pastimes with Rādhā at Vraja have been described in the Padma and Brahmavaivarta Purāṇas, which are comparatively of later period. Padma Purāṇa, which is at least earlier than Brahmavaivarta, mentioned and criticised the doctrine of Illusion, as propounded by Śaṅkara.[21]

By about the seventh century A. D. Rādhā came to be recognized as the Śakti of Vāsudeva. She has been mentioned in Hāla's Gāthā Sapta Śatī—which does not seem to be earlier than the sixth century A. D.

In the preceding pages, an attempt has been made to trace the early history of the Triad. The inclusion of Subhadrā, took place at latest by the fifth century A. D. Had the conception of Rādhā developed by that time-- Subhadrā would have been forestalled by Rādhā, as the Śakti of Krishṇa-Jagannāth.

Period of the Completion of the Puri Triad

From the field of guess-work we shall, with relief, now turn to the inscriptions. Early Vaishṇavism prevailed in Kaliṅga in about the sixth century A. D. when the Māṭhar chiefs were ruling there.

Early Vaishnavism in Kalinga

Mr. Satyanarain Rajguru quotes from an inscription of Pravañjana Varmā to show his devotion to the feet of Nārā-

19. Utkal Khanda, in the Skanda Purana. XIX. 17.

20. *Ibid* XIX. 11-15.

21. Padma Purana, Uttar Khanda, XXV, 7.

yaṇa.[22] Fleet edited another inscription of Pravañjana Varmā—the Lord of Kaliṅga.[23] Here the king has been described as "Parama-Bhāgavata".

In the seventh and eighth century A. D. the Śailodbhava kings reigned in "Koṅgada-maṇḍala"—which may be roughly identified as the tract round the Chilka lake and northern part of the Ganjam district. So far five inscriptions of the Śailodbhava kings have received the attention of the scholars—"the Ganjam plates of Śaśānka's feudatory being the earliest".[24] This feudal vassal, Mādhavarāja II of the Ganjam plates,[25] is also known from his copper-plate record found at Khurda.[26] He was the grandfather of Madhyamarāja I, of the Tekkali copper-plates of king Madhyamarāja III. This king was the son of Petavyāllopa, who was probably the brother of Madhyamarāja II.[27]

The Sailodbhava Kings of Kongada-mandala

Pundit Gopavandhu Vidyabhusan has recently published a new Tekkali-plate of Madhyamarāja III.[28] King Dharmarāja's fame "could not be contained in the three worlds, even as the legs of Hari in the Vāmana incarnation". This so-called famous king was succeeded by Madhyamarāja II, about whom it is said that Lakshmī, the consort of Madhusudan "has to-day like a veritable house-wife taken shelter under Mānabhīta's (Dharmarāja) son and has forgotten all her previously enjoyed felicities" (Lines 9-12.)

A New Copper-plate of Madhyamaraja III

In the 8th century Kara kings reigned in Northern Toshala[29] and in Southern Toshala.[30]

The Kara Kings of Toshala

22. Utkal Sahitya—Vaisakh, 1338.

23. Fleet: Indian Antiquary, 1884. Mr. Rajguru suggests the date of the Mathar kings mentioned above. Fleet is silent on this point.

24. Tekkali Plate of Madhyamaraja III. J. B. O. R. S. Vol. IV. Pt. II.

25. Epigraphica Indica. Vol. VI, pp. 143-146.

26. J. A. S. B. 1904. Pt. I.

27. History of Orissa, I, p. 135.

28. The Prachi, III, Pt. :III.

29. Neulpur Plate of Subhakardeva I—Epigraphica Indica, XV.

30. Chaurasi Plate of Sivakaradeva II. *Ibid.* XIV.

The kingdom to the north of Koṅgada was known as Southern Toshala. Pandit Vinayak Misra suggests that "Guheśvar Pātaka" was the capital of the Kara dynasty and he seeks to identify a suburb of Jajpur town, with the afore-named capital. [31]

The Kara Kings of Toshala

The early Kara kings were decidedly Buddhist, but the later Kara monarchs were eclectic in their belief though leaning towards Śaivism. While editing a copper-plate grant of Daṇḍi-Mahādevi, the late H. Panday observes that her seal, besides having usual Śaivite emblems, has the representation in relief of a conch-shell. This, in his opinion, represents Vishṇu. "The same emblems" he writes "appear on the seals of all the copper-plate grants of this dynasty, namely, a couchant bull, the representations of the sun and the moon and the conch-shell."[32]

The Grant of Dandi Mahadevi

Tribhuvana Mahādevi (who probably was the grandmother of Daṇḍi-Mahādevi) describes herself as "Parama Vaishṇavi", (A devoted follower of Vishṇu) and further informs that "she sat on the Lion-throne like Kātyāyanī, with her feet placed on the heads of the Mahā-Sāmantās." [33] The end of the Kara dynasty is wrapped in obscurity.

The Grant of Tribhuvana Mahadevi

When the curtain rises again, towards the end of the 9th century A. D., Janmejaya Mahābhavagupta is found to be ruling in the south-eastern part of Mahākośala, which R. D. Banerjee seeks to identify with modern Sonepur-Patna states. But according to the tradition, he ruled over whole of Orissa. He styled himself "The lord of three Kaliṅgas" and "Māharājādhirāja."[34] Mr. P. Acharya points out that the

The Rise of the Somavamsi Kings of Mahakosala

31. J. B. O. R. S. Vol. XVI. Pt. I.

32. An Inscription of Dandi-Mahadevi. J. B. O. R. S. Vol. V. Pt. IV. In one of her grants Dandi Mahadevi calls herself "a devout worshipper of Mahesvara". Epigraphica Indica, Vol. VI. Edited by Kielhorn.

33. J. B. O. R. S. Vol. II. Pt. IV. Edited by H. P. Shastri.

34. Mursima Copper-Plate. Epi. Indica, III, p. 341.

epithet "Tri-kaliṅgādhipati" was indiscriminately used by the Somavaṁśi kings of Eastern Kośala, early Gaṅga kings of Kaliṅganagara[35] and by Udayotakeśari of the Brahmeśvara temple inscription.[36] Thus it is difficult to attach any special significance to that biruda, in Janmejaya Mahābhavagupta's case.

To quote R. D. Banerjee again :

"The evidence of the inscriptions prove clearly and definitely that Mahābhavagupta I Janmejaya had no control over any part of Orissa proper."[37] Banerjee's categorical statement is opposed by the prevailing tradition that Janmejaya built the fort of Chauduar near Cuttack.

In all likelihood, Yajāti Mahāśivagupta, the son of Janmejaya, conquered Orissa proper. Even R. D. Banerjee concedes that much.[38] Yajāti Mahāśivagupta is usually identified with Yajāti-Keśari of the tradition, who played the role of a second Indradumnya. According to the Jagannāth temple chronicles, he restored the Puri Triad, who were secreted as a result of "Mogala" incursion.

Yajati Mahasiva-Gupta

Yajati Kesari.

Hunter, who has relied on the Pānji, writes in this connexion ; "Jagannath makes his first historical appearance in the year 318 A.D. when the priests fled with the sacred image leaving an empty city to Red-Arm and his buccaneers. For 150 years it remained buried in the western jungles, till a pious prince drove out the foreigners and brought back the sacred Log".[39]

The Incursion of Raktavahu, the Mogala Chief

R. D. Banerjee suggests that "the so-called Mughal invasion of Orissa was really the conquest of the country by the Kushān foreigners".[40] Yajāti Mahāśivagupta, with whom

35. Epigraphica Indica, Vol. VI.
36. See Utkal Sahitya. Vol. XXVIII.
37. History of Orissa. Vol. 1, p. 212.
38. History of Orissa, Vol. I, p. 219.
39. Orissa, Vol. I, p. 85.
40. History of Orissa, Vol, I, p. 113

"the pious prince" of Hunter's statement is usually identified, flourished as late as in the tenth century A. D. Clearly, Hunter's date is inadmissible. The Puri Triad was completed by the inclusion of Subhadrā ; and then the images were lost in oblivion and were subsequently restored by Yajāti. These events require a length of time, for which Hunter's reckoning proves inadequate. On the other hand, if Yajāti Mahāśivagupta was really the king who recovered the deities—then the invaders cannot, by any stretch of imagination, be the Kuśāns.

Prof. A. B. Mohanty opines[41] that the so-called Mogalas were really the Hūṇas. His suggestion seems to be fairly probable. The existence of the Hūṇas, as a disturbing factor, is mentioned by the Garuḍa Pillar inscription at Mangalbāḍi, belonging to the 9th century A.D. King Devapāla is credited with the conquest of the Hūṇas and Utkalas, (उत्कीलितोत्कल कुल० हृत हूण गर्व०) in this inscription.

The Restoration of the Triad

The Temple-chronicles describe how Yajāti recovered the hidden images. "In his 11th Anka he asked the Sannyasis and Brāhmanas, 'where existeth Jagannāth, the tutelary deity of the kings of Orissā' ? They replied that from beyond the seas came the Mogalas. The Lord was taken to Sonepur but we know not, whither hath He been secreted." Then the king repaired to Sonepur and elicited from inquiry that the images might have been buried under a banyan tree, which was revered by the ancestors of the people. The king caused the tree to be cut down and unearthed the images. Forthwith the images were taken back to Puri, and duly installed in a newly constructed temple.

Early References to Jagannath Temple

In the 9th century, Śaṅkarāchārya visited the temple of Jagannāth and established the Śaivite form of worship. Chāndbhaṭṭa in his Prithvirāj Raso refers to the Somavaṁśī king Mukunda Deva, who was said to be a great devotee of Jagannāth.[42] In the Nagpur

41. Introduction, Types of Ancient Oriya Prose and Poetry.
42. "Yajati Kesari", Nababharat, Mesha—1344.

incription of Lakshma Deva of Malava country, dating 1104 A. D., Purusottam Kshetra has been mentioned. In about 1137 A. D. one person, Manoratha by name, set out for the Purusottam Kshetra (Govindapur Sasan Grant of 1137-38 A.D).[43]

Bhimaratha Mahābhavagupta was the son and successor of Yajāti Mahāśivagupta.[44] Mukunda Deva and Karṇakeśarī (mentioned in Rāmacharita) were in all probability Somavaṁśī kings. For the rest, all is dark about the Somavaṁśī kings of Orissa.

From the plains, we now move to the Orissan highlands where ruled the Bhañja chiefs. Raṇabhañja I flourished in about the 11th century A.D. [45] In his copper-plate grants Raṇabhañja professes devotion to Vishṇu, Śiva and the goddess Stambheśvarī. Rānaka Raṇabhañja and Śatrubhañja similarly call themselves "the devout follower of Vishṇu" in their charters ; while "they had not omitted to insert verses in praise of Śiva, which became customary with their ancestors".

The Bhanja Kings

Thus a study of the history of the Early Vaishṇavism in Orissa reveals that Vishṇu hardly received exclusive devotion. The Śailodbhavas, the later Karas, the Somavaṁśī kings and finally the Karas offered homage to Vishṇu along with other gods.

Early Vaishṇavism had serious rivals in Buddhism and Śaivism and was sometimes eclipsed by them. Buddhism and Śaivism left indelible impression on the conception of Jagannāth. The history of Jagannāth will be incomplete without reference to the history of Early Buddhism and Śaivism in Orissa.

Saivism and Buddhism in Orissa

Early Buddhism in Orissa

In all probability, Buddhism spread to Orissa, as a result of the missionary propaganda of Aśoka.

43. See, M. M. Chakravarti's Article J. A. S. B., 1896. Pt. I.
44. Orissa in the Making, p. 160.
45. Orissa in the Making, p. 129.

It is stated by Tāranath, the Buddhist pilgrim, that the great Buddhist scholar Nāgārjuna (who was a contemporary of Kanishka) visited Orissa, and converted Muñja, the king of that country, into Buddhism. He constructed many monasteries in Orissa.[46] The theory of the Unconditioned Void, as expounded by Nāgārjuna, influenced the religious philosophy of Orissa.

Nagarjuna

With some alterations, the Mādhyamika philosophy prevailed in Orissa as the Nāgāntaka school of Philosophy. Scholars like Manjuśrī, Bodhaśrī and Chandra gomi preached Buddhism in Orissa.

Buddhism in the Seventh Century Orissa

Hiuentsiang, the great Chinese pilgrim, visited Orissa between 629-45 A. D. He found Buddhism in a thriving condition, in Mahākośala or the western region of Natural Orissa. He tells us that Nāgārjuna was at one time the resident of a monastery, situated outside the capital city of Mahakośala. The Saṅghārāma of Puse-po-kili (Pushpa-pura) has been vividly described by the traveller.

The conquest of Orissa by the Buddhist Emperor Harsha in C. 643 A. D., gave impetus to the growth of Buddhism. The Udayagiri and Lalitgiri hills in the Cuttack District became flourishing seats of the "Great Vehicle" (Mahāyāna) in the 7th and 8th century A. D.

The Bonai plate of Maharaja Udaya Varāha shows him to be a devout worshipper of Sugata (Buddha).[47]

Buddhism in Orissa reached the zenith of prosperity in the 8th century A. D. when the early Kara kings were ruling in South Orissa. 'The first group of Kara kings were decidedly Buddhist". The first king of this group, Kshemaṅkara by name, is called a lay-worshipper (Paramopāsaka.) His son Śivakara is styled the devout worshipper of Tathāgata, and his son Śubhakara is addressed as the devout Buddhist (Parama

Buddhism in the eighth Century Orissa

46. Taranath's Account, The Journal of the Dept. of Letters, Calcutta University, Vol. I, p. 28.

47. J. B. O. R. S. Vol. VI.

Saugata).[48] Śubhakara zealously espoused the cause of his faith. In 795 A. D. Emperor Te-Tsong of China received the last section of Avataṁsaka from Śubhakara "Kesari", the king of Odra country, "who had deep faith in Sovereign Law and who followed the practice of Mahāyāna."[49]

It is quite likely that the Buddhist form of worship prevailed in the temple of Jagannāth, in South Toshala, during the regime of the early Kara kings.

This inference brings to the forefront that much-discussed question—"Was Jagannāth originally a Buddhist deity ?" Hunter is of opinion that he was, and that "Vaisnavism at Puri is but the successor of the older Buddhistic creed." In the following paragraphs of discussion, which may be considered as a critical digression, we intend to examine the points raised in favour of the Buddhist origin of Jagannāth.

The Alleged Buddhist Origin of Jagannath

There is a story that the Divine Log (Dāru Brahma) consisted of the skeletal bones of Krishṇa (Vishṇu) and charred remains of Neem Wood.[50]

Vishnu Panjara

Hamilton, who wrote his account in 1820, relied on the version of Nārada Saṁvāda in Bengali. After the passing away of Krishṇa, he writes, "Some unknown persons, having collected the bones of that incarnation, put them into a box. About that time a king named Indradumnya was performing austere worship to Vishṇu who directed him to form the image of Jagannāth and to put the bones into its belly."

Hamilton's "Hindostan"

It has been suggested that the so-called Vishṇu-Pañjara was in reality the sacred Tooth of :Buddha. But there is no cogent evidence to support such a hypothesis. Vishṇu-Pañjara is mentioned in Garuḍa Purāṇa (Chap. XIII) but

48. History of Orissa, Vol. I, p. 147.

49. Epigraphica Indica. Vol. XV.

50. See, "Jagannath Mahatmya" & "Jagannath Vijay."—The Catalogue of MSS. Bangiya Sahitya Parishad.

there are no references to the skeletal bones of Krishṇa or to the Tooth of Buddha. Thus the story of Vishṇu-Pañjara has no historical basis.

The Story of Datha (Dhatu) Vamsa

Dr. Rajendra Lal Mitra is of opinion that the image of Jagannāth contains the sacred Tooth of Buddha and the quotes the story of Dāṭhā-vaṁsa in support of his statement.[51]

The substance of the story of Dāṭhā-(Dhatu) vaṁsa is as follows :

Kshemamuni collected the left big Tooth of Buddha from his funeral pyre. He presented the Tooth to Brahmadutta, king of Kaliṅga, who built a temple over the sacred relic. The place, wherein the temple stood, became known as Dantapuram. The fame of the Tooth was noised abroad and Dantakumāra, the Prince of Ujjaini, came to Kaliṅga to offer worship to the Tooth. He married Hema-mālā, the daughter of Guhasiva, the king of Kaliṅga, and was appointed as the custodian of the Tooth. Now Kaliṅga was invaded by another king, who sought to obtain the priceless relic. Guhasiva was defeated and killed. Dantakumāra and Hema-mālā fled to Ceylon, taking the sacred Tooth along with them. King Mahāsena of Ceylon received the Tooth and built a temple for it.

Dāṭhā-vaṁsa abounds in episodes, as rich in romance as the tales of the Epics are. Dhamma-Kitti, the author of this book, flourished in Ceylon in the 12th century A. D. when the widow of king Parākrama was reigning.[52] Thus he was separated from the time and place of the event by a long distance. The author seldom troubled himself about the historical accuracy of his statements. Lastly, the sacred Tooth was taken away for good to Ceylon. Even Dhamma Kitti concedes this. Thus the image of Jagannāth cannot possibly contain the relic of Buddha, when the relic was duly installed in a Ceylonese temple. In the face of

51. The Antiquities of Orissa, Vol. II, pp. 105-106.

52. Account of the Tooth relic of Ceylon.—G. Turnour. J. A. S. B., 1837.

these facts, the theory of Raja R. L. Mitra possesses little inherent plausibility.

According to some scholars, the Puri Triad "have been copied from the Buddha Stūpa indicative of five elements".[53]

Jagannath's Resemblance to Buddhist Chaitya or Stupa

But Colonel Sykes opines that "the uncouth figures of Jagannāth, etc., were more like Chaityas than beings with human form". Thus the scholars are at variance whether the Triad resemble the Stūpa or the Chaitya!

Traditions are unanimous that the prototype of Jagannāth was worshipped by the Śavaras; though as Hunter poignantly

The Savara Worshippers of Proto-Jagannth

remarks, "Vasu the fowler would now be driven out from the doors of the temple dedicated to his god".[54] The Śavaras are mentioned in Post-Vedic Texts, such as Aiteraya Brāhmaṇa (XVIII. 2), and Pañchaviṁśa Brāhmaṇa. The Śavara origin of Jagannāth is

The Savara Origin of the Image of Jagannath

probably the cause of his deformed shape. Religion dawned in the mind of the primitive people through terror; terror of evil, of death and hunger. This led Man to propitiate the objects of terror.

A deformed uncouth figure instils that required feeling of fear. The proto-Jagannāth deity was absorbed into the Brahmanical religion and identified with Krishṇa-Vāsudeva. The images of Balarām and Subhadrā had perhaps similar origins or they were designed in conformity to the shape of Jagannāth. Such a hypothesis will be more consistent than that of the alleged Buddhist origin. If Jagannāth's image was originally designed to be an image of Buddha then it would have been shaped to resemble Buddha and not something which looks like a Stūpa or Chaitya.

It has also been contended that the Triad resemble the Buddhist Tri-Ratna. "The individual figures of the Triad bear

The Triad's Alleged Resemblance to Tri-Ratna

definite resemblance to the 'Tri-Ratna' or the Disc-crescent symbol of the Buddhist system and this has been very ably pointed out by

53. Orissa and Her Remains, p. 405.

54. Orissa. Vol. I, p. 136.

General Cunningham in his books, "Bhilsa Topes" and the "Stūpa of Bharhut."[55] But the conception of Trinity is not peculiar to Buddhism. M. M. Ganguly expresses elsewhere his belief that "the figure of Tri-Ratna has been copied from the tri-lateral syllable Aum." Varāhamihira in his Vrihat Saṁhitā refers to the Trinity formed by Baladeva, Ekānaṁsā and Krishṇa.

Other reasons are also advanced to prove the Buddhist origin of the Puri Triad. It is pointed out that the temple of Jagannāth faces the east contrary to the Hindu canons of temple building ; that the caste distinctions are absent within the temple precincts ; and that the sister-brother relation between the presiding god and the goddess goes against the spirit of the Hindu theology.

But almost all the temples in Orissa face towards the east. Secondly, the caste distinctions are absent so far as the partaking of oblations is concerned. The untouchables are not allowed to enter into the temple. Lastly, we have already explained the reason why the sister came to be worshipped along with Jagannāth. The Brahmanical texts, such as Nilādri Mahodaya, (chapter on 'Pratimā Nirmāṇa) likewise give reasons for the odd shapes of the Puri Triad. The sanctity of the oblation (Mahā-Prasāda) has been extolled in several old texts.[56]

Untenability of the Theory of Buddhist Origin

Thus we reject the theory of Buddhist origin of the Puri Triad.

Though we deny that Jagannāth was originally a Buddhist god, we cannot ignore the fact that the worship and later mythology of Jagannāth point out unmistakable Buddhist influence.

Hunter opines that the Car-festival is a distinct Buddhist contribution. He refers to the description of the Car-festival in Fa-hien's account. "This was in the fifth century A. D. ; but the account applies so exactly to the Car-festival at the present day

The Car-Festival in Buddhism

55. Orissa and Her Remains,—M. M. Ganguly, p. 406.

56. See M. M. Sadasiv Misra—Jagannath Temple, p. 30 and "Jagannath is not Buddha," Sahakara XVI. No. 7.

that one of the most accurate of Indian observers pronounces the latter to be merely a copy. Certain it is that in its leading doctrines the worship of Jagannāth bears the impress of the ancient Buddhistic faith."[57]

The ancient Cars were not the monopoly of the Buddhists. The Cars of the Easterners (Prāchyas) have been mentioned in Lāṭyāyana Srauta Sūtra (VIII. 6.9). In Rāmāyaṇa, it has been stated that Rāma had witnessed the Indra-ratha festival—a Car-procession with an image of Indra.

But it is more than improbable that the devotees of Jagannāth had ever seen a Prāchyaratha or Indra-ratha. Thus we believe that the Car-festival of Jagannāth was borrowed from Buddhism. It might have been introduced in the regime of the Buddhist Kara kings. But this is a hypothesis and nothing more.

In the 9th and 10th century A. D. the Buddhist Pāla kings of Bengal—like Dharmapāla,[58] Devapāla,[59] and Rāmapāla[60] exercised suzerainty over Orissa. The Buddhist Pāla kings tried their best to arrest the decline of Buddhism.

The Pala Suzerainty over Orissa

At this time, flourished Rāmāi Pundit who tried to synthesise the different creeds by preaching the Dharma cult. Dharma Thākur was the son of Adi-Buddha and was Vishṇu himself. Rāmāi Pundit was the priest of Lāusena—the Sāmanta chief under Devapāla. Dharma Pujā Vidhān and Śūnya-Purāṇ are attributed to Rāmāi's authorship. It is stated in Dharma Purāṇ of Mayurbhaṭṭa that Dharmadās, the son of Rāmāi, converted Rañjit, the king of Kaliṅga,[61] into the new creed.

Ramai Pundit and the Dharma Cult

N. N. Vasu traces the influence of the Dharma cult in

57. Orissa, Vol. I, p. 132.
58. Bhagalpur Inscription of Narayan Pala.
59. Garuda Pillar Inscription at Mangalbadi.
60. Rama Charita—Chap. III, Sl. 45.
61. Mayurbhatta flourished probably in the 11th century. He was the court-poet of Lausena's grandson. Ranjit may be tentatively identified with Rana-Stambha I—the Sulki chief.

the adaptation of the Nāgārjuniya Philosophy of the Void[62] and the theory of Creation[63], which prevailed in Orissa.

In Dharma Pujā Vidhān, we find perhaps the earliest literary reference to Jagannāth's identification with Buddha. "In the

Early Literary References to Jagannath as Buddha

ninth incarnation Hari dwelt on the sea-coast known by the name of Jagannāth."[64] "Appearing as Buddha on the sea-coast, O Lord, Thou lookest graciously".[65] Thus, Jagannāth is declared to be the 9th incarnation of Vishṇu. Jagannāth has also been mentioned in the mythology of the Dharmacult. He joined the marriage-festival of Ādyā and suffered mutilation of limbs for stealing wine.[66]

Early Saivism in Orissa

Like Buddhism, the Medieval Śaivism exercised great influence in Orissa and had left a permanent impression upon the

Saivism in Orissa

growing Vaishṇavism. The Māṇa overlords of south Toshala were worshippers of Maheśvara.[67] The Śailavaṁsī chiefs of Koṅgoda and Māṭhar chiefs of Kaliṅga professed devotion to Śiva and installed several Śiva images.[68]

The Eastern Gaṅga dynasty was established by Kāmārṇava in Kaliṅga "probably in the 7th century A. D."[69] These early

The Eastern Kings of Kalinga

Gaṅga kings were professedly Śaivite in faith.

Coming to the later Kara monarchs of Toshala, we find

62. Modern Buddhism in Orissa, pp. 111-12.

63. *Ibid.*, pp. 51 & 109,

64. "नवम मूर्तिने हरि जगन्नाथ नाम धरि जलधिर तीरे कैला वास
Dharma Puja-Vidhan, pp. 206-7.

65. "जलधिर तीरे स्थान बौद्ध रूपे भगवान हय्या तुमि कृपावलोकन"
Ibid.

66. The Gajan Song of Maldah. Quoted in Adyer Gambhira by Haridas Palit.

67. Patiakella Grant of Sivaraja, Epigraphica Indica, Vol. IX.

68. "Saivism in Orissa"—K. N. Mahapatra, Nababharata, Biccha, 1341.

69 "The Gangas of Kalinga"—S. N. Rajguru. Prachi Vol. I. Pt. IV.

that Śaivism was the prevailing faith, though other faiths had a share in the royal devotion. The inscriptions of Śubhakara Deva II[70], Daṇḍi Mahādevi[71], Gayāḍa Tuṅga[72] and Vinita Tuṅga[73] express their reverence for Maheśvara.

The Saivite Kings of the Kara Dynasty

From towards the end of the eighth century A. D., Śaivism gradually acquired a prominent position in Orissa. The temples of Siddheśvar, Parśurameśvar and Mukteśvar, which are the earliest extant temples in Orissa, belong to this century.[74]

The Rise of Saivism

In the ninth century A. D. Śaṅkarāchārya came to Puri and established therein the Bhogavardhana or Govardhana Math. Śaṅkarāchārya "was the name assumed by a Sannyasi born at Kaladi in the North of Travancore probably in the year 788 A.D."[75] It is told that Śaṅkarāchārya introduced the Śaivite form of worship in the Jagannāth temple and added many new items of bhoga to the existing ones.[76]

The advent of Sankaracharya

Śaṅkara's teachings undoubtedly stimulated the growth of Śaivism, which found expression in the temple of Liṅgarāja at Bhuvaneswar.

"The temple of Liṅgarāja represents the efflorescence of racial genius in all its inspiring dignity and classical grace". According to the Pānji, Yajāti Keśarī started the construction of the temple. B. C. Majumder opines that "Yajāti Mahāśivagupta flourished in the tenth century A. D."[77] The temple of Liṅgarāja, in the opinion of R. D. Banerjee and other Indian

The Temple of Lingaraja

70. The Hindol Plate of Subhakardeva, J. B. O. R. S., XVI, pp. 69-83.
71. A Copper-Plate Grant of Dandi-Mahadevi, J.B.O.R.S., Vol. V, Pt. IV.
72. Mayurbhanj Archaeological Survey Report. Vol. I, p. 150.
73. J.B.O.R.S. Vol. VI.
74. History of Orissa. Vol. II, pp. 341 & 356.
75. Outlines of the Religious Literature of India—Dr. J. N. Farquhar, p. 171.
76. "The Historical Sanctity of Jagannath," Bichitra, Jaistha, 1341.
77. Orissa in the Making, p. 171.

scholars, was constructed in the tenth century A.D.[78] Yajāti *Mahāśivagupta* declares himself as "Param-Māheśvara" in his inscriptions.

The construction of the temple was completed by Lalāṭendu Keśari. He is a real enigma to the historians and lives only in traditions.[79]

Kolāvatī, the mother of Udyotakeśarī, built the temple of Brahmeśvar. Mahādevi Vijayā, the queen of Raṇabhañja gave away lands for the worship of Vijayeśvar Śiva.[80]

Like Śaivism, Śaktism also flourished in Orissa on the eve of the Gaṅga conquest. "The Śringāra sculpture may be the

Tantrism in Orissa

outcome of Tāntric influence by whom sexuality was given an abhorrent preference". R. D. Banerjee opines that Tāntric temples of Baudh belong to the group of early temples, which precede the tenth century.

The Śākta Tāntrists conceive Jagannāth as Bhairava and

Vimala

Vimalā as Bhairavī. ("Vimalā Bhairavī Jatra Jagannāthastu Bhairavaḥ). The Mādla Pānji states that Yajāti Kesari reared the temple of Vimalā. Jagannāth's oblation of rice is offered to Vimalā and to no other deity.[81]

Goddess Stambheśvari has been mentioned by Ranaka

Stambhesvari

Raṇabhañja as the Bhairavi of Mahādeva.[82] She has also been alluded in Kulastambha's grant to Bhaṭṭa Brihaspati, who was a "devout worshipper of Vishṇu".[83]

The Māranjmurā Charter of Yajāti Mahāśivagupta extols

Bhagavati Bhadrambika

Bhagavati Pañchambari Bhadrāmbikā, of Pattan Suvarṇapura.[84]

78. "Coomaraswamy and R. P. Chanda are substantially correct in placing it to the tenth century A.D." History of Orissa. Vol. II, p. 356.
79. K. N. Mahapatra, a research-scholar of Orissa, seeks to identify Lalatendu Kesari with Udyota-Kesari of the Brahmesvar temple inscription. Sahakara, Vol. XVI, No. 3.
80. Epigraphica Indica Vol. XX.
81. "The Historical Sanctity of Jagannath", Vichitra, Jaistha, 1341.
82. J. B. O. R. S. Vol. II. Pt. II.
83. J. B. O. R. S. Vol. II. Pt. IV.
84. J. B. O. R. S. Vol. II. Pt. I.

Conclusion

It is natural at the conclusion of the conspectus, to pause and look back. Fragmentary as are the collected scraps of evidence on which the preceding outlines have been constructed, yet we are now enabled to make some conjectures that may not be far from truth. In the period under review Vaishṇavism certainly existed in Orissa, but had by no means acquired an exalted position. Nevertheless the growing influence and status of Jagannāth facilitated the rise of Vaishṇavism as the State religion.

Intolerance, the bane of religious zeal, seldom stained the early religious history of Orissa. The spirit of rare catholicity had been personified in Yajāti Mahāśivagupta. He restored Jagannāth out of oblivion and built a temple for him.

This very king reared the temple of Vimalā, started the construction of the Liṅgarāja temple and adored Bhagavati Bhadrāmbikā. Similarly, Tribhuvana Mahādevi, though a devout worshipper of Vishṇu, compared herself with Kātyāyanī. The emblem of conch-shell, which is a representation of Vishṇu, appears on the seals of the Śaivite Kara kings. The Vishṇuite Bhañja kings like Ranaka Raṇabhañja and Śatrubhañja did not neglect to insert the customary verses in honour of Śiva in their charters. The figures of Gaja-Lakshmī are to be found on the doorways of the Medieval Śaivite temples. More interesting are the twin temples at Gandharādi, which are assigned to the early group of the Medieval temples by R. D. Banerjee. One temple was dedicated to Siddheśvar Śiva and the other to Nila-Mādhava Vishṇu.

From the eleventh century A. D. the predominance of Vaishṇavism over the sister sects in Orissa was a *fait accompli.* It was Rāmānuja who rehabilitated the conception of Jagannāth. The deity of the "Blue Abode" became the State deity of Orissa—an event which was signalized by the magnificent temple reared by Choḍagaṅga and his sons. But the old associations of Jagannāth were not rejected. Vaishṇavism absorbed elements which were essentially Śaivite or Buddhistic in spirit. Thus :flourished the Medieval Vaishṇavism. It held ground up to the 16th century, when appeared the Chaitanya Movement. Because of its heterogeneous elements, the Old School of Vaishṇavism was denounced by Neo-Vaishṇavism. The Modern Vaishaṇvism in Orissa is based upon the teachings of the Chaitanya Movement.

CHAPTER II

THE HISTORY OF MEDIEVAL VAISHNAVISM UNDER THE GANGA KINGS

The Eastern Gaṅgas came from Gaṅgavāḍi in Mysore and reigned in Kaliṅga (South of Koṅgada) for more than two centuries, before they conquered Orissa proper.[85] The Gaṅgas of Kaliṅga professed Śaivism and Gokarneśvar on the Mahendragiri was their tutelary deity. Kāmārṇava I and Vajrahasta invoked that deity in their inscriptions. Kāmārṇava II built the temple of Madhukeśvara. Rājarāja I married Rājasundarī—the daughter of the Chola king Kulottuṅga. The issue of this marriage was Anantavarmana Choḍagaṅga.[86] The Korṇi copper-plates of Choḍagaṅga state that the king ascended the throne of Kaliṅga in the Śaka year 999=1078 A. D.[87]

The Mādlā Pānji narrates the story of the conquest of Orissa, with a touch of romance. Suvarṇakeśarī, the last king of the Keśari dynasty, is said to have rejected the overture of Choḍagaṅga, who sought the hands of Nandikā, the daughter of the Keśarī king. The Vizagapatam land-grant of the Śaka year 1040-1118 A. D. states that Choḍagaṅga "replaced the fallen lord of Utkala in his kingdom in the Eastern region and then the waning lord of Veṅgī in the Western region and propped up their failing fortunes".[88]

The Conquest of Orissa by Chodaganga

In the opinion of R. D. Banerjee, Choḍagaṅga did not personally rule over Orissa. He allowed "some local king" to reign there as his vassal. Thus he tries to account for the

85. History of Orissa, Vol. II, p. 372 ; Vol. I, pp. 237 and 239.

86. Vizagapatam land-grant of Chodaganga of 1118 A.D.

87. "Initial year of the Ganga Era".—V. Misra. Journal of Orissa Academy Vol. I. Pt. II.

88. History of Orissa, Vol. I, p. 249.

total absence of Choḍagaṅga's inscriptions in Northern Orissa.

In his early inscriptions, Choḍagaṅga expressed his devotion to Śiva. In 1081 A.D. he granted land in honour of the deity Rājrājeśvara. Choḍagaṅga and his queen visited the Śiva temple at Drākshārām and donated some lamps. Late in life, he came under the influence of Vaishṇavism. He repaired the Kūrma temple at Śrıkūrmam. His Korṇi copper-plates begin with an invocation of Lakshmī.

But his crowning achievement was the work he began on the eve of his life—the construction of the temple of Jagannāth. What was the motive behind this superb attempt ? Tradition records that Yajāti-Keśarī built the pre-Gaṅga temple of Jagannāth. The temple-chroniclers tried to show that the aforenamed pious king flourished as early as the 5th century A.D. The Pānji has been stereotyped in accordance with this view, and so Aniyaṅkabhīma is made to declare that the existing temple has become very old.[89] But if Yajāti Keśari is identical with Mahāśivagupta Yajāti, who lived in the tenth century A.D., then the existing temple was hardly old enough to deserve reconstruction.

A Possible Reason for the Temple Construction

Yajāti Mahāśivagupta was a Śaivite king, and it can be hardly expected of him to raise a sky-scraping temple for the Vishṇuite deity. Choḍagaṅga and his sons espoused the cause of Vaishṇavism and with the proverbial zeal of enthusiasts, they erected an immense and gigantic structure—as "the magnificent assertion of autocratic devotion".[90] It is quite possible that Choḍagaṅga's enthusiasm was aroused, as he came into contact with some great personality. The first name which strikes us in this connection is that of Rāmānuja, apostle of the Śrī-cult.

The first apostle in the preceptorial list of the Śrī-

89. "ययाति राजा योउँ पाटल तोलाइ पर्मेश्वरंकु विजे कराइ अछन्ति, से पाटल गोटि अति बइषम होइला । एहा भाङ्गि अर हाथ उच्च प्रासाद गोटिए तोलाइबा पर्मेश्वरंकु "

Madla Panji.

90. Orissa, Vol, I, p. 100.

Vaishṇavas was Nātha-Muni, who probably flourished in the beginning of the tenth century A.D.

The Sri-Vaishnavas

Śailapūrṇa was the chief disciple of Yamunācharya—the fourth in the apostolic succession. Rāmānuja was the sister's son of Śailapūrṇa. He is said to have been born in the year 1017 A.D.[91] at Perumbūdūr 26 miles to the west of Madras. Rāmānuja became the mohunt of the Śrī-Raṅgam temple.

Rāmānuja, like Śaṅkarāchārya, started on a mission to preach his faith. At Puri, he established two maths—one in his own name and the other in the name of his cousin and disciple Govinda. Rāmānuja was known to his disciples as "Mannāth". He wanted to confer that name on Govinda, but the latter hesitated to accept the designation of his Guru.

Ramanuja at Puri

Rāmānuja then translated Mannāth into Tamil as "Em-peru-Mān-ār". Shortening it into 'Embār' he gave the designation to Govinda, and named the second math after him.[92] Later on, he met the Raja of Orissa who was impressed by his exposition of Vedānta.

Rāmānuja's work in the Puri Temple has been described by Anantācharya in Prapannāmrita. Winning the Raja over, he next sought to alter the Smārta form of worship that prevailed in the temple of Jagannāth. But he encountered stiff opposition from the Servitors of the temple. Rāmānuja had had the divine service performed by other Brāhmins—according to the Pāñcharātra rite, which was observed in the Śrī-Raṅgam temple. Consternation and disgrace stared at the face of the priests and at nightfall they assembled before the altar of Jagannāth. "Hark

Ramanuja in the Puri Temple

91. Prapannamrita—canto 115, Sloka XXVII.
"Ramanuja is a monist no less than Sankara, but his monism is Visishtadvaita—one that recognises attributes of God as real, that cognizes Brahman as carrying plurality within itself, and the world which is the manifestation of his power as something real."
Indian Theism, p. 104.

92. Life of Ramanuja—Ramkrishnananda. Embār is now corrupted into Emār.

thee, O Lord" they cried. "The Yatindra seeketh to introduce changes in the form of Thy worship. We belong to the old school and we abhor such changes. Save us, we beseech Thee, from this imperious Sannyasi. Otherwise we will die before Thee." The deity was moved at this supplication and he appeared before the Yatindra in a vision and advised him not to insist on changes. But Rāmānuja was adamant. Jagannāth then got him removed overnight to a distance of hundred Yojanas—to Kūrmakshetra.

It is stated that at Kūrmakshetra, the presiding deity was worshipped at that time according to Smārta principles.

Ramanuja at Kurmakshetra

Rāmānuja never tasted food before offering oblation to Vishṇu. He fasted rather than offer worship to a Śaivite deity. At night Kūrma-Nārāyaṇa appeared before him in dream and explained his proper identity to him. Next day Rāmānuja cleared away the popular mistake and worshipped the Kūrma image befittingly.

When did Rāmānuja come to Orissa? In 1098 A. D. Rāmānuja was persecuted by Kulottuṅga Chola and retired to Mysore. A record found in his monastery at Melkota in Mysore makes it clear that he lived there up to 1122 A. D.[93] He returned to Śrī-Raṅgam where he died in 1137 A. D. A reasonable conjecture will be that Rāmānuja visited Orissa between 1122 and 1137 A. D. and Choḍagaṅga came into contact with him during this period. But the force of this remark is impaired by the statement of Anantāchārya that Rāmānuja was born in 1017 A. D. It is improbable that he lived for 120 years. Thus we reject the latter statement. Anantāchārya hardly cared for historical accuracy in his book and the date given by him seems to be a wrong one.

Rāmānuja was the last of the Ālwars.[94] The famous

93. J. R. A. S. 1915, p. 147. See "Ramanuja"—Outlines of the Religious Literature of India by Dr. J. N. Farquhar.

94. Alwar=Those who are immersed in devotion.

temple of Ālālnāth or Ālwarnāth is situated in the village of Brahmagiri, about 16 miles to the South of Puri. Lakshmī, Rukmiṇī and Saraswatī are now worshipped along with Ālālnāth. Thus the worship of Ālālnāth has now lost the distinctive spirit of Śrī-Vaishṇavism. According to the Temple chronicles, Madana Mahādeva, the brother of Anaṅgabhima Deva, built the temple of Ālālnāth.[95]

Alalnath

The temple of Lakshmī within the temple precinct of Jagannāth was probably constructed as a result of Rāmānuja's influence. "The only structure of the same date as the Vimāna and Jagmohana of the Jagannāth temple" writes R. D. Banerjee "is the temple of Lakshmī inside the inner compound."[96] The Vimāna and Jagmohana, referred to above, were constructed by Choḍagaṅga.[97]

The Temple of Lakshmi

As regards the date of the Jagannāth temple, R. D. Banerjee has accepted the opinion of M. M. Chakravarty.[98] Chakravarty quotes the following passage from the Copper plates of the Gaṅga kings of Orissa.

Date of the Temple of Jagannath

"What king can be named that could erect a temple to such a god as Purusottama ? This task which had been hitherto neglected by previous kings was fulfilled by Gaṅgeśvara. The Ocean is the birth place of Lakshmī. So thinking in his father-in-law's place (the Ocean) Vishṇu lodged with some shame, though he got full adoration. Thus ashamed, the god Purusottama was glad to get this new house and Lakshmī gladly preferred living in her husband's new house to living in her father's house." M. M. Chakravarty identifies Gaṅgeśvara with Choḍagaṅga. He then refers to the Govindapur

95. See Purusottam Chandrika—" derived fromt he palm-writings direct" (Hunter). Alalnath has been mentioned in Chaitanya Charitamrita, II 1. 22. & 2. 63 ; III. 2. 132 & 9. 33.

96. History of Orissa, Vol. II, p. 376.

97. *Ibid.* Vol. I, p. 251.

98. See his monograph, "The Date of the Jagannath Temple in Puri". J. A. S. B. 1898. No. 4.

inscription and Nagpur inscription of Lakshmadeva and points out that "both these inscriptions show that the temple might have been there, say in 1090 A. D." "and might have been built between 1085-90 A. D."

But the temple was not constructed for the first time by Choḍagaṅga. Traditions affirm that Saṅkarāchārya visited the temple and Yajāti Mahāśivagupta reared a new temple for Jagannāth.

There are no grounds for dismissing the traditions as baseless. The afore-named inscriptions seem to refer to the existing Pre-Gaṅga temple of Jagannāth. The construction was not completed in the reign of Choḍagaṅga. The work was continued in the reigns of his sons and was finished by Anaṅgabhima II, the youngest of them. The Pānji categorically points out Anaṅgabhima II, to be the builder of the temple and our suggestion is the only possible explanation of such a statement.

Choḍagaṅga was succeeded by his sons Kāmārṇava and Rāghava, about whom we know next to nothing. Rāghava was succeeded by his brother Rājarāja II (1170-90).

Svapneśvara Deva, the brother-in-law of Rājarāja II, built a temple in honour of Megheśvara, *i. e.*, the Lord of Kailāśa.

The Meghesvara Temple Inscription

Svapneśvar compared himself with Vishṇu, who is the consort of Lakshmi, destroyer of Vali in the Vāmana incarnation, favourite of the Gopāla clan, doer of every exploit and who held the earth up in the Vishakasena and Varāha incarnations (V. 18).[99] Krishṇa does not appear as the Supreme Being, nor Rādhā has been mentioned. Lakshmi rising out of the churned ocean has been compared with Suramā, the sister of Svapneśvara Deva (Sl. 6 & 7). Lakshmi and Nārāyaṇa have been frequently mentioned, which may be due to the indirect influence of the Rāmānuja Movement.

Rājarāja II was succeeded by his brother Aniyaṅka or

99. Meghesvara Temple Inscription—Epigraphica Indica, Vol. VI.

Anaṅgabhima II. 1190-98

Anaṅgahhīma II. He has been given the sole credit for the construction of the Jagannāth temple, in the Mādlā Pānji.

Gathering his courtiers he expressed before them his desire to build a temple to Jagannāth. He wanted to replace the dilapidated Keśarī temple by a gigantic structure, reared to the height of hundred cubits. The courtiers supported his proposal but suggested a height of 90 cubits. The resolution plus the amendment was then carried into effect. The Vimāna of the temple is 214′-8″" high above the road-level.[100]

The date of the completion of the temple can be fixed up almost with precision. According to the tradition, the date is

Date of the Completion of the Temple

"शकाब्दे रन्ध्र शुभ्रांशु रूप नक्षत्र नायके प्रासाद कारयामासानङ्ग भीमेन धीमता"। Randhra=8 Subhrāṁsu=1 Rūpa=1 Nakshatra Nāyaka=1. Reversing the digits we find the Saka year 1118=1197 A. D. The amount spent on the construction of the temple was equivalent to a million of gold māḍhas (1 māḍha=about half a tola). The jewellery given to the deities amounted to two lakhs and a half of gold māḍhas. Thus the total expense came up to six lakhs and twenty-five thousands of gold tolās. In the fifteenth Aṅka of the king, on the tenth day of the waxing moon in the month of Phalgun, the deities were installed in the newly constructed temple.

The temple of Jagannāth bears silent witness to the glorious days of yore. There it stands, calm, severe and sombre—a symbol of eternity defying the ravages of time. Generations after generations of devout Hindus have gone to the holy Purusottam Kshetra to offer worship and to die there perchance—"being lulled to their last sleep by the roar of the eternal ocean".

Anaṅgabhima II was succeeded by Rājarāja III (1198-1211) and after him Anaṅgabhima III (1211-38) ascended the throne.

Anaṅgabhīma III's daughter Chandrikā was devoted to Vishṇu and she erected a Vishṇu temple on the Vindu-Saro-

100. Orissa and Her Remains, p. 417.

vara (1.8) "at Ekāmra, (Bhuvaneswar) and offered worship with great magnificence to Baladeva, Krishṇa and Subhadrā".[101]

The Inscription of Chandrika Devi

Mr. K. N. Mahapatra has tried to prove that it is the original inscription of the temple of Ananta-Vāsudeva and the present inscription in the temple-wall is a spurious one.[102] Mr. Mahapatra deserves praise for his critical observation, in spite of his uncalled for tirade against the Bengalis.

The existing inscription on the western compound-wall of Ananta-Vāsudeva was incised by order of Bhavadeva Bhaṭṭa,

The Inscription of the Bhavadeva Bhatta

who was the minister of king Harivarma Deva (V.16). In his inscription there is no reference to Subhadrā, Ekāmra-Kānana or Vindu-Sarovara. It is further stated that the pious minister had a tank excavated in the water-less tract in Rāḍha country (V. 26). There is no cogent reason why he should construct a temple at Bhuvaneswar, far away from his country. Thus the temple, in which he installed the images of Nārāyaṇa, Ananta and Nrisiṁha, was in all probability, built in the Rāḍha country.

The existence of Bhavadeva Bhaṭṭa's inscription at Bhuvaneswar can be explained in this way. Colonel Stuart was an officer under the East India Company. He was notorious for his craze for images and was nick-named as 'Hindu Stuart'. In about 1810 he visited Bhuvaneswar and removed some inscriptions from the temple walls. In 1837 when Major Kittoe went to Bhuvaneswar, the priests complained before him and the Major agreed to return the inscriptions. He sent from the museum of the Asiatic Society of Bengal, the inscriptions of Bhavadeva Bhaṭṭa and of the Brahmeśvara temple. Through some mistake or other, the outer wall of the Ananta-Vāsudeva temple was selected for both these inscriptions.

101. Bhuvaneswar Inscription of Royal Asiatic Society—Epigraphica Indica, XIII.

102. Prachi, III. Pt. I & Sahakara, Vol. XV. No. 6. For the inscription, see Epigraphica Indica, VI.

Dr. R. L. Mitra found the Brahmeśvara slab in the temple-wall of Ananta-Vāsudeva "in the very place where the slab of Megheśvara is located now".[103] The Brahmeśvara slab is now missing. Thus in the last quarter of the 19th century, somebody took away the inscription of Uddyota Keśari and replaced it by the slab of Megheśvara, so as to avoid publicity. The inscription of Chandrikā Devi was taken to England by Stuart and subsequently found its way to the museum of Royal Asiatic Society. Thus at present the temple of Ananta-Vāsudeva contains two inscriptions—one giving a wrong identity and the other has nothing to do with the temple.

Anaṅgabhīma III was succeeded by Narasiṁha I. He will be remembered by posterity as the builder of the

Narasimha I
1238-64.

Koṇārka temple—"now standing in ruins which still testify to its former grandeur, unrivalled by any other temple in the world." Many land-grants of the successors of Narasiṁha I refer to his glorious work.

The Early History of Konarka

Arka-Kshetra acquired celebrity even before Narasiṁha I's time. In Śāmba-Purāṇa, which is not later than the eleventh century, the sanctity of Koṇārka has been extolled.[104] The Sun-god at Koṇārka has been mentioned :as "Koṇāditya" in Brahma-Purāṇa (Chap. 44). There is a reference to "Sūrya-Kshetra" of Orissa in the description of Skanda's pilgrimage in Śiva Purāṇa.[105] It is stated in the Mādlā Pānji, that Purandara Keśarī built a temple at Arka-Kshetra and gave lands to the Brahmins to settle there. Anaṅgabhīma Deva of the Gaṅga dynasty increased the royal

103. Orissa and Her Remains, p. 330.

104. The Castes and Sects of Bengal. Vol. II. The Chapter on the Brahmans of Sakadvipa.

105. Orissa and Her Remains, p. 439.

grant for the oblation of the Koṇārka deity.[106] We know from the temple archives that the Koṇārka temple was completed in the 17th year of Narasiṁha I's reign. According to Ain-i-Akberi of Abul Fazl, "its cost was defrayed by twelve years' revenue of the province."

The Sun-Worship in Ancient Orissa

The Sun-worship also prevailed in ancient Orissa. We have already referred to the figure of the Sun-god with four horses in the rear-wall of Ananta-Gumphā. There is a similar representation of the Sun in the wall of a small temple within the Liṅgarāja temple precincts.[107]. At Koṇārka the Sun-god is represented with seven horses. Foreign influence is distinctly visible in the Koṇārka statues of the Sun-god—"wearing kilts or boots reaching a little below the knee-cap".[108]

These boots resemble the Nepali or Tibetan boots. Mr. Nirmal Kumar Basu opines that this booted representation of the Sun-god exactly corresponds with the conception of Sūrya in Brihat Saṁhitā[109] of Varāhamihira who was "a Brahmin of Śakadvipa."[110]

Jajpur was another centre of heliolatry. Sun-pillars, crowned by the sacred Vulture, existed there and were subsequently disfigured or destroyed by the Muslims. The flight of steps leading to the Vaitaraṇī from the Varāha temple "exhibits a granite bas-relief of the Sun-god seated on his celestial car and drawn by seven prancing horses".[111] There is a small Garuḍa pillar within the temple-precincts of Jagannāth, sanctified by the touch of Chaitanya.

Vishṇu was conceived as a Sun-god *par excellence* in the

106. Konaraker Bibaran, p. 4.
107. Orissa and Her Remains, p. 365.
108. Orissa and Her Remains, p. 451.
109. "कुर्य्यादुदीच्य वेश० त० गूढ पादावुरोयावत्"
Quoted in Konaraker Bibaran, p. 98.
110. "History of the Brahmans of Sakadvipa."—The Castes & Sects of Bengal, Vol. II.
111. Hunter's Orissa, Vol, I, p. 285.

Rigveda. He has been praised for his three strides.[112] Dr. Macnicol is of opinion that Vishṇu's rise into eminence was largely due to the fact that "he was a Sun-god with a Sun-god's association of light, life and blessedness."[113] Later on, evolved the conception of Sūrya-Nārāyaṇa.

Vishnu as a Solar Deity

Bhāgavatism from the very beginning was associated with heliolatry. "All the legends dealing with the origin of the Bhāgavata religion are connected in some way or other with the Sun".[114] Vāsudeva-Krishṇa was the disciple of Ghora Āṅgirasa and the Āṅgirasas were the priests of the Sun. Krishṇa appropriated Garuḍa (Eagle Vehicle) and Chakra (discus) of Vishṇu, which are "connected with solar legends." The Sun-worship received fresh impetus as a result of 'Maga' (Śaka-Hunish) influence. The legend of the advent of the Magas centred round Śāmba, a son of Krishṇa. He was afflicted with leprosy by the curse of his father and got cured by worshipping Mitra—the Sun-god. The deity asked him to fetch Maga Brahmins from Śakadvīpa ; as competent priests for conducting the Sun-worship were not locally available.

N. N. Vasu has copiously quoted from Maga-vyakti in his book, The Castes and Sects of Bengal (Vol. II). Maga-vyakti is written in Sanskrit by Krishṇadās Misra. It is stated that the Magas were divided into 12 Ādityas, 12 Maṇḍalas and 7 Arkas. Koṇa was a caste of the Arka class of Maga Brāhmins and had thus been highly praised by Krishṇadās Misra.

Magavyakti by Krishnadas Misra

"All the Maga Brahmans of Koṇāraka had achieved eminence. They lived by the sea and their heart was pure. The gods and sages used to offer worship to Koṇāraka (deity).

112. R.V. I, 22, 17.
"Vishnu seems to have been originally conceived as the Sun, not in his general character but as the swiftly moving luminary, which with vast strides traverses the three worlds". Macdonell, History of the Sanskrit Literature, p. 80.

113. Indian Theism, p. 34.

114. Early History of the Vaishnava Sect, p. 90.

The Koṇārakas were ontologists and followed the path of virtue. They devoted themselves to the worship of the god 'Chandraśekhara' (Śiva). The whole world was illuminated by the light of their fame."[115] The description is quoted as given in the text without any criticism, as nothing useful will come out of it.

Reference to Konarka in Sarala Mahabharata

Sāralā Dasa refers to Koṇārka in his Mahābhārata, which is the earliest reference to that place in Oriya literature. "Agastya said that the demon Arka was killed at the Agni-Koṇa (S. E. direction) of Jambūdvipa (India) by Sūrya-Nārāyaṇa. Towards the south (of that place) is the sea and the river Chandrabhāgā flows to the north of that place. The river Ganges (secretly) exists there with the accumulated virtue of all the holy places. Because the demon was killed at the Agni-Koṇa, the place became famous as Koṇārka".[116] In India, sanctity is conceived by the remoteness of antiquity and thus the epic hero Arjuna is made to exalt Purusottama and Koṇārka Kshetras.[117]

Abandonment of the Konarka Temple

According to the Jagannāth temple chronicles, the temple of Koṇārka was profaned by Kālāpāhāḍ and other Muhammadans. The Sun-temple is reported to have been abandoned in 1627-28 A. D., by order of Mukunda Deva II.[118] In this connection, we are tempted to quote Hunter's inimitable language :

"The Priests abandoned the desecrated shrine and migrated with their god to Puri. Certain it is, that the great shrine at

115. "History of the Brahmans of Sakadvipa"—The Castes & Sects of Bengal, Vol. II, pp. 83-84.

116. अगस्ति बोलन्ति जम्बुद्वीप अग्नि कोणे
अर्क दैत्य नाशिले विरञ्चि नारायणे ॥
दक्षिणे महोदधि उत्तरे चन्द्रभागा
कोटिए तीर्थ घेनि सेठारे छन्ति गङ्गा ॥

* * *

पृथ्वी अग्नि कोणे यहुँ दैत्य हेला हत
तेणु से कोणार्क नामे होइला विख्यात ॥

Santi Parva, Sarala Mbh.

117. Drona Parva, Sarala Mbh.

118. J. B. O. R. S., Vol. III. Pt. II—Article of M. M. Chakravarty.

Puri has a little temple to the Sun within its all-embracing walls and the exquisite polygonal tower which Abul Fazl mentions as outside the Koṇrak edifice now stands in front of the Lion-Gate of Jagannāth."[119]

The Aruṇa Pillar was brought to Puri, in the last quarter of the 18th century, by order of Brahmachāri Gossain—the religious head of the Marathas in Orissa.[120]

There is a small temple of Dharmarāja within the temple precincts of Jagannāth. The servitors of the temple point out the image of Dharmarāja, as the original image of Sūrya of Koārka. Mr. Nirmal Basu seeks to identify another image (which is within the Dharmarāja temple but is screened by Dharmarāja) with the lost Sūrya image of Koṇārka.[121]

The Sūrya temple at Koṇārka stands as the very culmination of aesthetic beauty. A spirit of loneliness reigns where life once vibrated with strong pulsation. Gone are those men who thought that the best appreciation of divinity lay in the cultivation of the sense of beauty.

Bhanu Deva I
1264-78

Narasiṁha I was succeeded by Bhānu Deva I. He filled up the river Bāṅki, which used to flow between the main temple and the Gunḍichā house, thus obstructing the Car-procession. Bhānu Deva is also credited with the construction of the bridge named Aṭharanālā.

Narasimha II
1278-1306

Narasiṁha II succeeded Bhānu Deva I to the throne. According to Narahari-Yati Stotra—a part of Stotra-Mahodadhi—Narahari Tīrtha acted as the regent of Narasiṁha II in Kaliṅga, while the king was a minor.[122] Copper plates of Narasiṁha II are discovered

119. Hunter's Orissa Vol. I, p. 200.

120. मरहट्टाङ्क गुरु ब्रह्मचारी गोसाईं······कोणार्क क्षेत्रर मुगुनि पथ्यर खम्ब आणि सिंघद्वार चकड़ारे रखाइले Madla Panji.

121. Konaraker Bibaran, p. 9.

122. See History of Orissa, Vol. I, p. 270 and Gaudiya, Vol. VI, No. 14.

at Kenduapatna in the Cuttack District. They are recorded in the Śaka years 1217-18.

Narasiṁha II was succeeded by Purusottama as is known from an inscription of Bhānu Deva II, which has been recently found. He ruled for seven years. R. D. Banerjee, however, considers him to be a usurper.[123] Bhānu Deva II (1313-1328) was a son of Narasiṁha II and his wife Chola Devi. After Bhānu Deva the following kings ascended the throne, viz., Narasiṁha III (1328-52), Bhānu Deva III (1352-78) and Narasiṁha IV (1379-1425). Narasiṁha IV was "the last known king of the Eastern Gaṅga dynasty". Five inscriptions of his time are found at Kūrmakshetra. "We know from the inscriptions at Śrī-Kurmam that Narasiṁha IV was recognized as the king of Orissa till the Śaka year 1346=1425 A. D."[124] According to the Pānji, the last king of his dynasty was Matta Bhānudeva or Bhānu Deva IV, who was succeeded by Kapilendra in 1435 A. D.

The Later Ganga Kings

The Vishnusvami And Sri Cults in Orissa

From the eleventh century A. D. Puri became a centre of the Vishṇusvāmi cult which was founded by Devatanu Vishṇusvāmi. Śrīdhar Svami, and Lakshmīdhar, the author of Śrīnāma Kaumudi, belonged to this sect. They lived at Puri at an uncertain date.[125]. Śrīdhar is famous for his Bhāvārtha Dipikā commentary of the Bhāgavata, in which he has quoted the opinion of Vishṇusvāmi in two places. (I. 7. 6 & III. 12. 2) According to a tradition, Śrīdhar's home was in Northern Orissa. There is a family at Mareijñā near Remuṇā in Balasore, which claims to be the descendants of Śrīdhar Svami.

123. History of Orissa, Vol. I, p. 280. Orissa in the Making, p. 203.

124. History of Orissa, Vol. I, p. 287.

125. Gaudiya Vol. IV No. 46 & Vol. VIII. No. 8. Hemadri of the 13th century A. D. has referred to the opinion of Sridhar Svami, in his commentary on Mukta-phala by Bopadeva. Thus Sridhar's floruit cannot be later than the 13th century.

Puri has a little temple to the Sun within its all-embracing walls and the exquisite polygonal tower which Abul Fazl mentions as outside the Koṇrak edifice now stands in front of the Lion-Gate of Jagannāth."[119]

The Aruṇa Pillar was brought to Puri, in the last quarter of the 18th century, by order of Brahmachāri Gossain—the religious head of the Marathas in Orissa.[120]

There is a small temple of Dharmarāja within the temple precincts of Jagannāth. The servitors of the temple point out the image of Dharmarāja, as the original image of Sūrya of Koārka. Mr. Nirmal Basu seeks to identify another image (which is within the Dharmarāja temple but is screened by Dharmarāja) with the lost Sūrya image of Koṇārka.[121]

The Sūrya temple at Koṇārka stands as the very culmination of aesthetic beauty. A spirit of loneliness reigns where life once vibrated with strong pulsation. Gone are those men who thought that the best appreciation of divinity lay in the cultivation of the sense of beauty.

Narasiṁha I was succeeded by Bhānu Deva I. He filled up the river Bāṅki, which used to flow between the main temple and the Guṇḍichā house, thus obstructing the Car-procession. Bhānu Deva is also credited with the construction of the bridge named Aṭharanālā.

Bhanu Deva I
1264-78

Narasiṁha II succeeded Bhānu Deva I to the throne. According to Narahari-Yati Stotra—a part of Stotra-Mahodadhi—Narahari Tīrtha acted as the regent of Narasiṁha II in Kaliṅga, while the king was a minor.[122] Copper plates of Narasiṁha II are discovered

Narasimha II
1278-1306

119. Hunter's Orissa Vol. I, p. 200.

120. मरहट्टाङ्क गुरु ब्रह्मचारी गोसाईं······कोणार्क क्षेत्रर मुगुनि पथर खम्ब आणि सिंहद्वार चकडारे रखाइले Madla Panji.

121. Konaraker Bibaran, p. 9.

122. See History of Orissa, Vol. I, p. 270 and Gaudiya, Vol. VI, No. 14.

at Kenduapatna in the Cuttack District. They are recorded in the Śaka years 1217-18.

The Later Ganga Kings

Narasiṁha II was succeeded by Purusottama as is known from an inscription of Bhānu Deva II, which has been recently found. He ruled for seven years. R. D. Banerjee, however, considers him to be a usurper.[123] Bhānu Deva II (1313-1328) was a son of Narasiṁha II and his wife Chola Devi. After Bhānu Deva the following kings ascended the throne, viz., Narasiṁha III (1328-52), Bhānu Deva III (1352-78) and Narasiṁha IV (1379-1425). Narasiṁha IV was "the last known king of the Eastern Gaṅga dynasty". Five inscriptions of his time are found at Kūrmakshetra. "We know from the inscriptions at Śrī-Kurmam that Narasiṁha IV was recognized as the king of Orissa till the Śaka year 1346=1425 A. D."[124] According to the Pānji, the last king of his dynasty was Matta Bhānudeva or Bhānu Deva IV, who was succeeded by Kapilendra in 1435 A. D.

The Vishnusvami And Sri Cults in Orissa

From the eleventh century A. D. Puri became a centre of the Vishṇusvāmi cult which was founded by Devatanu Vishṇusvāmi. Śrīdhar Svami, and Lakshmīdhar, the author of Śrīnāma Kaumudi, belonged to this sect. They lived at Puri at an uncertain date.[125]. Śrīdhar is famous for his Bhāvārtha Dīpikā commentary of the Bhāgavata, in which he has quoted the opinion of Vishṇusvāmi in two places. (I. 7. 6 & III. 12. 2) According to a tradition, Śrīdhar's home was in Northern Orissa. There is a family at Mareijñā near Remuṇā in Balasore, which claims to be the descendants of Śrīdhar Svami.

123. History of Orissa, Vol. I, p. 280. Orissa in the Making, p. 203.

124. History of Orissa, Vol. I, p. 287.

125. Gaudiya Vol. IV No. 46 & Vol. VIII. No. 8. Hemadri of the 13th century A. D. has referred to the opinion of Sridhar Svami, in his commentary on Mukta-phala by Bopadeva. Thus Sridhar's floruit cannot be later than the 13th century.

But the family records, supporting such a claim, are now lost.[126]

The sectarian Mantras of the Vishṇusvāmi sect are, "Om Rāma-Krishṇāya namah" and "Om Rāma-Krishṇa Hari." It is to be noticed that the name of Rāma precedes the name of Hari. The Mantra of sixteen namas (consisting of 8 Hari, 4 Rāma, and 4 Krishṇa words) prevailed in Orissa, even before the Chaitanya Age. The names of Rāma were placed before the names of Krishṇa. Later on, Krishṇa turned the tables. Jagannātha Dasa, the author of the Oriya Bhāgavata, has followed the interpretations of Śrīdhar Svami. This fact has been acknowledged in the last canto of Jagannātha's book.

The Influence of Ramanuja

Rāmānuja's influence upon the religious opinion of Orissa did not wholly die out. From the 12th century A. D. Jagannāth was considered exclusively as a Vishṇuite deity.

Lakshmī was invoked for benediction in the inscriptions of the Gaṅga kings. Yaśobhañja, the son of Rāyabhañja II, described himself as a Śrī Vaishṇava. Ālālnāth and Kūrmanāth received increased attention of the Vaishṇavas.

As Jagannāth was identified with Vishṇu, the incarnations of that deity now enjoyed the full glare of publicity. The Tortoise, Nrisiṁha or Man-Lion, Parśurāma and Boar incarnations were highly honoured by the Gaṅga and early Solar kings. Krishṇa was regarded only as an incarnation of Vishṇu.

Sāralā Dasa, a contemporary of Kapilendra Deva, constantly invoked Jagannāth for benediction, in his translation of the Mahābhārata in Oriya. "But the poet has painted the character of Krishṇa in a contemptible light in many places of his book."[127]. He would have certainly hesitated, had he not thought of Krishṇa as merely a Vishṇuite incarna-

126. See Utkal Sahitya, Sravan 1309 & The Vaitarani Vol, III. No. 2.

127. Sarala Dasa Charit—Mrityunjaya Rath, p. 84.

tion, while Jagannāth was to him the embodiment of the Absolute Being.

The increased influence of Lakshmi led to the introduction of new festivals in the Jagannāth temple, like "Herā Pañchami" and "Chandana Yātrā."

CHAPTER III.

"THE HISTORY OF VAISHNAVISM IN ORISSA UNDER KAPILENDRA DEVA AND PURUSHOTTAMA"

Unlike the Gaṅga kings, Kapilendra Deva was "a genuine son of the soil of Orissa with Oriya for his speech." It was during the shortlived dynastic rule of the Solar kings that "Orissa attained the highest glory in all directions."[128]

The temple archives record a story which accounts for the accession of Kapilendra Deva. It is stated that Jagannāth informed the son-less king Mattabhānudeva to nominate as his successor that person who lived upon the remains of Jagannāth's oblations, left in the discarded earthen pots. That man was no other than Kapila—a Kshatriya scion of the Solar family (Sūrya-Vaṁsa). The Raja met him near the temple of Vimalā and was struck by his manly appearance. Kapila was appointed as a retainer. Further promotions came in quick succession and he became a minister—after a successful treaty negotiation with a Muslim chief, possibly a Sultan of the Bahmani kingdom.

The Story of Kapilendra Deva's Accession

R. D. Banerjee, on the other hand, makes the prosaic statement that Kapilendra, the minister of the last Gaṅga king, effected a *coup-d'etat* after the king's death. "Kapilendra's inscription shows his reign to have begun in Śaka year 1356 or A. D. 1434-35". [129] Obviously, we can not fully rely upon Mādlā Pānji. Nevertheless the general purport of the story possibly embodies truth. Kapilendra was perhaps accepted as the nominee of Jagannāth and this divine selection might have made the coup an easy task.

128. Orissa in the Making, p. 212.

129. See "The Eastern Ganga Kings of Orissa." J. A. S. B., 1903

According to a tradition, Kapilendra built the outer wall of the Jagannāth temple.[130] R. D. Banerjee mentions some of the inscriptions of Kapilendra, incised on the temple-walls of Jagannāth.[131] The first inscription records that the Gajapati "came to worship Jagannāth and ordered exemption of the tax on salt and cowrie shells." The second one informs that the king made a gift of a number of utensils and ornaments "out of the devotion to the lotus-feet of Lord Jagannāth." "A supply of gold was brought by a number of officers and placed with other offerings in the audience-hall." Another inscription orders for the performance of the dances at the time of the evening dhupa up to the time of Baḍa-Singāra (bed time). Besides dancing, four Vaishṇava singers will sing from Jaydeva's Gita-Govinda. In another inscription, the king gives vent to his feelings :

Kapilendra's Devotion to Jagannath

"O Jagannāth, thou knowest everything of mine, both external and internal. Whatever precious things I have, I will bestow upon the Brahmanas as much as I can." "Thus he humbles himself before Jagannāth."[132] A rebellion of minor importance occurred in the reign of Kapilendra. Some of the rebel Zamindars were helped by the king's officers.

Kapilendra expresses his wrath before Jagannāth. "I will treat them as they deserve. Lord Jagannāth, judge the correctness or incorrectness of mine (actions)."

These temple-inscriptions of Kapilendra shed light on the history of Jagannāth. The king succeeds to the throne, on the recommendation of Jagannāth. He freely invokes divine curse for his purpose—"whoever violateth this, rebeleth against Jagannāth." (Jagannāthaṅka droha karai). The temple was enriched by lavish gifts of utensils and ornaments of gold. Jagannāth was now honoured

The Increased Influence of Jagannath

130. This fact has also been mentioned in a copy of the Madla Panji, quoted in Types of Ancient Oriya Prose and Poetry.
131. History of Orissa, I, pp. 300-01.
132. "Uriya Inscriptions of the 15th and 16th Century," M.M. Chakravarty, J.A.S.B., 1893 No. I.

as the State-deity of Orissa and enjoyed a share in the spoils. The situation was different when the Eastern Gaṅga kings ruled over Orissa. Jagannāth did not monopolise their attention, as these kings did not depend upon Jagannāth's dispensation for their claims on the throne. But Kapilendra and his son Purushottama had that necessity, and thus there was a closer relation between the political head of the State and the State-deity.

The reference to Gita-Govinda in the inscription of Kapilendra is interesting. The book received an early ovation in Orissa though Rādhā-idea, the quintessence of its theme, was not popular in the Pre-Chaitanya Age. According to a tradition, a king named Purushottama composed a new Gīta-Govinda to excel the original one.[133] There is some difficulty in identifying the aforesaid king Purushottama, if we accept the story of rivalry to be true. Mr. Bhagavan Pati has written a series of articles in "Sahakār" (Vol. X) proving that Jaydeva was an Oriya by birth, as has been mentioned in Sanskrit Bhakta-mālā. (Canto XXXIX). He seeks to identify Purushottama, the author of Abhinava Gīta-Govinda, with Rājarāja II, the son of Choḍagaṅga. The Pānji indeed refers to such a name of Rājarāja II. But there was another Purushottama of the Gaṅga dynasty, who ruled before Bhānu Deva II. Thus the task of identification is not an easy affair.

Gita Govinda and King Purushottama

Later on, an inscription of Pratāprudra insisted that the female dancers and the four Vaishṇava singers of the temple will sing no other song than "Gita-Govinda of Barathākur."[134]

Kapilendra was succeeded by his son Purushottama Deva in 1464 A. D. Though he had eighteen (!) legitimate sons, he selected the illegitimate son (Phul-bibāhi putra) Purushottama for the throne. It is told that Jagannāth himself recommended him to the king through dream.

Purushottama Deva 1464-97

As usual, there is a story behind Purushottama's accession.

133. See Dardhyata Bhakti—Rama Dasa.

134. "Uriya Inscriptions of the 15th and 16th Century." J. A. S. B. 1893

The version of Gaṅgavaṁsānucharita has a touch of romance and narrates the complete story, which is not to be found in the Pānji. The legitimate sons questioned the dispensation of Jagannāth, in favour of Purushottama. They demanded that Purushottama must undergo an ordeal to prove that he was the "chosen one". Purushottama agreed and on the appointed day he stood before them unarmed, calmly reciting the name of the Lord. The brothers hurled deadly weapons aiming at him, but by divine grace Purushottama remained unscathed. The brothers then resigned to their fate without further protest. They left their ancestral home to seek their fortune elsewhere.

Story of The Ordeal

Recently there is a growing feeling among the Oriya scholars that Purushottama of the Solar dynasty was not a bastard. They are of opinion that Purushottama the dāsi-putra was really the son of Kapila-Bhānudeva I.[135] The weak point of the argument is that it can not be made to square with the evidence of the inscription of Bhānudeva II. Purushottama of the inscription ascended the throne, after Narasiṁha II, and not after Narasiṁha's father Bhānu Deva I. Moreover, other sons of Narasiṁha II were not disinherited and Bhānu Deva II was a lawful heir to the throne.

Was Purushottama Really Illegitimate?

It is stated in Gaṅgavaṁśānucharita that Hamira Deva was the disinherited eldest son of Kapilendra. Raja of Tekkali has edited the Oruganti Copper-plate of "Amviradeva Kumar Mahapatra". By astronomical calculation he finds the date of the copper-plate to be 1459 A. D.[136] The date of Purushottama's accession to the throne is, as already stated, 1464 A. D.[137]

Hamira Deva.

135. Raja of Tekkali—Sahakara, Vol. XV, Nos. 9 & 10. Gopavandhu Vidyabhusan—Prachi, Vol. II, pt. I.

136. Sahakara, Vol. XVII, No. 9. Firishta states that Ambar Rai, a son of Kapilendra, sought the assistance of the Bahmani Sultan Muhammad III to gain the throne.

137. According to R. D. Banerjee, Purushottama ascended the throne in 1470 A. D. But the date given in The Historical Inscriptions of S. India seems to be more probable and is mentioned above.

Purushottama is famous as the hero of the Kāñchī episode. He was anxious to marry Padmāvatī, the beautiful princess of Kāñchī. But the Raja of Kāñchī refused to marry his daughter to the Maharaja of Orissa "because the Maharajas were in habit of performing the duties of sweeper (Chandāla) before the image of Jagannāth, on its being brought forth from the temple annually at Ratha-Jatra."

The Kanchi Episode.

The Kāñchī king was a devoted worshipper of Gaṇeśa and had no respect for Jagannāth. Naturally he misunderstood the Gajapati's duty as sweeper of Jagannāth.

"The Gajapati monarch became very wroth at the refusal and swore that to revenge the slight cast at him he would obtain the damsel by force and marry her to a real sweeper. He accordingly marched with a large army but was forced to retire."[138] The Gajapati now sought the assistance of Jagannāth "to avenge the insult offered to the deity himself in the person of his worshipper." Assured of divine help the king marched again. At Māṇikapātaṇā a milkmaid named Māṇika appeared before the king and produced a ring which, she said, was deposited by two generals of the king. Mounted on horseback they were accompanying the expedition; and being thirsty they purchased curd from her and gave the ring in lieu of the price. They asked her to get the price from the king in exchange of the ring. The king could easily guess from the ring that these generals were no other than Jagannāth and Balarām themselves. The king marched forward and inflicted a crushing defeat on the Kāñchī monarch. It is said that Jagannāth and Balarām assisted in storming the citadel of Kāñchī. The jewelled throne of Kāñchī monarch was taken away as the trophy and dedicated to Jagannāth. The princess was brought to Puri and Purushottama intended to marry her to a sweeper. But a story of romance forbids such an unpleasant conclusion and eventually the princess was given

138. Sterling's Orissa, p. 129.

away in marriage to the king—while he was acting as a sweeper during the Car-festival.

In spite of the supernatural elements, the story undoubtedly contains a good deal of truth, though some of the informations supplied by the story do not stand historical scrutiny. At this point it may not be out of place to examine the Kāñchi episode critically.

(1) The Ratnavedi

According to the story, the golden throne of Kāñchi was dedicated to Jagannāth. The dais of Jagannāth contains "the bizarre arabesque of the decadent Hoysala type."[139]

(2) The Representation Of The Divine Horsemen

"The incidents of the Kāñchi-Kāverī expedition were recorded in the Mādlā Pānji. It is on a wall of the audience-hall of the temple of Puri that the pictorial representation of the incident appears."[140] These wall-representations were depicted probably by order of Purushottama himself. In Vedā-Parikramā of Balarāma Dasa we come across the following lines "After (visiting) this, you will find the representations of the two brothers galloping valiantly towards Kāñchi up to the Kāveri—on the walls of the Jagamohana."[141]

(3) The Matrimonial Relation With The Kanchi King

Pratāprudra in his book Sarasvatī-Vilāsa mentions that his mother's name was Rupāmvikā and Padmāvatī was the name of one of his wives. In the Anantavaram inscription of the same king,[142] we find that his father Purushottama vanquished

139. History of Orissa, Vol. I, p. 316.

140. B. C. Majumdar: "The Early Oriya Writers," Ashutosh Jubilee, Vol. III.

141. एथु अनन्तरे जगमोहनरे देखिब वेनि भाइङ्कि
वीर ये घोड़ारे चढ़िण सत्वरे काञ्चि कावेरि पाइङ्कि

Balarama Dasa lived in the reigns of Purushottama and Prataprudra.

142. See the Article of S. N. Rajguru—Utkal Sahitya, Pousa 1337. Purushottama sacked Kanchi or Conjevaram in 1464 or 1469 A. D. (Historical Inscriptions of S. India, p. 224) Nrisimha is evidently Saluva Narasimha who ruled in the Arcot district under the Vijayanagara kings.

Nrisiṁha—the king of the Karṇāṭa country. (Nrisiṁha nripati karṇāṭa deśādhavah) Popular tradition names the Kāñchi king Kalevara.[143]

The Udaygiri (in the Nellore district) inscription of Krishṇa-deva Rāya (reign—1510—c. 1530 A. D.) records his victory over Pratāprudra in the Śaka year 1436-1514 A. D. Tirumalappa Raya,[144] the uncle of the Gajapati, was taken into custody. Tarini Charan Rath opines that "this Tirumalappa Raya was obviously a maternal uncle of the Orissan king."[145]

(4) The Conquest Of Vidyanagara

The Anantavaram inscription states that Vidyānagari was "the city of the king of Karṇāṭa" (stanza 8). Purusottama discomfited king Nrisiṁha of Karṇāṭa (stanza 13). Purusottama brought the image of Gopala from Vidyānagar as a trophy.[146] Vidyānagari or Vidyānagar was the old name of Vijayanagara. Purushottama probably plundered this city. It is clear that the Karṇāṭa expedition of Purushottama formed the kernel of the romance.

Purushottama's Devotion to Jagannath.

Purushottama was a devout worshipper of Jagannāth. "If the Mādlā Pānji is to be believed, Purushottama erected the Bhoga-maṇḍapa or the Hall of refection being in fact the third Maṇḍapa in the temple of Jagannāth."[147] Some of his inscriptions are incised on the temple-walls of Jagannāth. Purushottama advises the kings of Orissa—as long as the world lasts—"to make gifts to the Brahmaṇas with peaceful and attentive mind."

The usual curse is laid down for those who will not comply with this advice. In another temple-inscription, he bestows land "for the festival etc. of other gods, goddesses and

143. See Kanchi-Kaveri by Kapilesvara Vidyabhusan.

144. The name is given as "Tirumalkanti *alias* Raghava Raya" in Sewel and Aiyangar's The Historical Inscriptions of Southern India, p. 239.

145. J. B. O. R. S. Vol. V, pt I.

146. Chaitanya Bhagavat, II, 6.

147. History of Orissa, Vol. I, p. 319.

Mahādeva." "He will be a rebel against Jagannāth—who takes away these gifts."[148]

In the prologue of his book, Abhinava Veṇīsaṁharaṇam, the king offers homage to the feet of Nārāyaṇa. In his Drākshārām inscription he styles himself the devout worshipper of Vishṇu, the Boar of the earth (Dharaṇi-Varāha) and the worshipper of the feet of Rāmachandra.[149]

The Piety of Purushottama.

148. "Uriya Inscriptions of the 15th and 16th Century A. D."—J. A. S. B. 1893. No. 1.

149. Utkal Sahitya—Article of S. N. Rajguru, Pous 1337.

CHAPTER IV

RELIGIOUS CONDITION OF ORISSA ON THE EVE OF THE CHAITANYA AGE

We are now approaching the Chaitanya Age which culminated in the final triumph of the cult of Rādhā-Krishṇa. The Gaṅga kings and the kings of the Solar dynasty in the fifteenth century, worshipped the deities without discrimination and this eclecticism left indelible impress on the 16th century Vaishṇavism in Orissa.

Worship of the Incarnations of Vishnu

Nrisimha

The incarnations of Vishṇu had their due share in royal devotion. In Gaṅga-Vaṁsānucharita of Vāsudeva Rath, who flourished about four hundred years ago, king Narasiṁha I had been described as the incarnation of Man-Lion. (Narasiṁhāvatāra). The evidence of Narasiṁha I's devotion to Man-Lion is borne by an inscription in the Nrisiṁha temple at Simāchalam. The king built the Dancing-hall and another Maṇḍapa of the temple in 1267-68 A. D. Narahari Tīrtha, the regent of Narasiṁha II in Kaliṅga, reared the temple of Yogānanda Nri-Siṁha at Śrī-Kūrmam. One of his inscriptions is incised on the temple-wall of Lakshmī-Nrisiṁha at Simāchalam.

Kurma

The temple of Kūrma at Śrī-Kūrmam gradually became the chief Vishṇuite shrine in Kaliṅga. Narahari Tīrtha was a patron of this temple. Several inscriptions in that temple record gifts by him. Viśvanātha, a feudatory of Bhānu Deva II, "gave forty coins to Vishṇu in Kūrmakshetra." The temple also enjoyed the royal beneficence, as has been attested by several votive records. Bhānu Deva III presented the image of his father Narasiṁha III and of his step-mother to the Kūrma temple.

Narahari Tīrtha, the regent of Narasiṁha II, obtained the

images of Rāma and Sitā from the treasury of Kaliṅga and sent them to his Guru Ānanda Tīrtha—better known as Maddhācharya—the founder of the Māddha sect of Vaishṇavism. A temple of Rāma-Chaṇḍī has been unearthed near the Koṇārka temple. Legends of Rāma worship are prevalent in Orissa, as elsewhere. It is stated that Rāma, while on his way back to Ayodhyā after the rescue of Sitā, had to break the journey at a pleasant (ramaṇīya) spot, as Sitā experienced menses. She wished for a bath, and in the absence of a river Rāma pierced the soil seven times by his arrows. A river appeared which was named the Saptaśarā. The place was subsequently known as Remuṇā. Rāma worshipped the local Chaṇḍī and Śiva images which were renamed Rāmachaṇḍī and Rāmeśvar Śiva respectively.[150] Achyutānanda in his Śūnyasaṁhitā (canto XI) refers to Daṇḍakāraṇya, situated to the east of the river Prāchī.

Rama

According to the tradition, Vishṇu was propitiated by Brahmā, when the Vedas were stolen, by performing Aśwamedha sacrifice. After the ceremony, Vishṇu came out of the sacrificial altar in the form of a Boar and recovered the Vedas. That place of sacrifice was subsequently known as "Jajñiyapura" or Jajpur. Kāśī Misra, the preceptor of Pratāprudra, reared a temple of Varāha at Jajpur. Chaitanya, on his way to Puri, visited the deity.[151]

Boar

Kapilendra Deva composed Paraśurāma-Vijaya drama. The stage manager of the play states that the king was an incarnation of Paraśurāma and "thus cherishes great love for the god Paraśurāma."[152]

Parasurama

Keśava has been mentioned as the friend of the Gopa's, in the Megheśvara temple inscription.

Kesava

150. Gopinath Charitamrita—Vinod Chaitanya Das.
151. Chaitanya Bhagavata, 11. 5
152. The Prachi, Vol. III, pt. 2.

SAIVISM IN THE 15TH CENTURY ORISSA

Śaivism was by no means a dying faith in the 15th century Orissa. Śiva temples of Parśurāmeśvara, Bhāskareśvara, Brahmeśvara, Mukteśvara and Liṅgarāja were already old by this time. Svapneśvar Deva, the brother-in-law of Rajaraja II, reared the temple of Megheśvara. Govinda, the minister of Anaṅgabhima II, built the Chhāteśvara temple in the district of Cuttack. Anaṅgabhima III was a devotee of Liṅgarāja, which is known from his three inscriptions discovered on the temple-walls of Liṅgarāja. [153] The chief queen of Bhānudeva I gave land to Bhimeśvar Śiva at Drākshārām in the Godavari District.[154] An inscription of Narasiṁha IV, found at Math Tiramali, begins with a salutation to Śiva.[155]

Sāralā Dasa, the contemporary of Kapilendra, refers to several Śiva images in his Mahābhārata. He refers to

Siva images mentioned in Sarala Mbh.

Uttareśvara on the river Murāj (Ādya Parva), Yamveśvara (Ādya Parva) and Mārkaṇḍeśvara at Puri (Mushali Parva) and to Nācheśvara image at Ekāmra Tīrtha (Bhuvanesvar). He also mentions the eight Śiva images on the banks of the river Prāchi. (Mushali Parva)

Kapilendra Deva continued the traditional eclecticism of

Saivism under the Solar Kings–Kapilendra

the Orissan kings. At Muṇṇur in South Arcot, land was granted for the oblation and necessary repairs of two Śiva temples.[156] The Gajapati granted land for maintaining proper service of Liṅgarāja and recorded this fact on the jamb of the western doorway of the temple. Liṅgarāja has been addressed as the god Bhuvaneśvar.

King Purushottama reverently speaks of the festival in honour of the goddess Durgā, in his book Abhinava-Veṇī-

Purushottama.

saṁharaṇam. The Potāvaram grant of the king informs about the gift of the village Potāvaram to Liṅgodbhava Mahādeva—"for the purpose of

153. History of Orissa, Vol. I, pp. 261-62
154. "The Draksharam Ins. of Alla Devi"—Sahakara, XVIII. No. 3
155. "The Inscription of Narasimha IV", J. A. S. B. 1895.
156. History of Orissa, I, p. 294.

personal enjoyment, stage entertainments and other splendours of the god."[157]

Mention has already been made of the Śākta goddess Vimalā. Virajā of Jajpur was already famous by the 14th century A. D. and she has been extolled by Sāralā Dasa.[158] He also mentions these four Śākta goddesses, namely, Vāseli, Charchikā, Ugratārā and Dākeśvari.[159] Vāseli is near Patāmuṇḍi and Charchikā is at Bāṅki, both in the district of Cuttack.

Saktism in the 15th Century.

Sāralā Dasa received inspiration from Sāralā Chaṇḍi of Jhankaḍ. In this connection it is significant to note that the poet describes this decidedly Śākta goddess as a Vishṇuite deity.[160]

Sāralā Chaṇḍi has been conceived as a Bhairavī and the destroyer of the demon Mahishāsura.[161]

LATER BUDDHISM IN ORISSA

Buddhism, on the other hand, was in moribund condition in the 15th Century Orissa. It suffered more from assimilation by Hinduism than from persecution. The Buddhists drifted towards Hinduism, when they found elements of Buddhistic principles within the four corners of Hinduism. The Vishṇuite faith particularly attracted them, as Jagannāth was identified with Buddha. The temple-chronicles have indeed mentioned a story of persecution of the Buddhists.

Buddhism in the 15th Century Orissa.

The Buddhists, it has been stated, lived in the rock-cut caves during the reign of Madana Mahādeva, the brother of Anaṅgabhima Deva. One day the king had a heated discus-

157. History of Orissa Vol. I, p. 316.
158. Sarala Mahabharata, Drona Parva.
159. *Ibid.*
160. "उत्तरे फक्कड नामे अछि ग्रामखरिड
विजे तहिं माहेश्वरी श्रीसारलाचरिड
महा योगेश्वरी सेहि परम वैष्णवी"
Sarala Mbh. Adya Parva.
Jhankad is situated near the sea in the district of Cuttack.
161. Vilanka Ramayana—Sarala Dasa.

sion with his queen. She espoused the cause of the Buddhists who, in her opinion, were omniscient. The king claimed omniscience for the Brahmins. "It was at last determined to make another formal trial of their relative skill as men of science and magicians. Accordingly, a snake was put secretly into an earthen jar, the mouth of which being covered up, the vessel was produced in a great assembly at that place. Both the parties were then asked what the jar contained."[162] The Buddhists with their superior knowledge of occult art could correctly guess the existence of the snake within the jar. The Brahmins declared that the vessel contained nothing but a heap of ashes. The lid was subsequently uncovered and the prediction of the Brahmins was found to be true. The king ordered the massacre of the Buddhists. Sterling opines that this Raja was Pratāprudra.

The Account of Iswara Dasa.

This story is also mentioned in Chaitanya Bhāgavata by Īśwara Dasa—which was composed towards the end of the sixteenth or in the beginning of the next century. It is stated that the Buddhists numbered seven hundred in the reign of the Keśarī kings,[163] one of whom killed 616 of them. The remnants found a patron in Padmāvatī, the queen of Anaṅgabhīma. The king sided with the Brahmins. The trial of the snake within the jar then followed. Thirty-two of the Buddhists were clubbed to death and the surviving few fled to Bāṅki and took shelter in the caves of the Mahā-Parvata hill. The Buddhists were looked down as "unbelievers in the Vedas." The leader of the Buddhists was Vīrasiṁha, whose career will be discussed in the end of this chapter.

Buddhist Śarākis even now live at village Ragaḍi near

162. Sterling's Orissa, p. 132. Sterling has not strictly followed the version of the Panji. He adds that the Raja destroyed all the writings of the Buddhists except the MSS. of Virasimha and Amarasimha.

163. सात शत आनबौद केशरी राजा सङ्गे बाद

Chaitanya Bhagavata, Chap. III.

Bāṅki, Nuāpatnā in Tigiria State and at village Māniābandha in Barambā State, which are all near the Mahāparvata hill. Bāṅki Government Estate is in the district of Cuttack. The Śāstra of the Śarākis shows that their ancestors lived at Nandigrām in the Burdwan district (Bardhamāna Śarāka Deśa). These ancestors came to Puri, perhaps as a result of the Muhammadan persecution, in the reign of Gajapati Pratāprudra. The Buddhists (Bauddhaputra) were worsted in the trial of the snake-within-the-jar and only a few escaped with their lives.

The Buddhists of Orissa of he present days.

M. M. Haraprasad Sastri, first of all, drew the attention of the scholars regarding the Śarākis, who are weavers by profession. "The Śarāki Tantis," he writes, "who not only inhabit the Tributary mahals of Cuttack, but are to be found in the settled districts of Cuttack and Puri, still worship Buddha along with the Brahminic gods in all their religious ceremonies and the word Śarāki is simply a Prakrit form of the word Śrāvaka. The Sarākis are to be found in Bankura and Burdwan too."[164] Thus the history of the Śarākis indicates an early immigration of Buddhist monks from Bengal. Their surnames, *viz.*, Dutta, Bardhan, Chanda, Dev, Nandi, etc. are unmistakably of Bengali origin. Barring that they are now Oriyas in every sense.

Systems of Buddhist philosophy prevailed in Orissa in modified forms. Mādhurī Dasa, a young Vaishṇava cenobite, learnt Nāgāntaka and Yogāntaka philosophy from his preceptor. Nāgāntaka has been identified with the Svābhāvika School, "which is a later development of the Mādhyamika School inaugurated by Nāgārjuna."[165] The Yogāntaka School, according to N. N. Vasu, was "a compromise between the ancient Yogāchāra and the Vedāntā philosophy.[166] Buddhist philosophy was studied by the Vaishṇavas like Mādhurī Dasa. Krishṇa himself is said to

Nagantaka and Yogantaka Philosophy of Buddhism

164. Introduction, Modern Buddhism in Orissa.

165. Modern Buddhism in Orissa, p 124

166. Modern Buddhism in Orissa, p. 123

have expounded Nāgānta (ka) and Yogānta (ka) philosophy.[167] Virasiṁha, the exponent of Nāgānta philosophy, is stated to be a devotee of Krishṇa.

But in the sixteenth century, Buddhist philosophy was regarded to be an occult art. Nāgāntaka and Yogāntaka theories were placed in the same category with the Tāntric principles of expelling and killing.[168] It is also admitted that the knowledge of Nāgānta philosophy is sham and does not lead to salvation.[169] Gradually, the Buddhists of Orissa began to worship the Vishṇuite gods such as Nrisiṁha and Jagannāth.

The Siddhacharyas in Orissa

Like the Śaivite and Buddhistic deities, the Siddhācharyas too were adored in Orissa. The list of Siddhācharyas is quite fanciful and both Buddhistic and Nāthist Gurus are included. The Siddhācharyas are conventionally 84 in number. The list is found in the Tengur texts of Tibet, Java texts and in Varṇana Ratnākara of Kaviśekhara Jyotirīśvara.

The Oriya tradition refers to the following Siddhāchāryas:—

Hāḍipā, Kānhupā, Tantipā, Chowrangināth, Gorakshanāth, Matsyendranāth and Lui.

Hadipa.

The real name of Hāḍipā was Vālapāda or Jālandharnāth.[170] Thus he was a Nāthist Guru. He has been mentioned in the following books in Oriya :—

1. Govinda Chandra Tikā—ascribed to Yaśovanta Mallika of the 16th century.

167. श्रीहरि करुणा येणु साधु ब्रह्मज्ञान ॥
प्रभुङ्क श्रीमुखुं आज्ञा होइछि माधुरी
नागान्त वेदान्त ये योगान्त आदि करि ॥

Sunya Samhita, XI.

168. तारण मारण नागान्तक योगान्तक—Sunya Samhita, XI.

169. नागान्ति बिधा पढि छथ भक्ति
एमाने लोढि न पाइवे गति ॥

—Ibid.

170. Govinda Chandra Gita—Durlabh Mallik. See also, "The legend of Raja Gopinath"—Gopal Haldar. Proceedings of the 6th Oriental Conference.

2. Tikā Govinda Chandra—The author Uddhava Dasa has not taken the trouble of informing about his floruit. Hāḍipā was cursed by Brahmā, to live the life of a scavenger.[171]

The name of Hāḍipā is inseparably associated with that of Raja Gopichānd or Govindachandra. This Raja flourished probably in Eastern Bengal, on the eve of the Muhammadan conquest. But "Gopichand remains as obscure as ever—nothing could have made him survive in folk-memory but for his renunciation and connection above all, with great Nātha-Siddhas".[172] The story of his renunciation is popular in Orissa. The mendicants of the Yogi caste sing that story, while playing on 'Kendrā' (an indigenous musical instrument). The genealogical table, according to the Oriya version, is as follows :—

Raja Gopichandra.

Ripuchandra=Muktā Devī
|
Godamā=Govinda Chandra=Rodamā
(Guṇavatī) (Rūpavatī)

Muktādei asked her son to renounce the worldly pleasures which are but transitory. She cited the instance of Govinda's father. "All the elephants and horses and the beautiful dresses formerly belonged to thy father. But alas, my son ! at the time of his death he expired on a wretched couch."[173] She advised him to serve as a disciple, the scavenger who daily cleansed the palace-latrine.[174]

Dr. D. C. Sen has labelled few lines from this book as the Mayurbhanj ballad and has arbitrarily included them in Vanga Sahitya Parichaya, Pt. I. The king was at first unwilling. But he soon discovered that Hāḍipā was not a common man.

171. Govinda Chandra Tika, p. 7.

172. The legend of Raja Gopichand—Gopal Haldar.

173. एहि हाति घोड़ा एहि पाट योड़ा
तोहरि वापर थिला
मरि गला वेले गोविन्द चन्द्रे
छिड़ा पलङ्करे गला A Ballad

174. Govinda Chandra Tika, p. 6

Sixty-four Siddhas came down from the sky to meet him. Forthwith he became the disciple of Hāḍipā.

Kanhupa.

Kānhupā is curiously stated to be the Guru of Hāḍipā, as Hāḍipā says to Muktā Dei.[175] In Gorakshavijay of Sheikh Faizulla Marhum, Kānhupā is described as the disciple of Hāḍipā.[176] Kānhupā or Krishṇācharya is mentioned in the Tibetan Tengur, and Varṇanaratnākara.[177]

Chowranginath.

Chowrangināth came down from the sky along with Matsyendranāth, to witness the occult powers of Hāḍipā.[178]

Tantipa.

Chowrangināth and Tantipā are mentioned in Varṇanaratnākara. He challenged Gorakshanāth to a trial of occult feats but had to admit defeat.[179]

Gorakshanath.

The prince among the Nāthas was Gorakshanāth (to be mentioned hereinafter as G. N.). M. M. Haraprasad Sastri agrees with Wassiljew, who proves from Tibetan sources that G. N. flourished in the 9th century A. D.[180]

In his book Haṭha-yoga Pradīpaka G. N. expounded the principles of Haṭha-yoga, which "deals with strange bodily postures, purification of the channels of the body, modes of breath-regulation and exercises in which posture, breathing and attention are combined."[181]

G. N. has been mentioned in the following Oriya books.

1. The Mbh. of Sāralā Dasa—floruit, the 15th century.

2. Śūnya Saṁhitā—Achyutānanda Dasa—floruit, the 16th century.

175. Govinda Chandra Tika, p. 29.
176. Goraksha Vijay, p. 10.
177. Bangiya Sahitya Parishad magazine, 1329 B. S. No. I.
178. "मत्सेन्द्र चउरङ्गीनाथ मिलि गले भासि"
Govinda Chandra Tika, p. 10.
179. Tika Govinda Chandra, pp. 59-60.
180. J. B. O. R. S. Vol. V, pt. IV.
181. Outlines of the Religious Literature of India, p. 253.

3. Govinda Chandra Tīkā.

4. Parache Gitā—Dvārakā Dasa—floruit, the 17th century.

5. Chaitanya Bhāgavata—Īśwara Dasa—floruit, possibly first half of the 17th century.

6. Saptāṅga Yogasāra—ascribed to Balarāma Dasa of the 16th century.

G. N. has been represented as the Guru of Muktā Dei and the foremost Siddha among the sixty-four, which is the conventional number for the Siddhas in Orissan tradition.

G. N. was deified, before the time of Sāralā Dasa. Nakula of the Epic met him at 'Kadali' forest. G. N. said, "Hark thee my son. An Avadhūta I am, of the name of Gorekh. Ādyanath belongeth to the clan of Nirañjana (Nirañjana Gotrī). His disciple is Matsyendranāth. Knowest thou, that I am the disciple of Matsyendranāth. Thus before thee, I disclose the account of mine heritage."[182]

Reference to G. N. in Sarala Mbh.

Nakula fell at G. N.'s feet and solicited the knowledge of Yoga. "G. N. imparted the knowledge of 'stambhana' (suppression of a faculty of body by muscular process). He explained how internal air was to be drawn upwards and how motionless air was to be inhaled."[183] Śakuni, the notorious dice player, calls G. N. the Siddha to mind for Siddhi *i.e.* success.[184] He invokes the Siddha again, while handing over the dice (to Yudhisṭhira).[185]

Mādhurī Dasa, a young Vaishṇava cenobite, visited a forest towards the east of the river Prāchī in the Puri district. Thither he was accosted by a resident of the forest who said, "Behold O Mādhurī, the cave of Gorekh. Sitting in Yoga posture he worships the

Reference to G. N. in Sunya Samhita.

182. Sarala Mbh. Sabha Parva.
183. Sarala Mbh Sabha Parva.
184. "सुमरे मने शकुनि गोरेख ये यति
Sabha Parva.
185. "गोरेख सुमरि देले करे पथा काढि" Vana Parva.

supportless" (*i.e.* the Void). Another cenobite taught him "the occult art of Gorakhnāth."

In Chaitanya Bhāgavata of Īśwara Dasa, G. N. is said to have assumed the form of a cat to pay a visit to infant

Reference to G. N. in Chaitanya Bhagavata.

Chaitanya at Navadwipa. He sought to taste the leavings of Chaitanya's meal. The Lord knew that and gave the cat rice mixed with ghee. G. N. partook of the meal and took a portion of it for other Siddhas.[186]

In Parache Gītā of Dvārakā Dasa (Chap. I), Krishṇa taught the 'Haṁsa Mantra' to Arjuna. That esoteric knowledge was

Reference to G. N. in Parache Gita.

known only to eleven persons, beginning from Krishṇa himself. The last four recipients were Śiva, Pārvatī, Matsyendranāth and G. N. respectively. In Saptāṅga-Yoga Sarā, Mallikānāth, a disciple of G. N., asks his Guru to explain "Ghaṭa-Yoga".[187]

Matsyendranāth was the preceptor of G. N. He himself was the disciple of Ādyanāth.[188] It is said that Ādi-Buddha

Matsyendranath

asked him to descend to the earth.[189] But in many Oriya texts Matsyendranāth has been described as Ādi or First Nāth. In Saptāṅga Yoga Sāra, G. N. informs Mallikānāth that Machhendra, the first Nāth, was his Guru.[190] In Govinda Chandra Tīkā, Tantipā says:—"Bowest thou at the feet of Machhendra, the first Nāth."

Our old friend Mādhurī Dasa learnt about the "Sākshī-

Lui or Lohidas

Mantra" of Lohidās and Kapila. He also beheld the Math of Lohidās, whose attention was absorbed in the meditation of the Void.[191]

N. N. Vasu identifies Lohidās with Lohichandra, the son

186. Iswara Dasa's Chaitanya Bhagbata, LXIV.

187. घट योग स्वामी मोते कहिवा विस्तारि"।
मल्लिका मुखु गोरेख पमन्त शुणिले ।

Saptanga Yogasara.

188. See the footnote No. 182.—Sarala Mbh. Sabha Parba

189. Bangiya Sahitya Parisad Patrika, 1328 B. S. No. 2

190. आदिनाथ योगी ये मच्छेन्द्र मोर गुरु"—Saptanga Yogasara.

191. Sunya Samhita, XI.

of Raja Harichandra, who preached the Dharma cult.[192] But Lohidās had practised the Nāthist principle of shutting up the body from air, so that the mind will be in unison with the Void. We are of opinion that he was really 'Lui' the Siddha. The surname "Dāsa" need not perplex us, as in the Oriya texts of the Vishṇuite sect it has been used indiscriminately. Lui or Luipād was the earliest Siddhāchārya and heads the Java list.[193]

Nāthism is not Vaishṇavism. Nevertheless, there is a close similarity in the system of Yoga which appertains both to Nāthism and the Medieval Vaishṇavism in Orissa. In Nāmaratna Gītā of Dinakrishṇa Dasa, G. N. is exalted as a devout Vaishṇava. In Parache Gitā, Krishṇa explains Haṁsa Mantra to Arjuna. The same patient listner hears from him about air-controlling by sixty-four postures (mudrās) of Yoga.[194]

Nathism and the Medieval Vaishnavism

In the sixteenth century, leading Vaishṇavas like Yaśovanta Dasa and Balarāma Dasa composed books on the legend of Govinda Chandra, and on the supposed dialogue of G. N. and Mallikānāth. They would have hardly done so, had there been rigid lines of demarcation between Vaishṇavism and Nāthism. Without this background, any attempt of delineating the Philosophy of the Medieval Vaishṇavism will be defective.

192. Modern Buddhism in Orissa, p 123
193. J. B O. R. S. Vol. V, Pt IV.
194 Sarala Mbh. Mushali Parva.

APPENDIX

VIRASIMHA

The name of Vira Simha has been rescued from oblivion by collecting scraps of evidence from several texts. The references are not always trustworthy and in some cases conflicting. One wishes for more light on the veiled history of this great Buddhist scholar. According to Iśwara Dasa, he lived in the reign of Anaṅgabhima Deva, which seems to be erroneous. He was a Brahmin of the name of Vinod Misra, and was a devotee of Nrisimha.[195] Later on, he became a Buddhist and assumed the name Vira Simha. By profession he was a physician.[196] He became the leader of the Buddhists but continued to profess devotion for Nrisimha.

One day the queen Padmāvati went to offer worship to the image. At the temple, she met Vira Simha. She overheard his philosophical expositions and began to weep. "Why dost thou weep", questioned the Buddhist leader. "Hast thou mercy upon me" replied the queen, "and let me serve thee". But the Brahmins were loath to tolerate the ascendancy of Vira Simha. Forthwith they repaired to the king's palace and reported, "There is a Buddhist Brahmin, heterodox in his conduct. The chief queen hath received religious instruction from such a person."[197] Hearing this, the king became angry. He reprimanded his wife for her action but Padmāvati held her ground.

The trial of the snake-within-the-jar subsequently followed, and Vira Simha escaped with the skin of his teeth from being clubbed to death. He took shelter in the Daṇḍakāraṇya forest, whilst his Bengali followers fled to the hills near Bāṅki.

His hermitage in that forest was visited by Mādhuri Dasa,

195. Iswara Dasa's Chaitanya Bhagavata—Chap. 53.

196. "वद्य शास्त्रे वीरसिंह सकल शास्त्र वीरमय"—Ibid.

197. वडदे वोलि विप्रवर वर्णे घटन्ति अनाचार
ताहाङ्क ठारु उपदेश होइले तीर राणी हंस"

who was thus informed by his guide, "Here is the hermitage of Vira Siṁha, the descendant of Bharadwāja. By virtue of his occult powers he can control air within his body. Vira Siṁha's method of Yoga is different from that of Lohidās. Vira Siṁha knows the intricate philosophy of Nāgānta Vidyā. He travels hundred yojanas at his will. He visits Krishṇa every day and serves him."[198] Mādhuri Dasa could torment his own spiritual mentor by exercising the occult art (Ājñyā) of Vira Siṁha. He wrote the Mantra in the shape of a figure (of his Guru). Then thinking of that person he placed the sheet on fire. The Guru felt unbearable pain all over his body.[199]

Reference to Vira Simha in Sunya Samhita.

Hearing of the advent of Chaitanya, Vira Siṁha repaired to Puri. "After the Nrisiṁha incarnation, the Lord manifested Himself again, in the incarnation of Buddha. Chaitanya was but the embodiment of Buddha."[200] Vīrasiṁha could realize the truth and forthwith he cast himself at the feet of the Master.

Vira Simha and Chaitanya

This fact shows that he was a contemporary of King Pratāprudra, and the Buddhists were persecuted by this king. Moreover, Padmāvati was the name of a wife of Pratāprudra.[201] We do not know of any consort of Anaṅgabhima II or III, bearing this name. Perhaps Iśwara Dasa invented the name

198. वीरसिंह आश्रम ए भारद्वाज वाल
याईं आसि साधन्ति से तपी वारांगुन

* * * * * *

वीरसिंह विपरीत आज्ञाकारी प्यान्ति
विषम सन्धि नागान्त विद्या से जाणन्ति ॥
इच्छाए यान्ति तपी शए युण क्षणे
श्रीकृष्ण नियोगी से आसन्ति प्रतिदिने Sunya Samhita XI

12 Angulas are associated with Air-controlling. See Sunya Samhita IV

199. Sunya Samhita XI

200. चैतन्य विष्णु अवतार वहिले बउध शरीर
नृसिंह अवतार हरि बउध तहुँ अवतरि
Iswara Dasa's Chaitanya Bhagavata, LXV

201. वीररुद्रोऽपि पद्माश्लिष्ट तनुः कटक नगरीं
पद्मा पद्मालयेला महिलाभिस्समं सम्मानयन्
Sarasvati Vilasa

of Anaṅgabhima, to pass Vira Simha as a Methuselah. The foregoing incident in all probability took place in the early part of the King's reign, before the advent of the Master ; otherwise the Gauḍiya writers would have gladly narrated this story of the Buddhist persecution.

There is a booklet in Oriya, which is ascribed to Vira Siṁha. In one MS. the concluding line is :—"Thus saith the Buddhist Vira Siṁha of the Drāviḍa country." In this Chautiśā book, Vira Siṁha gives religious instruction to Nacchindra or Lakshmidhara. Lolla Lakshmidhara was an Andhra scholar in the court of Raja Pratāprudra. He wrote the commentary of Saundarya Lahari.[202] He might be the Lakshmidhara of the Chautiśā.

Virasimha Chautisa

202. The article of S. N. Rajguru. Utkal Sahitya, Paus, 337

CHAPTER V

"RADHA AND KRISHNA IDEA IN ORISSA, BEFORE THE CHAITANYA AGE"

"The personality which we have attributed to God is that perfection of personality, which is only adumbrated in ourselves. We cannot use categories which we do not possess. Our thinking must be anthropomorphic because we are men."

W. R. Matthews—"Studies in Christian Philosophy", p. 193

Krishṇa is such an anthropomorphic conception of Godhead. But before the advent of Chaitanya—Krishṇa was seldom conceived as the Supreme and Absolute Being, in Orissa. Vishṇu, "favourite with the Gopāla clan", has been mentioned in the Megheśvara Temple inscription. Chandrikā Devī, the daughter of Anaṅgabhīma III, reared a temple of Bāla-Krishṇa-Subhadrā. Krishṇa was regarded as an incarnation only, though revered in honoured way.

Sāralā Dasa's portrayal of Krishṇa's character justifies such a hypothesis. In some places of the book he expresses his devotion to Krishṇa. Thus he seeks inspiration from Krishṇa (Āśramik Parva) and gets his mind absorbed in the contemplation of Krishṇa (Droṇa Parva). "But the poet has depicted Krishṇa not always as one possessing supernatural prowess and a deity—but in many places, as an insincere self-applauding person revelling in vile plans."[203] Thus, Krishṇa by blinking, signs Dhrishṭa-dumnya to kill Droṇa. Krishṇa's head was decapitated by Śiva and was replaced by a cow's head, thus forming the image of Gomukhī Keśava.[204]

Portrayal of Krishna by Sarala Dasa

203. Sarala Charita, Mrityunjaya Rath, p 84.
204. Sarala Mbh. Mushali Parva.

THE WORSHIP OF GOPALA-KRISHNA IN ORISSA

Krishṇa as 'Gopāla', is worshipped through the feelings of affection and companionship. Mention has already been made of the image of Gopāla the witness (Sākshi-Gopāla). Nityānanda, while on pilgrimage, came to Cuttack and bowed before the image of Sākshi-Gopāla. On his way to Puri Chaitanya visited the temple of Sākshi-Gopāla, and Nityānanda narrated the story of the image before the Master.

Sakshi Gopala.

In days gone by, there lived two Brahmins at Vidyānagar, who set out on a pilgrimage. At Vrindāvana they visited the Gopāla temple. The young Brahmin rendered great service to the elderly one and the latter reciprocated by swearing before the image of Gopāla that he would wed his daughter to the younger Brahmin. But when they went back, the promise was not kept as the young Brahmin belonged to a lower rank. The story goes that Gopāla travelled to Vidyānagar to bear witness regarding the unfulfilled promise. The king of Vidyānagar built a temple for Gopāla. When Raja Purushottama plundered Vidyānagar, he brought the image to Cuttack for daily worship. His chief queen offered many ornaments including a valuable nose-ring to the deity. The image is said to be "two-handed" (Chaitanya Charitāmrita, II, 5) "very old," (Chaitanya Chandrodaya, VI) "flute playing." (Kāñchi Kāveri).

Story of Gopala the Witness.

Mādhavendra Puri, the preceptor of Chaitanya's Guru Iśwar Puri, was an ardent devotee of Gopāla.[205] He recovered the image of Gopāla from a grove at Vrindāvana and at the god's bidding Mādhavendra set off for Puri to bring sandal-paste.

Kshirachora Gopinath.

At Remuṇā (near Balasore) he did obeisance to the

205. Madhavendra Puri was a Sannyasi of the Maddha School. But the followers of Vallabhacharya claim that he entrusted Madhavendra with worship of the Gopala image, (The Materials for the Biography of Chaitanya, pp. 391-396).

image of Gopināth. Thither he tasted the oblation of Kshira (thickened and sweetened milk).

"The Puri only thought that if I can get a little of the kshira unasked, I may learn its taste for the purpose of establishing it as my Gopāl's bhog."[206]

But the longing shamed him. In the night, Gopināth appeared before his priest in dream and said:—"Up, priest; and open my door. I have kept a pot of kshira for the hermit. You will find it concealed under the skirt of my lower garment." The servitor handed over the pot of kshira to Mādhavendra. From that time, the image came to be known as 'Gopināth who stole the kshira.'

Faring forth Mādhavendra reached Puri. Thither he collected sandal and camphor for Gopāla's sake. While on his way back to Vrindāvana, Mādhavendra again halted at Remuṇā. Gopāla ordered him in dream, to anoint Gopināth's body with sandal and camphor. He carried out the order. "Mādhavendra passed away at Remuṇā. His burial mound and wooden sandals are even now worshipped there."[207]

The early history of Gopināth is not to be found in the Gauḍiya texts. It is given in Gopināth Charitāmrita, whose author Vinod Chaitanya Babaji served in the temple of Gopināth for a long time. He has taken much trouble to collect all the traditions regarding Gopināth; leaving to the readers the task of separating the kernel from the husk.

The Early History of Gopinath.

It is stated that king Lāṅguliya Narasiṁha Deva had for a long time no son to succeed him. So he started on pilgrimage. At Chitra-kūta, he worshipped the image installed by Rāma. The image communicated this message to him in dream. "Madana Gopāla is my name. I long to go to a lovely (ramaṇiya) place." The king set off for his own kingdom, taking the

206. Chaitanya Charitamrita II, 4 (Sir J. N. Sarkar's translation).

207. "Kshira-chora Gopinath," Bharatvarsha, Kartik 1330.
"Madhavendra and Chaitanya were initiated in the Gopala Mantra of 10 Letters."

image with him. At the time of installation, the queen gave the image the name of "Gopināth"; the image being surrounded by the figures of Ashṭa-Sakhī (eight female associates of Krishṇa). The deity was installed at Remuṇā, as he desired.

Significance of the Name of Gopinath.

Much ink has been spilled on the name of Gopināth. "The idea behind the worship of Gopināth is the feeling of Gopī" writes Rai Bahadur R. P. Chanda, "and as Rādhā is chief among the Gopīs, the main idea behind the worship of Gopināth is that of Rādhā."[208] But Gopī images are not to be found with the image of Gopināth. Murāri Gupta states in his Kaḍchā that it is an image of Gopāla-Krishṇa.[209] "The image is two-handed like that of Sākshi-Gopāla."[210] According to Gopināth Charitāmrita, his previous name was Madana Gopāla. These facts lead us to suppose that Gopīnāth was originally a Gopāla image.

Image of Madan Gopala.

The copper-plate grant of king Purushottama in favour of Poteśvar Bhaṭṭa (an ancestor of the Muslim Bhuyan family of Balasore) shows that the king sought for the benediction of Madana Gopala. (Śrī Madana-Gopāla śaranaṁ mama).[211] Thus we find that the worship of Gopāla-Krishṇa flourished in the sixteenth-century Orissa.

Jagannāth's dress as Vāla-Gopāla fascinated the Master. He recited a sloka in honour of Jagannāth, conceived as Gopāla.[212] During the Herā-Pañchami festival, Jagannāth is regarded as Krishṇa—the young cowherd. It is said that Jagannāth-Krishṇa longs at that time for the disport of Vrindāvana. So he repairs to the Gunḍichā house, which resembles the abode of the Gopīs.

208. "Vaishnavism in Bengal"—Udayan, Pous, 1341.

209. "रेमुणायां महापुर्य्यां दुष्टै गोपाल देवकम्"

Murari Gupta's Kadcha—III, 6,

210. Chaitanya Chandrodaya—Canto VI.

211. J. B. O. R. S. Vol. IV.

212. Quoted in Chaitanya Bhagavat, III, 2.

The Mode of Consort-service

We now refer to the mode of consort-service. (Madhura-rasa Upāsanā).

"The votary serves Krishṇa as a lover, offering him his or her own person." Mādhavendra was the precursor of Chaitanya in the service of Krishṇa through conjugal passion.[213] Before him, the consort mode of devotion was unknown also in Bengal.[214]

Gopi-Bhava.

Madhura-rasa Upāsanā can be treated from two aspects, *viz.*, Gopī-bhāva and Rādhā-bhāva. (Bhāva =Idea).

"Krishṇa alone is the object of devotion and the mode of service through conjugal love by which the damsels of Braja adored him—is the only true form of service."[215]

In Chaitanya Charitāmrita (II. 8), Rāmānanda explains the feelings of the milkmaids before the Master. The Gopīs share between themselves Krishṇa's passion as the lover. Even Lakshmī does not enjoy, "the favour shown by the Supreme Being to the fair ones of Vrindāvana."

Gopī-idea has been described in the chapters on Rāsa sport in Canto X of the Bhāgavata. Krishṇa dallies with the milkmaids and favours one. Later on, attempts were made to identify the favourite Gopī as Rādhā herself.

Radha-Bhava.

Rādhā-idea is the perfected conception of the consort-service. The conception of Krishṇa as the amorous lover of the cowherd girls almost fades away from mind. It is the quintessence of love, being the supreme emotion (Mahā-bhāva) of which Rādhā is the embodiment.

But Rādhā's love is impatient of partnership. The supreme love is to be directed towards one channel only. The Master

213. Harmonist, Feb. 4, 1935. See also Bhakti Ratnakar, V,

214. Chaitanya Bhagavat, III, 4.

215. "आराध्यो भगवान् व्रजेश तनयस्तद्धाम वृंदावनं
रम्या काचिदुपासना व्रजवधूवर्गेण या कल्पिता।"
Viswanath Chakravarti.

questioned Rāmānanda Rai, "A love that extends to others than the beloved, is not deep enough. If you can show that for Rādhā's sake Krishṇa openly forsook the other Gopī's, then I shall know that he passionately loved her." In answer to his question, Rāmānanda quoted from Gita-Govinda. Rādhā left the Rāsa arena out of sensitiveness and wounded pride, when she found Krishṇa disporting with the Gopī damsels. Krishṇa came to know of this. He forsook the damsels of Braja, carrying in mind the memory of Rādhā.[216] A thousand million Gopīs could not satiate his passion.

The milkmaids, according to the Radha-idea, play a role of renunciation. Thus explains Rāmānanda Rai, "The Sakhīs do not wish for Krishṇa's embrace, but they exert themselves to make Krishṇa embrace Rādhā. Thereby they gain a pleasure ten million times sweeter than that of selfish enjoyment."

"The right of direct dalliance with Krishṇa is reserved for Sri Radhika."[217]

The Development of Radha-idea

Rādhā-idea and Gopi-idea developed both in North and South India. Vishṇusvāmi looked upon Rādhā as the chief among the Gopīs. Līlāśuka Vilvamaṅgala, the author of the famous Krishṇa-Karṇāmrita, (lit. the Slokas which are felt like nectar in the ears of Krishṇa) belonged to this sect. His real name was Pustanam Namburī,[218] though he was popularly known by his assumed name. He was imbued with Gopi-idea whilst he addressed Krīshṇa in the Slokas. "The world has nothing like the Karṇāmrita which kindles pure devotion to Krishṇa." The Master brought a manuscript of the Karṇāmrita from the south.

Radha-Idea in the Vishnusvami Sect

But Rādhā-idea came to Orissa from the north and not

216. कंसारिरपि संसार वासनाबद्ध शृङ्खलाम् ।
राधामाधाय हृदये तत्याज व्रजसुन्दरीः ॥१॥
Gita-Govinda, III.

217. The Erotic principles and Unalloyed devotion, p. 20

218. Article of A. L. Seal. Prabasi, Sravan, 1322.

from the south. The conception of Rādhā has been given a prominent place in the teachings of Nimbārka. He was a Telugu but he settled at Vrindāvana. His floruit cannot be precisely determined, though he seems to have lived before Maddhācharya of the 13th century. Rādhā has been extolled as the eternal consort of Krishṇa, by Nimbārka. But he gives prominence to "Svakiya-vada" also, which conceives Krishṇa as the husband of Rukmiṇi

Jaydeva.

Rādhā-idea is perfected, perhaps for the first time, in Gita-Govinda of Jaydeva who lived in the 12th century. Rāmānanda Rai quoted from this book before the Master, to show the superiority of Rādhā over other Gopis.

Vidyapati and Chandidas.

Rāmānanda studied the songs of Vidyāpati and also Śri Krishṇa Kirtan of (Baḍu) Chanḍidās. Vidyāpati was an early exponent of Rādhā-idea. In the "Māthur" songs of Vidyāpati, Rādhā turns herself into Mādhava due to constant thought of him. Śri Krishṇa Kirtan belongs to a period not later than the 12th century A. D. The poet has risen to philosophical height in the padas (songs) dealing with 'separation' (Viraha).

Chaitanya.

The idea of consort-service received its fullest exposition from the Master himself. It has been stated that Rādhā herself descended into this world as the embodiment of separation from Krishṇa. (Vipralambha Vigraha). Externally he was Krishṇa, because the anthropomorphic incarnations of the Godhead are always conceived as male Beings. Thus Chaitanya was the incarnation of both Rādhā and Krishṇa.[219] But mentally he imitated Rādhā. "Chaitanya like Chanḍidās's Rādhā fainted at the sight of dark blue cloud which brought to his memory the lovely colour of Krishṇa."[220]

Rādhā-idea spread to Orissa due to the influence and

219. "राधा भाव-द्युति सुवलितं कृष्णस्वरूपम्"—Rupa Goswami's Kadcha
See also Advaita's exposition in Isan Nagar's Advaita Prakas, XX

220. Chaitanya and His Age, p. 29

teaching of the Master. Formerly it was not popular in Orissa, though Gita-Govinda was recited before Jagannāth at the time of Bara-siṅgāra ceremony.[221] Only a few persons, like Rāmānanda Rai and possibly Mādhavī Dasi, were already acquainted with this idea. Rāmānanda had a sound knowledge of Brajabuli literature, which mainly deals with the amour of Rādhā-Krishṇa.

Radha-idea in Orissa.

Rāmānanda recited a pada (song) in the Braja dialect before the Master, depicting the 'kalahāntaritā' feeling of Rādhā. Possibly excepting a pada of *Yaśorāj Khan, which* refers to Sultan Hussain Shah of Bengal, the pada of Rāmānanda is the earliest extant one in the Braja dialect.

There is no reference to the Master in Rāmānanda's Jagannāth Ballabha drama. This shows that the drama was composed before he met the Master. In the drama he has described the devotion of Inclination-led type and the feelings of Rādhā.

Rāmānanda's knowledge of Rādhā-idea was derived from the study of the devotional poems of Jaydeva, Vidyāpati and Chaṇḍidās. Possibly he was helped by Rāghavendra Puri, who was known to be a disciple of Mādhavendra Puri. It seems that at the time of the Master's first advent, there was no competent Vaishṇava at Puri who could talk on Rādhā-idea. So Sārbabhauma had to recommend the name of Rai Rāmānanda, living far away on the bank of the Godavari.

Efforts have been made to trace the existence of Rādhā-idea in Orissa, before the advent of the Master. In Padyāvali, the anthology of Rūpa Goswami, six Slokas of a Raja Purushottama have been quoted. One of these, distinctly refers to Rādhā. (No. 163) Another Sloka describes Krishṇa in the embrace of the Gopis. (No. 293) It has been suggested that he was a King of Orissa.

Purushottama of the Solar dynasty supplicates indeed, for blessings from the amorous union of Rādhā and Krishṇa, in his Abhinava Veṇisaṁharaṇam. He also praises "the captivat-

221. See the Jagannath Temple Inscription of Kapilendra, dated 1450 A. D.

ing lock of hair of Rādhā." But the prologue of his book informs us that the king was a devout worshipper of the goddess Durgā and devoted to the feet of Nārāyaṇa. Thus his devotion to Rādhā-Krishṇa was a customary one.

It is told that king Pratāprudra brought the Rādhā-Kānta image from Kāñchi, as ordered by Krishṇa in dream.[222] Narahari Chakravarti quotes the following story in his book, Bhakti-Ratnākar. A Brahmin lived, in days gone by, at Rādhānagar, a village in Orissa. He worshipped an image of Rādhā in the mode of Vātsalya rasa, (affection). After his death the image was removed and kept within the temple precincts of Jagannāth. There it passed as an image of Lakshmī. Rādhā informed Purushottama Baḍajenā, the son of Pratāprudra, to send the image to Vrindāvana. The prince carried out the behest. These stories are based on dreams and thus do not deserve serious consideration.

222. Gambhirai Sri Gauranga—By Rasik Vidyabhusan, pp. 3-5.

CHAPTER VI.

THE VAISHNAVA WRITERS OF THE MEDIEVAL SCHOOL OF VAISHNAVISM IN ORISSA

Before we proceed further, some amount of knowledge regarding these Vaishṇava writers and their important writings will be necessary. The history of the Chaitanya Age depends to a great extent on the literary sources. We should be conscious of the fact that the Master spent three-fourth of his life of asceticism in Orissa and passed away at Puri. Moreover, the obscure history of the Medieval School of Vaishṇavism can not be reconstructed without the help of Oriya literary sources. Thus the old Oriya literature deserves our close attention. We shall mention the writers in order of sequence. The list is not exhaustive, but is a discriminating one according to our requirements.

Vatsa Dasa & Markanda Dasa.

Vatsa Dasa—Kalasā Chautiśā of this writer is the earliest known book of verse in Oriya literature. There is a reference to this book in the Mahābhārata of Sāralā Dasa.[223] The poet has described the marriage of Śiva with Pārvatī, to which Vishṇu was a spectator.

Mārkaṇḍa composed Keśava Koili "which is based on an incident of the Bhagavata. Śri-Krishṇa had gone to Mathurā leaving his mother Yaśodā. Yośodā felt unhappy at the separation and poured out her grief addressing the cuckoo."[224] Jagannātha Dasa of the 16th century composed a spiritual commentary on Keśava Koili. Thus the book was at least a century old to acquire such importance.

Śāralā Dasa was a cultivator by caste[225] and his real

223. See Introduction—Types of Ancient Oriya Prose and Poetry.

224. "The Language and Literature of Orissa"—M. M. Chakravarti, J. A. S. B. 1898, No. 4.

225. "जन्मे कृषिकारी मुं न जाणे शास्त्रविधि"

Chandi Purana.

name was Siddheśvar Pariḍā. He named himself after Sāralā Chaṇḍī, his tutelary goddess, by whose grace he was able to compose the Mahābhārata in Oriya.[226] Sāralā Dasa was a contemporary of Kapilendra.[227] Besides the Mahābhārata, two other books of the poet have been found out. Vilaṅkā Rāmāyaṇa is based on imagination. Rāma failed to kill Sahasra Rāvaṇa—a feat which was performed by Sitā by the grace of Sāralā Chaṇḍī. Śiva also enjoyed the esteem of the poet and the graphic description of Pārvatī's marriage with Śiva in Chaṇḍī Purāṇa bears out this fact.

Sarala Dasa.

In the opinion of B. C. Majumdar,[228] Bhīmā Dhīvara flourished in the fifteenth century. The book narrates the popular theme of Śakuni's dice-playing and subsequent humiliation of Draupadī. Her modesty was saved by Krishṇa, "the consort of Rukmiṇī and Satyabhāmā."

Bhima Dhivara.

Prof. A. B. Mohanty has edited Rāma-bibhā (the marriage of Rāma) by this poet, who in his opinion flourished towards the end of the fifteenth century.

Arjuna Dasa

Chaitanya Dasa composed Nirguṇa Māhātmya and Vishṇugarbha Purāṇa. The first one was composed at Kharial, in the reign of Pratāprudra[229]—possibly before the advent of Chaitanya. Prof. Mohanty points out that in the chapter 16 of the book, Rāma's expiation for killing Rāvaṇa (he being a Brahmin) has been described.

Chaitanya Dasa

This statement is at variance with the original story of the Rāmāyaṇa. But Chaitanya Dasa's version was followed by Balarāma Dasa in the Laṅkā Kāṇḍa of his Rāmāyaṇa.[230]

226. Adya Parva. Sarala Mbh.

227. "कलिकाल धंसन भोगेया कोटि पूजा ।
प्रयामिते खटइ कपिलेश्वर महाराजा ॥

Adya Parva.

228. Introduction, Typical Selection from Oriya Literature, Vol. I.

229. Nirguna Mahatmya, XVI.

230. See the Introduction, Nirguna Mahatmya.

Chaitanya Dasa's floruit can be determined in another way. His conception of Krishṇa can be best judged from a passage which borders on vulgarity. "In the Dvāpara Yuga, Vishṇu was again born in the mundane region. He abducted many damsels by force, after killing the Asuras. Not being afraid of sin, he enjoyed the damsels of the royal and cowherd families. He kidnapped his sister and cohabited with her. He killed cow and woman and his maternal uncle Kaṁsa."[231] Thus he depicts Krishṇa as a shameless profligate. He would not have dared to do so, after the advent of the Master—when the tide of devotion for Krishṇa reached its highest level.

Chaitanya Dasa's Conception of Krishna

Now we will refer to five great Oriya Vaishṇavas, who were disciples of the Master, and exponents of the philosophy of the Orissan Vaishṇavism. They were generally known as five Associates. (Pañcha Sakhā).

Balarama Dasa

Balarāma Dasa was one of the greatest figures among the Vaishṇavas in the sixteenth century Orissa. Just as Sārāla Dasa is celebrated as the author of Oriya Mahābhārata, similarly, Balarāma lives in the memory of the people as the author of the Rāmāyaṇa in Oriya. In the last but one colophon, the poet tells that he was the son of Somanātha Mahapatra, who was a minister of the State.

Mahāmāyā was his mother's name.[232] He was a Karaṇa by

231. "द्वापर युगर वेभार विष्णु जन्मिले मर्त्तपुर ॥
असुर कुलकु संहारि शतेक कन्या वले हरि ॥
राजकुमार। गोपनारी रमिले पापकु न डरि ॥
सोहोद्र माइक्कि हरिले भउणी संङ्गे घर कले ॥
गोवध स्तिरी वध कले कंस मउलांकु नाशिले ॥

The 'references are interesting. Krishna killed Naraka Asura and took away the princesses, whom Naraka held captive. He killed the cow-demon Dhenuka and the Demoness Putana. He forcibly abducted and married Mitravinda, the daughter of Rajadhidevi, his aunt. He also married Madra, his cousin.

232. But according to Chhatris Gupta Gita, XXXV, the mother's name was Jambuvati.

caste.[233] In the last but one colophon of the Rāmāyaṇa, the poet says that at the time of the completion of the book he was thirty years old.

The Works of Balarama Dasa

Jagamohana Rāmāyaṇa—Balarāma Dasa's Rāmāyaṇa was named "Jagamohana"[234] in honour of Jagannāth. "The Purusha, who fascinates the world, is beyond destruction and is formless. Before him manifests the sin-less Sun-Bird."[235] His father was a devotee of Jagannāth. "So Jagannāth was kind to him and inspired him to compose the book."[236]

In Ādi-Kāṇḍa, Vishṇu *alias* Jagannāth has been exalted as a king, with Rukmiṇī and Satyabhāmā as queens and Baladeva as minister.

Vedānta-sāra Gupta Gitā—We are of opinion that N. N. Vasu mentions this very book as Praṇava Gupta Gitā. Both the texts begin with the following incident, though the wordings do not always tally. We find that the Brahmins were discussing Vedānta at Mukti-Maṇḍapa. Balarāma Dasa was brought before the king Pratāprudra, because he ventured to participate in the discussion. He imparted Mantra into the ear of an idiot and caused him to talk on "Praṇava."

Gupta Gitā—This book contains a dialogue between Krishṇa and Arjuna. In the last chapter the poet refers to Virajā and Varāhanāth of Jajpur and to Haṭeśvar Śiva.

Chhatris Gupta Gitā—In the last but one chapter, it is stated that Balarāma could finish only the first chapter. The remaining chapters were completed by another Balarāma Dasa, son of Rāma Dasa, who was born in the second regnal year of king Mukunda Deva II. (1657-1690).

Virāṭa Gitā and Brahmāṇḍa Bhūgola—Krishṇa expounds

233. "मुदि हीन पापी विशेष शूद्र योनि"
colophon in Lanka Kanda. See also Sunya Samhita, I.

234. "जगमोहन बोलि ए रामायण नाम"—Sundara Kanda.

235. "जगमोहन पुरुष अव्यय अरूप
अग्रतरे वैनतेय विहग अपाप"
Last but one colophon.

236. Lanka Kanda, Jagmohan Ramayana.

the Yoga philosophy before Arjuna. In both of these books, Mother Void (Mātā Śūnya) has been described.

Gaṇeśa Bibhūti Tikā—N. N. Vasu thinks it to be a composition of Balarāma.[237] The name of the author is not given in the text. The C. P. C. publication attributes the authorship to Bhupati Bhañja of uncertain date.

Amarakosha Gitā—Krishṇa has been spared this time. So Śiva explains the Yoga to Pārvatī. Pratāprudra is mentioned, because of the reverence shown by him to the Vaishṇavas.[238]

Mriguṇi Stuti—The poet invokes the benediction of Rāma in the beginning of the poem. The eight chief consorts of Krishṇa are mentioned.

Saptāṅga Yoga Sāra—Mention has already been made of this book. It is ascribed to Balarāma Dasa, though there is no definite evidence for his authorship in the text.

Lakshmī Purāṇa—Lakshmī, within the Jagannāth temple precincts, is the object of the poet's devotion.

Vaulā Adhyāya—Vaulā was a cow, who was saved from the clutches of a tiger by Lakshmī, the chief queen of Jagannāth.

Kānta Koili—Captive Sītā bewails her lot and weeps for Rāma.

Vata Avakāśa—Jagannāth holds a court which was attended by all the deities of Orissa. No less than 26 Śiva delegates attended the conference, while 76 Śākta goddesses of Orissa participated. It is strange that the Vishṇuite delegates were comparatively fewer in number. They were Varāhanāth, Gopīnāth, Ālālnāth, Nrisiṁha images of Jiyaḍ and Ahoval and the twelve Mādhava images of the Prāchī banks.

Jagannātha Dasa is perhaps the most celebrated Oriya Vaishṇava. In Orissa, his memory will be always cherished as the translator of the Bhāgavata in Oriya. His parents were Bhagavāna Dasa Purāṇapaṇḍā and Padmāvatī. He was born on Radhāshṭami day at

Jagannatha Dasa.

237. Modern Buddhism in Orissa, pp. 15, 73.

238. "प्रतापरुद्र महाराजा वैष्णवे करे दिव्य पूजा"

Amarakosha Gita, Chap. VII.

Kapileśvarpur near Puri. His father used to read the Purāṇas in the temple of Jagannāth. Jagannātha Dasa took up his father's profession. It is stated in Jagannātha Charitāmrita (the biography of J. Dasa) that he used to expound the Purāṇas under a banyan tree, towards the southern enclosure of the Jagannāth temple.

At the age of eighteen, he for the first time met the Master. He was reading from the Bhāgavata, "When Chaitanya along with his companions came to that place, and halted there. He was pleased with the exposition of the Purāṇas."[239] The Master came to Puri, for the first time in 1510 A. D. Thus Jagannātha Dasa was born not before 1491 A. D.

The Works of Jagannatha Dasa.

Numerous books are sold in the Bazaar as compositions of Jagannātha Dasa. We shall refer only to a few books. Kamala-lochana Chautiśā—The poet invokes Krishṇa, the Lotus-eyed.

Beḍā-Parikramā—The shrines within the limits of Puri have been described. The following Vishṇuite deities are mentioned in this connection:—Vatakrishṇa, Nila Mādhava, Nrisiṁhanāth and Kshetrapāla. There is also reference to the temple of Mahā-Lakshmī. It is stated that Raja Pratāprudra worshipped Jagannāth, with the help of thirty-six classes of servitors.[240]

Brahma Gītā—This book is written in prose. Herein the writer expounds the Vedanta philosophy for the Brahmins.

The Translation of the Bhāgavata—Jagannātha Dasa's memory will be cherished for ever by his countrymen as the translator of the Bhāgavata in Oriya. Sāralā Dasa translated the Bhāgavata, as he states in Chaṇḍi Purāṇa. Balarāma Dasa dealt with it in Brahmāṇḍa Bhūgola. But it was Jagannātha Dasa's translation which made it popular in Orissa.

239. "एहि समये श्री चैतन्य सङ्गते घेनि सखागण
बट तलेया विजे कले पुराण शुणि तोष हेले

Jagannatha Charitamrita, Chap. II.

240. "रुद्र ये प्रताप खटे धूप दीप छत्तिशा नियोग घेनि"

Beda Parikrama

Allegations against Jagannatha Dasa.

Unfortunately, the translation of Jagannātha Dasa has been severely censured by the Gauḍiya Vaishṇavas.[241] It has been alleged that:

(1) The translation was vitiated by Māya-vāda or the doctrine of illusion.

(2) The poet added five more chapters in his translation, wherein he had expressed heretical ideas.

(3) He incorporated new facts in his book which have materially altered the subject-matter of the book.

Criticism of the allegations against Jagannatha Dasa.

Such allegations, arising out of sectarian animosity, have unjustly lowered the fame of this great Oriya Vaishṇava. We know of Oriya Vaishṇavas of the Gauḍiya school, who denounce their own national poet. A detailed examination of the book will ;show that many of these charges are baseless. In the third and the tenth cantos the poet has subdivided the chapters of the original text.[242] Thus, though there is an increase in the number of chapters, no substantial increase in the subject-matter has been attempted. Canto XI seems to be the poet's last composition. The subsequent canto was added by one, Mahādeva Dasa by name. (See Canto XII, Chaps. 1 & 13).

Discrepancies with the Original Text.

It must be admitted that Jagannātha Dasa did not literally translate the original text. Some of these discrepancies may be cited:

(1) The cowherd boys including Krishṇa and Balarāma, all resembled alike, and Akrūra failed to pick out Krishṇa and Balarām due to the veil of illusion. Krishṇa understood his feelings and removed the veil. This incident is not to be found in the original text.

(2) Sudām is sent by Krishṇa with the news of Krishṇa's impending return. The Sanskrit text is silent on this.

(3) The text refers to a conversation between Nanda and Akrūra. But Jagannātha Dasa does not mention this matter.

241. See Gaudiya magazine:—Vol. II, 33: Vol. IX, 24.

242. Chapters 1, 34, 36, 45, 58 and 68 of Canto X of the original text have been doubled.

(4) The translation has more elaborately dealt with the list of the kings, who sided with Kaṁsa.

(5) There is a slight deviation in the story of Kaṁsa's death, as given in the translation.

(6) But the most important difference lies in the reference to the Gopī, who was taken away from the assembly of the milkmaids by Krishṇa. (X. 29. 43)

The Gauḍiya Vaishṇavas maintain that this favourite Gopī was no other than Rādhā herself.[243] There are a few more slokas in the canto X of the Bhāgavata, which are interpreted as referring to Rādhā indirectly. (A) "वध्वा: पदै: सुपृक्तानि विलोक्यार्त्ता: समब्रुवन्" (X. 30. 22) Sanātan Goswami in his Vaishṇava Toshaṇī commentary has taken the word "Vadhū" to stand for Rādhā herself.[244] (B) "जनयाराधितो नूनं भगवान् हरिरीश्वर:" (X. 30. 24). According to the interpretations of Sanātan Goswami and Viśwanath Chakravarti, these words refer to Rādhā.[245]

The alleged References to Radha in the Bhagavata.

(c) The second sloka of this chapter contains the word "Ramāpati." Sanātan Goswami interprets Ramā to be Śrī Rādhā.

But Śrīdhar Svami in his standard commentary of the Bhāgavata nowhere refers to Rādhā. The silence of Śrīdhar on this point led Ballabh Bhaṭṭa to compose a more acceptable commentary. But the Master's rebuke damped his zeal. Jagannātha Dasa has generally followed Śrīdhar's commentary, a fact which he mentions in his book.

Jagannātha names the favourite Gopī Vrindāvatī. "A

243. See Vaishnava Toshani of Sanatan Goswami and also Sarartha Darsini of Viswanath Chakravarti. But Sridhar Svami in his Bhavartha Dipika and Jiva Goswami in his Krama Sandarbha are silent on this point.

244. "वध्वाः श्री राधायास्तस्या एव" etc.

245. "राधयति आराधतीति राधेति नामकरणञ्चदर्शितं॰"

Vaishnav Toshani Tika.

"ततश्च राधयत्याराधयतीति राधा इति नाम व्यक्तिर्बभूव"

Sarartha Darsini Tika.

Vrindavati.

Gopī named Vrindāvatī was standing near Krishṇa. She had practised asceticism previously. Holding her hand Krishṇa disappeared, after enslaving the mind of the Gopīs."[246] Vrindāvatī practised austerity to gain the attention of Krishṇa. This fact has been mentioned in Harivaṁsa, which was a popular book in Orissa and was translated by Achyutānanda Dasa. Later on, the account of Vrindāvatī was elaborated in Brahmavaivarta Purāṇa, which depicts her as proficient in the Yoga-Śāstra and as fortunate as Rādhā, being the leading Gopī. (राधा समा च सौभाग्याद् गोपी श्रेष्ठा बभूव ह) Vrindā is the protectress of Vrindāvana, and the mistress of the Kuñja.[247]

The probable reason of her selection was the significant fact that the favourite Gopī suffered disgrace in the long run. She seems to be a vain coquette, whose head was turned owing to the marked preference shown by Krishṇa. She had the audacity to ask Krishṇa to carry her on his shoulders. (X. 30. 32) So Jagannātha did not like to identify her with Rādhā. He has been followed by other writers of the Medieval School, on the Rāsa exploit of Rādhā and Krishṇa. Bhupati Pundit in his Prema Pañchāmrita, and Bhakta Charaṇa Dasa in his Mathurā Maṅgala not only identified the unnamed Gopī with Vrindāvatī ; but had also introduced Rādhā in their books. In Prema Pañchāmrita, Rādhā consoles Vrindāvatī after her sad plight.

Tulā Bhiṇā – In this book, Śiva explains the principles of Yoga to Pārvatī.

Gaja Nistāraṇa Gītā—It describes the well-known story of the rescue of the elephant from the clutches of the crocodile.

Kāliya Dalana—This book narrates the story of the humiliation of Kāliya serpent by Krishṇa.

246. "गोपी प वृन्दावती नामे थिला से कृष्ण सन्निधाने ।।
पूर्वे से अछि तप करि गोविन्द तार भुज धरि ।।
छन्दिले गोपीङ्कर मन कृष्ण होइले अन्तर्द्धान ।।"

J. Dasa's Bhagavata, Canto X, Chap. 30

247. Krishna Bhavanamrita—Viswanath Chakravarti Sl. 29

Artha Koili—Krishṇa philosophically interprets the stanzas of Keśava Koili before Arjuna. Yaśodā in the original text bewails that Keśava has gone to Mathurā and has not returned. Here the son has been compared with "Jiva-soul", which has not yet returned. Similarly Yaśodā says that Vrindāvana has lost all its charm, after the departure of Krishṇa. In this case Vrindāvana is identified with the body. When the soul departs, the body loses beauty.

M. M. Sadasiva Misra in his Life of Jagannātha Dasa has referred to a book, named Jagannātha Charita Sudhātraya. It is said to have been written by Jīva Goswamī. This book informs us that Jagannātha Dasa once showed his eight-handed form to king Pratāprudra. The book is undoubtedly a spurious one.

The Disciples of Jagannatha Dasa.

The chief disciples of Jagannātha Dasa numbered sixteen,[248] out of which only two names attract our attention. Gaurī, the Paṭṭa-Mahadevi, was his disciple. More interesting is the allusion to Kānhu Khuntiā. Is he identical with Kānāi Khuntiā of the Gauḍiya texts ?

The last days of Jagannatha Dasa.

According to a traditional story, Jagannātha was once ordered by Pratāprudra to vacate his Math,[249] where he was residing. Jagannātha refused to live within the jurisdiction of Pratāprudra's kingdom ; and by his occult knowledge he compelled the sea to recede to a distance of seven waves. (Sāta-lahari). In that extra-territorial plot of land he built Sāta-lahari Math, whither he died at the ripe age of sixty,[250] on the seventh day of the full moon in the month of Magh. It is told that his spirit got absorbed within the image of Jagannāth.

Achyutānanda was the son of Ānanda (or Dinavandhu,

248. Jagannatha Charitamrita, I.

249. Svami math, now known as Oriya math, This math is the principal gadi or seat of the Ati-badi sect.

250. See Jagannatha Charitamrita, XXIV and Life of Jagannatha Dasa, p. 35.

according to Śūnya Saṁhita, I) Mohanty, who was an officer of the king and got the designation of Khuntiā.[251] He was born at the village Tilkanā or Tripura, district Cuttack. He was probably a Gauḍa or milkman by caste. In Gopāla Math of Achyutānanda at Puri, the cowherd caste performs the daily worship. Achyutānanda himself indirectly admits his low origin in Śūnya Saṁhitā.[252]

Achyutananda Khuntia.

But in later texts, he is said to have belonged to Karaṇa caste.[253] According to Varṇatikā, his father was the Khuntiā of the Jagannāth temple. The Khuntias are in charge of the temple gates.[254] They supply dress and other articles for the decoration of the deities.[255]

At the time of his first meeting with Chaitanya, Achyuta was a little boy. From his boyhood he expressed indifference towards worldly affairs. After the first meeting, he stayed at home for eleven years. Then he repaired to Puri, and was initiated by Sanātana II at the instance of the Master. Later on, we find him as a constant companion of the Master. He was present in the Jagannāth temple, when the Master passed away. Pratāprudra tested his occult powers and was satisfied by his demonstration. He granted him a plot of land at the mouth of the river Bāṅki, at Puri. Thither Achyuta built a Math, known as Gopāla Math.

In the later part of his life, Achyutānanda lived for some

251. "आनन्द महान्ति करण ।।
खुयिटआ साङ्गिआ राजा देइ । राजार पात्र अटे सेहि ।। ताहार पुत्र ये अच्युत" ।
Iswara Dasa's Bhagavata, XLVI

252. "चित्रोत्पला तट निवासी । कहे अच्युत व्रजवंशी"
Sunya Samhita, I.

253. Iswara Dasa's Bhagavata, XLVI; Avatara Malika, & 84 Arts of Yasovanta. Ch. I.

254. M. M. Sadasiv Misra—Jagannath Temple p. 379. See also Varnatika Malika of Achyutananda.

255. Samachara Darpan—1, Oct. 1825. Quoted in Samvadpatre Sekaler Katha. Vol. I.

time under the patronage of Raja Padmanābha Narendra, who was stated to be the son-in-law of Telengā Mukunda Deva. A few years before his death he settled along with his wife Padmāvatī at Nembāla, (in Pergana Asuresvar, district Cuttack) on the river Chitrāṅgī (a tributary of the Chitrotpalā—a bifurcation of the Mahānadi.)

The last days of Achyutananda.

According to tradition, he died at an age of 108. Certain it is, that he died at a ripe age.

The Works of Achyutananda.

Śūnya Saṁhitā—Śūnya Saṁhitā is a masterpiece of the old Oriya literature. It was composed at Nembāla. Rādhā-idea gets a significant place in the book, because of its late composition. Due to the lapse of time, Achyutānanda's memory was not clear and thus he mentions Jiva Goswamī as one of the companions of the Master !

Aṇākāra Saṁhitā—Primordial (Anādi) Brahma once appeared before Achyuta as an ascetic and taught him the "Mantra beyond the Letters." (Aṇa-Akshara Mantra). Then he could realise that the Absolute is the source of all bliss and that he is formless. Shape is manifest when a form is assumed by the Formless One. [256]

Brahma Śāṅkuli Lekhana—This book treats of Haṭha Yoga (Ghaṭa Yoga) and mentions the theory of Vishṇu's womb (Vishṇugarbha).

Nirākara Saṁhitā—We have not come across this MS. N. N. Vasu quotes from this MS. in his book.

Navagujjari and Vyāllis Chaupadi · These are long poems in adoration of Rādhā and Krishṇa.

The Translation of Harivaṁśa—Harivaṁśa was a popular book in Orissa. Jagannātha Dasa utilized the conception of Vrindāvatī from this book. In the last chapter of the translation, he refers to his patron Padmanābha Narendra.[257]

256. "सर्व आदिमूल परम मङ्गल अणाकार बोलि सेहि ।
अणाकारटि आकाररे मिशिने तहिँस रूप प्रकाश ॥"
Anakara Samhita.

257. See, "The Language and Literature of Orissa," J. A. S. B. 1898 No. 4. And the Introduction—Anakara Samhita.

Brahma-Vidyā-Tattva-Jñyāna—This is a rare MS., written partly in Sanskrit, which contains a preceptorial list of the Master.

Gurubhakti Gītā—This book contains a wealth of information about the Medieval Vaishṇavism. As there is a reference to the Marathas towards the end of the book, Prof. A.B. Mohanty places the book in the 18th century.

Achyutānanda was supposed to possess preternatural insight as regards the future. This had an unfortunate effect, as numerous predictive booklets (Mālikā) passed for Achyutānanda's writings. A few contain some elements of truth and Avatāra Mālikā is one of them. Greatest mischief has been done in the case of Śūnya Saṁhitā, as several chapters containing predictions have been interpolated towards the end. Jñyāna-Sāgara, supposed to have been written by Achyutānanda, and spoken by Krishṇa to Arjuna—was actually composed in 1935, as the author confessed to us.

The Preceptor of Achyutananda.

Achyutānanda's preceptor was Sanātana Goswamī II, who has nothing to do with his worthier namesake. This preceptorial list is as follows :— Chaitanya—Sāraṅga Gossain — Śyāma—Rāmakrishṇa—Navakiśore—Sanātana II—Achyutānanda.[258]

Yasovanta Mallika.

Yaśovanta was the son of Jagu Mallika and Rekhā Dei of the village Aḍaṅga, district Cuttack. He belonged to Mahānayaka or Kshatriya caste.[259]

The Early Life of Yasovanta.

The early life of Yaśovanta has been described in 84 Arts of Yaśovanta (Yaśovanta Dāsaṅka Chaurāśi Ājñyā) by Sudarśana Dasa. Yaśovanta's father was a poor man. Privation compelled Yaśovanta to steal paddy. He was caught red-handed and produced before Raghurāma Jena, the Sāmanta chief of Aḍaṅga, who ordered the offender to be put on pike. Yaśovanta prayed Jagannāth for protection. Jagannāth listened to his supplica-

258. Sunya Samhita, I & Gurubhakti Gita, pt. I, I.

259. "चन्द्र व०शरे जात यशोवन्त क्षत्रिय कुल से कले पवित्र Avatara Malika.

tion and appeared in the body of Yaśovanta. Only Raghurāma was able to behold the vision. Thenceforth he, along with his wife Tilottamā, became disciples of Yaśovanta.

Sudarśana Dasa was a direct disciple of Yaśovanta. He writes that he was present at the time of Yaśovanta's death.

Sudarsana Dasa.

The word eighty-four, mentioned in his book, seems to be a conventional number.[260] Sudarśana lost all sense of reasoning while describing the supernatural powers of Yaśovanta. We find that Jagannāth always fulfilled his desires, however trivial they might be.

Another famous disciple was Sālabega. His father was a Muhammadan. He became a Vaishṇava and set out for Puri.

Salabega.

On the way he heard about the occult power of Yaśovanta. He put it to a test, and when convinced he hastened to take dust off Yaśovanta's feet.[261] This Yavana Sālabega may appear to be the Sālbeg of the Gauḍiya texts. There are two serious flaws in the way of accepting it.

Yavana Sālbeg of the Gauḍiya texts lived in the 17th century and his spiritual mentor was Śyāmānanda. Yaśovanta's

The Works of Yasovanta.

most important composition is Prema Bhakti Brahma Gitā, in which Krishṇa expounds the Yoga philosophy before Rādhā, and Arjuna. We have already referred to Govinda Chandra Tikā, dealing with the story of Govinda Chandra and Hāḍipā. Śiva Svarodaya is the translation of a Śaivite Tantra text.

The youngest and the least known among the five Associates was Ananta Dasa. His native village was Mehapur.

Ananta Mohanty.

His father Kapila Mohanty received the designation of "Mahāpātra" and was a Karaṇa by caste.[262] Ananta settled at Vālipātana, perganah Koṭhdesa, in the district of Puri.

260. At Balarama Dasa's command, a simpleton expounded 84 Mantras—Vedantasara Gupta Gita, I.

261. 84 Arts of Yasovanta. (Yasovanta Dasanka Chaurasi Ajnya) LXVI.

262. Iswara Dasa's Bhagavata, Chap. XLVI.

He is generally addressed as "Śiśu" (child). The reason for this appellation is to be found in Īśwara Dasa's book. Once Lakshmī and Nārāyaṇa were sitting in Vaikunṭha. Ananta and Jagannātha visited them. Jagannātha assumed the form of a "Sakhi" (female Associate) and attracted the attention of the divine couple. Not to be outwitted, Ananta assumed the form of Padmana (Pradyumnya)—the infant son of Lakshmī. For a time the ruse succeeded and he was caressed by the deities, who thought him to be the child Pradyumnya. Later on, they gave him the appellation of "Śiśu."

The Works of Ananta Dasa

Unfortunately, not a single book of Ananta has been published. In Rāsa MS., Chaitanya has been mentioned along with other four Associates.

Śūnya-Nāma-Bheda—Ananta Dasa has explained the Yoga postures in this MS.

Hetu-Udaya-Bhāgavata—The Mantras Hlim, Slim and Klim are elaborately explained in this MS.

Devadurlabha Dasa

Devadurlabha Dasa, the author of Rahasya-mañjarī flourished in the latter half of the sixteenth century. Rādhā-idea and the consort mode of devotion have been described in this book. But Rukmiṇi, and not Rādhā, is the heroine of this book.

Raja Govinda Bhanja

Raja Govinda Bhañja of Keonjhar probably lived in the beginning of the seventeenth century. In Bhakti Binoda he extols the erotic love of Rādhā and in Charaṇa Sudhā-Nidhi he reveres Chaitanya as the incarnation of Krishṇa.[263]

Chaitanya Bhagavata by Iswara Dasa.

Īśwara Dasa is already familiar with us, on account of his Bhāgavata. This unpublished and rare MS. is perhaps the most important text for research-work on the history of Vaishṇavism in Orissa—Śūnya Saṁhitā excepted. We had the opportunity of consulting

263. "चैतन्यावतारे प्रेम भक्ति देइ । गौरहरि रूप जगते देखाइ ॥"

Charana Sudhanidhi.

two MSS. Īśwara Dasa was not a historian but a credulous compiler, who laid hands on every available rumour and tradition.

Nevertheless, Īśwara Dasa's Bhāgavata has distinct value. Behind a mass of facts, loosely arranged and at times incredible, we glean valuable informations on the contemporary history of Vaishṇavism and allied sects in Orissa. Īśwara Dasa shows a wonderful capacity of gathering informations, however absurd they might be. Gorakshanāth, Nānak, Vira Siṁha, Sage Agastya, Chaitanya and Vīrabhadra (the son of Nityānanda) are all there, being introduced indiscriminately.

Importance of Iswara Dasa's Bhagavata.

The date of the book can be indirectly deduced. The poet says that after the completion of the book he came to Puri. The Brahmins and ascetics were busy on learned discussions at the Mukti Maṇḍapa, when the poet arrived there. The great sannyasi Vāsudeva Tīrtha, the embodiment of learning, was present there. The Vaishṇavas read some passages from Īśwara's book before the gathering. It elicited praise from the audience, Vāsudeva alone being dissentient. He could not believe that Chaitanya got actually absorbed within the image of Jagannāth. The Vaishṇavas tried their best to convince him but they failed.

The date of the book.

This incident shows that the work was completed at a time when the passing away of the Master was yet talked about. The book was written after the birth of Vīrabhadra, the son of Nityānanda, (Ch. 64); and the composition of Jagannātha Charitāmrita (Ch. 59). Jagannātha Charitāmrita refers to Chaitanya Charitāmrita. Thus Īśwara Dasa lived possibly in the first half of the 17th century.

The Bhāgavata of Īśwara Dasa is written in the form of a dialogue between the sage Agastya and an unnamed king of Sampurṇa nagara, (probably the capital of Videha). Īśwara borrows the sage from the Mahābhārata of Sāralā Dasa, where he is the story-teller to Vaivaśvata Manu. The account of the Master's life at Navadvipa does not deserve serious consideration, being based mainly on the Bazaar gossips.

In many places of the book we find lists of the devotees. These lists are pleasing, as they also contain the names of some devotees who are not mentioned in the Gauḍiya texts. Thus one kirtana party was attended by Uddatta (Uddhāran Dutta) Aditya (Advaita) Vakreśvar, Gauridās, Sundarānanda and also by the five Associates.[264] In another kirtan party, on the eve of the Master's passing away, Sārvabhauma, Gadādhar Pundit, Gauridās and the five Associates were present.[265] Īśwara Dasa includes even Jagāi and Mādhāi in his list of devotees at Puri. If we allow for a spice of poetical license, there is nevertheless a basis of hard fact in his statements. Īśwara Dasa mentions that Gadādhar Das (Pundit ?) was the embodiment of Rādhā, and he used to dress as a female.[266]

The followers of Chaitanya

Divākara was the fifth in the preceptorial descent from Jagannātha Dasa.[267] His surname was Miśra,[268] and he belonged to the Atibaḍi Sub-sect, founded by Jagannātha Dasa. After Īśwara Dasa's Chaitanya Bhāgavata, Divākara Miśra's Jagannātha (Dasa) Charitāmrita is the most important biography written by a Vaishṇava of the Medieval School. In one place of the book, he refers to the conversation between Rai Rāmānanda and the Master, as narrated in Chaitanya Charitāmrita.[269]

Jagannatha Charitamrita by Divakara Dasa

264. Iswara Dasa's Chaitanya Bhagavata, XLVIII.

265. Iswara Dasa's Chaitanya Bhagavata, LXIV.

266. "एमन्त वेश गदाधर। राधा वेश पटान्तर ॥
गदाधर स्त्री वेश होइ। चैतन्य गहने खटइ ॥"
Iswara Dasa's Chaitanya Bhagavata, LXII.

267. Jagannatha Charitamrita, Chapter I.

268. History of Oriya Literature by Tarini Rath, p. 15.

269. "चइतन्य चरित अमृत। गोदावरी कूल चरित ॥
राय रामानन्द पुछिले। शची कुमर आज्ञा कले ॥"
Jagannatha Charitamrita, XIII.

Divākara refers to the Gauḍiya followers of the Master with scant courtesy. He also writes that, "Nityānanda and the twelve Gopālas are born from the celestial Vaikuntha. They are ignorant of the principles of Madhura love."[270] According to Brahma Saṁhitā, Krishṇa in eternal form (Ananta) stays in Goloka. Thus Nityānanda, the embodiment of Ananta, was lacking in the knowledge of Madhura Rasa, which prevailed in Vrindāvana ! Nitya Guptamaṇi is a small Sanskrit book which is attributed to the authorship of Divākara Dasa.

Bhupati Pundita, the author of Prema-Pañchāmrita, lived

Bhupati Pundita towards the end of the 17th century A.D.

Dvārakā Dasa was born in the year 1662, in the fourth regnal year of Mukunda Deva II. He was the author of the

Dvaraka Dasa following books—Parachḗ Gitā, Govinda Gitā, Śaiva Purāṇa and a commentary of the Bhāgavata. Parachḗ Gitā was his most important composition. Dvārakā Dasa is identified with Balarāma Dasa II—the author of Chhatrisa Gupta Gitā.

Kārtika Dasa wrote Rukmiṇi-Bibhā (Rukmiṇi's marriage with Krishṇa) and Śaṅkara Dasa wrote Ushā-Vilāsa (the marriage of Ushā with Aniruddha, the son of Krishṇa) in the 17th century.

The 18th century marked a renaissance in the history of Oriya literature. The Medieval School of thought is reflected

The Oriya Literature in the 18th century. in only a few books, like Mathurā Maṅgala by Bhakta Charaṇa Dasa, Nāmaratna Gitā and Rasa-Kallola of Dīnakrishṇa Dasa. Dīnakrishṇa lived in the reign of Divyasiṁha II (1692-1718). In Nāmaratna Gitā (chapters 28-30) he describes the eternal Rāsa-Arena. The human Krishṇa enters into the Arena and is cursed by Nirākara Hari ! The 18th century saw the final and decisive

270. "नित्यानन्द आदि समेते । द्वादश गोपाल सङ्गते ॥
अमर वैकुण्ठु ए जात । ए न जाणन्ति प्रेम तत्त्व ॥"
Jagannatha Charitamrita, VIII.

triumph of Rādhā-idea in Orissa. Rādhā is the heroine in the following books. The list, it is to be borne in mind, is not exhaustive.

Vrindāvatī Dasi—Pūrṇatama Chandrodaya.

Abhimanyu Sāmanta Siṁhāra—Prīti-Chintāmaṇi
Vidagdha-Chintāmaṇi

Janārdana Dasa—Gopī-bhāshā.

Sadānanda Kavisūrya Brahmā—Chora Chintāmaṇi
Nāma Chintāmaṇi.
Prema Taraṅgiṇī

———

CHAPTER VII

THE PHILOSOPHY OF THE MEDIEVAL SCHOOL OF VAISHNAVISM IN ORISSA.

In this chapter we propose to deal with the philosophy of the Medieval School of Vaishṇavism. Unfortunately there is no clear-cut exposition of the philosophy. Contradictory statements make the situation embarrassing, and textual corruptions add to the difficulties. The reason for this drawback, lies in the nature of the Medieval Vaishṇavism itself. Theories were freely but unsystematically taken from other sects and absorbed. New interpretations were given to the borrowed ideas, so as to be acceptable by the community. Here we will discuss some of the distinctive features of the Medieval Vaishṇavism.

1. The Theory of the Void

The Void according to the Orissan philosophy is not nothingness. The spirit or Purusha, immanent in the Void, is conceived as the Void-Personified. He is known as the Alekh Purusha, *i.e.*, the Being who cannot be described in writing. In other words, expressions fail to describe him. Alekh-Purusha is identical with the Void.[271] He has got no shape or sign.[272] So he is known as the Unformed (Aṇākara) and the Eternal (Anādi Brahma). Chaitanya Dasa in Nirguṇa Māhātmya names him "Nirguṇa Purusha"—one who is not devoid of attributes but above and independent of attributes, of which the worlds are but manifestations.[273] As the Absolute manifests himself in the Void, he is also known as "Śūnya-Purusha."

271. "अलेख पुरुष शून्य दुइँ एकइ समान" Vishnu Garbha Purana, Chap. III.

272. "अलेख पुरुषर नाहि रूप वर्ण" Ibid.

273. Modern Buddhism in Orissa, p. 45.

Sunya Purusha.

Śūnya-Purusha possesses no shape or sign. He is the embodiment of the Void.[274] He has been vividly described in Śūnya Saṁhitā.

"O how great is the power of Śūnya Purusha! Though simply an abstraction, yet he is exercising royal power (over the universe). Śūnya-Purusha keeps himself aloof (from the created world) and reveals his play from the Void. * * * He has his abode on the Void and meditates on the Formless One, through worship of the Void. He worships with the aid of 32 Letters."[275]

The Alekh or Śūnya-Purusha thus corresponds with the attributeless Nirguṇa Brahman or Purusha of the Vedanta. Śūnya-Purusha is a transcendental entity, though he is supposed to perform worship of and meditate on the Void.

2. The Theory of Creation

Nirakara.

When Alekh Aṇākara assumed form, he was known as the formless Vishṇu.[276] "Nirākāra" is thus the creative aspect of Aṇākāra or the Unformed Absolute Being. According to the Vedānta, Īśvara is the creative aspect of the Brahman.

Mahavishnu

Nirākāra is also known as "Mahā-Vishṇu." In his womb Alekh created millions of universes.[277] Mahāvishṇu begot five more Vishṇus. The Gauḍiya Vaishṇava theology also mentions Mahāvishṇu.[278] In the third chapter of Vishṇugarbha Purāṇa, it has been stated that

274. "बाहार रूपरेख नाहिं शून्य पुरुष शून्यदेही"
Virata Gita, I.

275. "शून्य पुरुषर एतेक तेज शून्यटि होइ भोग करइ राज्य ॥
शून्य पुरुष अलगे रहिछि शून्य परे बसि लीला करुछि ॥
शून्य पुरुष शून्य परे रहे शून्य भजन निराकार ध्याये ॥
द्वात्रिंश अक्षर करे भजन शून्य पुरुष निराकार ध्यान ॥"
Sunya Samhita, VIII.

276. "अलेख अणाकार यहुँ आकार धइला
ताहाङ्कर नाम निराकार बिष्णु हेला ॥"
Vishnu Garbha Purana, II.

277. "एते बोलि अलेख महाबिष्णु मूर्ति हेला
बिष्णु गर्भे अनन्त कोटि ब्रह्माण्डमान कला ॥"
Vishnu Garbha Purana, IV.

278. Chaitanya Charitamrita, II, 21.

Brahmā comes out of the navel of Nirākāra. After 108 lives of Brahmā, Nirākāra gives up his existence. He is created again by Aṇākāra and the cycle of creation continues. Īśvara of the Vedānta similarly has a limited existence. For, according to Śaṅkara, his body is Māyā which is unreal. Īśvara exists so long the world exists and no longer.

Virata Purusha

Nirākāra is also known as "Virāṭa" Purusha. Virāṭa is the lustre of the Void.[279] Krishṇa says to Arjuna that he alone existed in the Great Void as Virāṭa Purusha.[280] Krishṇa also says that he will be omnipotent, and so he will be called Virāṭa Purusha.[281]

Adi-Brahma.

Nirākāra is to be identified with Ādi-Brahma. In Nirguṇa Māhātmya, Vishṇu confesses that, "only the great mysterious Anādi Brahma is greater than me. He is beyond description. Words like corporeal or formless fail to express him. I myself worship him and my abode is in his womb."[282] Nārāyaṇa originated from Anādi (Brahma) for mundane exploits.[283]

Vindu-Brahma

Vindu or Material Potency dropped from the Void.[284] Vindu-Brahma is the concrete aspect of Nirākāra.[285] The Tantras also speak of Vindu or Para (supreme) Vindu.

"Vindu implies both the Void and the Guṇa, for when Shiva becomes Vindurūpa, he is with Guṇa."[286] When Śakti[287]

279. "विराट ज्योतिरूपे थाइ" Brahmanda Bhugola. XXVIII.
280. "एका मुँ महाशून्ये थाइ। विराट रूपे थिलि मुहिँ ॥" Virata Gita, I.
281. "बले मुँ हेबि बलीयार। विराट नाम हेब मोर ॥" Prema Bhakti Brahma Gita, Chap. I.
282. Nirguna Mahatmya, XIII.
283. "अनादि ठारु नारायण हरि। संसार क्रीडा अर्थे अवतरि ॥" 36 Gupta Gita, VII.
284. "शून्यरु बिन्दु ये खसिला" Brahmanda Bhugola, LXVIII.
285. "बिन्दु-ब्रह्म रूपे बिजे से निरञ्जन" 36 Gupta Gita, VI.
286. Creation as explained in the Tantras—J. G. Woodroffe, p. 17.
287. "Shakti is the immanent aspect of one Brahman, who is Shiva-Shakti." Ibid. p. 9.

longs to create, she becomes massive (ghanībhuta) and appears as Vindu. The Orissan philosophy does not subordinate Vindu to Yogamāyā or Mahāmāyā.

Yogamāyā is the Ādi-Śakti. She is also known as Ardhamātrā, and she is immanent in the Void.[288] She is to be compared with Mūla-Prakriti of the Vedānta, who exists in association with the Spirit or Chit, and causes the Creation. In the Tantras, she is called Māyā-Śakti—who in the creative operation is the instrumental and material cause of the universe.

Yogamaya

Yogamāyā is Prakriti, and she was caused from the body of Krishṇa, as he informed Arjuna.[289]

She is the goddess and the Personified Great Void is the god; and thus the First Mother and Nirañjana are associates.[290]

She is Ādi-Śakti or the Primordial Energy.[291]

3. The Causation of Rama

We have already seen that Vindu or Material Potency dropped from the Void. Here we shall delineate the theory on the causation of the word Rāma (Rā+Ma).

The Vindu has been conceived as generative fluid. It fell into the womb of Yogamāyā—the First-Mother, and brought forth 'Rā' and 'Ma', denoting Rādhā and Krishṇa respectively. Yogamāyā's womb was ripe for conception. So it has been said :—

Birth of Radha and Krishna.

"Mother's lotus (womb, etc.) had been blossomed. In this the Father caused fertilization. * * * * The sperms got mixed

288. "से योगमाया आदि शक्ति । से अर्द्धमात्रा शून्ये स्थिति ॥"

Prema Bhakti Brahma Gita, I.

289. "मो देहुँ प्रकृति जन्मिला"

Prema Bhakti Brahma Gita, I.

290. "आदिमाता देवी से देवता महाशून्य ।
सखी तहिं आदिमाता सखा निरञ्जन ॥"

Ganesa Bibhuti, II.

291. "से आदिशक्तिटि महायोनि सर्वमाता"—Govinda Gita, V.
"तु आदिमाता शक्ति हेबु' —Prema Bhakti Brahma Gita, I.

with the ova, and caused the name Rāma. In Mother's lotus there were the ova. Thither the sperms appeared as Rādhā.[292]

Thus were born Rādhā and Krishṇa. Yogamāyā made a hole in her body. Through that opening she took out the twin and nourished them.[293]

From this standpoint Rādhā and Krishṇa are but the two parts of a seed.[294] The author of Gaṇeśa Bibhūti Tikā goes so far as to declare them to be brother and sister ! [295]

The nectar :of the nectars was showered from the Void and from the nectar was derived the male being, signified by the letter 'Ma.'[296] Similarly :—"The holiest of holy fluids, originating from the four Attributes (of the Absolute), caused the syllable 'Rā'—which denoted the name of Rādhikā."[297]

Significance of the Letters Ra and Ma.

The love fluid of Rādhā-Krishṇa became personified as "Premarūpā". She conceived and gave birth to "Tripurā." "She was called Tripurā, as her body was identical in the three universes. She was born with ten hands. She is Ādi-Durgā, the First Mother."[298]

Tripura.

292. "मातार पद्म फुटि थाई   नहिं पिता बीर्य्यरइ ॥

*   *   *

रजरे वीर्य्य जात हेला   राम नामटि बोलाइला ॥

मातार पद्मे रज थाइ   वीर्य्यटि राधा रूपे याइ ॥"

Prema Bhakti Brahma Gita, I

293. Prema Bhakti Brahma Gita, I, and Ganesa Bibhuti Tika, XVI.

294. "एक बीज बेनि फाल युगल अङ्गरे" Sunya Samhita, X.

295. "भाइ भग्नी राधाकृष्ण शुण मन देइ"

Ganesa Bibhuti Tika, XVI.

296. "सर्ब मधुङ्क मधु सार   से रस शून्यरु बाहार ।

सेहि से पुरुष ह्वरिले   'म' अक्षर बोलाइले ॥"

Prema Bhakti Brahma Gita, II.

297. "सर्ब पुण्यङ्क पुण्य रस ।   ये चारि कलारु प्रकाश ॥

से रसुं 'रा' अक्षर हेला ।   राधिका नाम बोलाइला ॥"

Prema Bhakti Brahma Gita, II.

298. Prema Bhakti Brahma Gita, III.

Yogamāyā told her to serve Rādhā-Krishṇa, who are sporting at the Rāsa-arena in the eternal region (Nitya sthala) with the Gopīs. She became the Guardian Angel of the eternal region. "Vishṇu has many forms. He is formless too, which is the most secret one. Ardhamātrā, the Primordial Energy, guards the gate."[299] Tripurā has been addressed as Ādi-Durgā in Premabhakti Brahma Gitā, and as Ādi-Śakti in Chhatriśa Gupta-Gitā. Achyutānanda, likewise, calls her Mahāmāyā and Mahā-Durgā.

Buddha-Mata.

Not content with this, he has provided her with eight female associates, one of whom was Buddha-Mātā. Thus did she accost Achyutānanda *alias* Sudām. "Whence hast thou come my son? Formless is this Rāsa-arena in Goloka. The worship of the Formless prevaileth here and only such a worshipper may enter." She revealed her identity as one of the eight female associates of Mahāmāyā Mahā-Durgā. It is to be noticed that no other writer uses this name, which was thus coined by Achyutānanda. It may be noted here that Balarāma Dasa addresses Ardhamātrā as Dharmamātrā.[300]

5. Radha-Krishna In The Eternal Region.

The following story is mentioned in Śūnya Saṁhitā, Chapter X.

Mundane Krishna and Nitya Radha.

Krishṇa in Dvārakā was pining, because of his separation from Rādhā. The eight Pāṭavaṁśis or chief queens asked the reason of his anguish. Krishṇa said, "I leave not for a moment Rādhā's side. Rādhā is in front (of me) and I am behind her as a lustful lover.

299. "एका विप्णु नाना रूप निरञ्जन महागोप्य
अर्द्धमात्रा आदिशक्ति द्वारे उदये"

36 Gupta Gita, II. See also Virata Gita, XXI.

300. "अर्द्दमात्रारे सर्व लीन"—Virata Gita, XII.

"प्रथमे महाशून्य अछि। ता तले धममात्रा गछि" ॥

Virata Gita, VIII.

We form one seed, being split into two component parts representing two separate entities."

"Eternal Rādhā," he added, "dwelleth in the Great eternal region."[301] The queens had misgivings and they said, "Sayest Thou, O Lord, that Rādhā dwelleth in Goloka, attended by eight Sakhis. Then wherefore didst Thou forsake her company? How couldst Thou relinquish Rādhā, who is one with Thee? Verily, the great men invent many lies, we being young women of gullible nature." The chief queens then pressed for a glimpse of Rādhā in the eternal region. Krishṇa had to send for his Vehicle, the Sun-Bird.

"How ambitious are these jealous Rājasika damsels," declared Krishṇa before Garuḍa, "they are desirous of gazing at (eternal) Rādhā."

Krishṇa at first did not like the proposed journey to the eternal region. "How wilt thou take them to that inaccessible place?" said he to Garuḍa. "Fear I, Krishṇa of the eternal region. We will be chastised and admission will be refused to us."[302] But his apprehensions were finally overcome by his longing to gaze at eternal Krishṇa—being lovingly united with Rādhā.[303] Sudām accompanied them.

While they were at a distance of two yojanas from the Rāsa-arena, they were blinded by the glare of countless suns. Further progress was impossible as Krishṇa, the chief consorts and Garuḍa fainted. Recovering consciousness, they hastened to go back. Sudām was more fortunate. He managed to push forward and crossed one more yojana. From a distance, he beheld Rādhā-Krishṇa in eternal Rāsa exploit. The eight

Failure of Krishna and his Consorts to reach the Eternal Arena.

301. "नित्यराधा महानित्य उपरे ता वास"

Sunya Samhita, X.

302. "केभन्ते दुर्गम पथे यिव तांकु घेनि।
महानित्य श्रीकृष्णंकु डरइ मुं पुणि॥
गले ये श्याकट हेव वारण पड़िव"।

Sunya Samhita, X.

303. "देखिवि मुं नित्य-कृष्ण प्रेम-राधा भक्त"

Sunya Samhita, X.

Sakhis are surrounding them and 1600 Gopi damsels are witnessing the exploit.

Buddha-Mātā came forward to meet him. She advised him to profess the Nirākāra Mantra and imparted instruction on it. Then she wended her way back to the eternal Rāsa-arena.[304] Sudām went back to Dvārakā and informed Krishṇa about the Mantra, he had received. Krishṇa congratulated him on his good fortune. This story with slight variation has been repeated in Rahasya Mañjarī of Devadurlabha Dasa.

Nirakara Mantra

According to Achyutānanda, the presiding deity in the eternal Rāsa-arena is formless. He has been indiscriminately addressed as Alekh and Nirākāra (-Krishṇa). "He is called Alekh," says Buddha-Mātā to Sudām, "he being invisible. The Nirākāra region has no shape. * * * Krishṇa is but the Void personified. Discriminating this, I advise you to worship the Formless One."[305]

Nirakara Krishna.

In Nāmaratna Gītā of Dīnakrishṇa Dasa (Chapters 18-20) Tripurā smuggles mundane Krishṇa into the eternal Arena, getting him dressed as a female. But he failed to keep up rhythm. 'Nirākāra Hari' came to know of the intruder and he cursed Tripurā for bringing in 'mortal' (Mānava) Krishṇa—who is but a transitory phase of Vishṇu (Mrityu aṅga Vishṇu kalā)—to the eternal Land.

Eternal And Mortal Krishna.

6. The Theory of Thirty-Two Letters.

The study of the thirty-two Letters is necessary for Krishṇa-worship. The process is that of an inverted pyramid.

First comes Alekh the Absolute, inexpressible by the Letters. (Aṇākshara)

304. "गले बुद्धमाता नित्य रासास मण्डपे"

305. "अलेख बोलन्ति तांकु न दिशन्ति येणु
निराकार मण्डल आकार नाहिं तेणु ॥
* * * * * *
शून्यवर बोलि सिना बोलन्ति कृष्णकु ।
पारि कहि देलु ध्याय तु निराकारंकु ॥"

Sunya Samhita, X.

From the effulgence, was caused Vindu-Brahma which along with Ardhamātrā formed Om or Ekākshara (one Letter).[306]

From one Letter, was derived two Letters Rā and Ma.[307]

Ra—Ma & Tri-Vija.

These two Letters denoted Rādhā and Krishṇa. Their love-ardour gave birth to Premarūpā or Chandrāvalī.[308]

Together they formed Tri-Vīja, which were represented by symbols. Thus :—

Krishṇa=Kāma Vīja=Klim.
Rādhā=Raja Vīja=Slim.
Chandrāvalī=Lajjā Vīja=Hlim.[309]

Gradually the three Letters were broken into component parts. In this way they formed "twice three Letters."[310] Thus :—

Klim=Ki+lam=Krishṇa.
Hlim=Hi+lam=Rāma.
Slim=Si+lam=Haré.

Tri-Vīja was expanded to six Letters.

These six Letters, when doubled, represented the six corners of the eternal Rāsa-arena—each corner being presided

Six Names of Twelve Letters

over by a Gopī. "Thus did six Śakhīs form the six Angles. Listen to the names of the six female associates—which I am going to relate. They are

306. "याहाकु अणाक्षर कहि । से विन्दु-ब्रह्म अछि वहि ॥ तहुँ जन्मिला एकाक्षर"
Prema Bhakti Brahma Gita, I.

"महाशून्य ये ज्योति रूप ज्योतिरु जात टूल रूप ॥
टूलरु अर्द्धमात्रा हेला मात्रारु ओंकार जन्मिला ॥
ओंकार-ब्रह्म ए जगत"

Tulabhina, I

307. "तहुँ जन्मिला वेनिक्षर सेहि राम नाम सार"
Prema Bhakti Brahma Gita, III.

308. "श्रीकृष्ण राधा चन्द्रावली ये नित्य तिनि रूपे केलि"
Prema Bhakti Brahma Gita, IV.

309. "ह्रीं वीज देहरे से चन्द्रावली परा"
Sunya Samhita, IV.

Chandravali's functions changed in the 18th century. In Mathura-mangala and Gopibhasa, she is engaged in arranging the meeting of Radha and Krishna.

310. "युगल तिनक्षर"
Prema-Bhakti Brahma Gita III. See also Tulabhina, I.

Subhadrā, Rañgadevī, Līlāvatī, Priyāvatī, Vrindāvatī and Ratnarekhā.[311]

Eight Names of Sixteen Letters.

The six Angles were subsequently expanded to eight Angles of sixteen Letters. (ह-रे रा-म ह-रे रा-म रा-म रा-म ह-रे ह-रे) Eight Gopīs preside over eight Angles. They are Sachalā, Lalitā, Haripriyā, Vimalā, Dhanyā, Śrīmatī, Padmā and Sukeśī. There are Four Haré and Four Rāma words.

Sixteen Names of Thirty-two Letters.

The eight words were subsequently expanded to sixteen words or names,[312] of thirty-two Letters. There are four Krishṇa, eight Haré, and four Rāma words in the Mantra of thirty-two Letters. The four Krishṇa words signify—Līlāñga, Stoka, Vāla and Śrī-Krishṇa. Four Haré words signify the Śaktis of Krishṇa, namely, Rādhā, Chandrāvalī, Dūti and Tripurā. The other four stand for the Śaktis of Rāma, namely, Rāmā, Rāmāyaṇī, Revatī and Yogamāyā. The four Rāma words denote—Virāṭa, Balabhadra, Śeshadeva and Ananta.

The Sixteen Gopis.

The sixteen words are represented by sixteen Gopīs. "Rādhā-Krishṇa disport themselves in the eternal Arena, along with sixteen (Sakhīs) bearing sixteen names." These sixteen names constitute thirty-two Letters.[313]

"Sixteen Sakhīs, dressed beautifully, form sixteen groups."[314] Madhura Rasa devotion is to be practised by imitating one of the sixteen Sakhīs.

The Influence of Chaitanya.

The influence of Chaitanya is distinctly visible in this theory, advocating Gopī-idea.

The names of the sixteen Sakhīs as given in Vedāntasāra

311. Prema Bhakti Brahma Gita, IV. Vedanta Sara Gupta Gita, XXI, mentions Nitya and Pramada instead of Lilavati and Priyavati.

312. "षड अक्षर नित्य नाम ।।
येथुँ होइला अष्ट कोण । आठस षोल नाम पुण ।।"
Prema Bhakti Brahma Gita, IV.

313. Prema Bhakti Brahma Gita, IV.

314. Vedantasara Gupta Gita, XXIV.

Gupta Gitā and Prema Bhakti Brahma Gitā do not agree, except in the cases of Śyāmalā and Chitra-rekhā. Evidently these are got-up lists to keep pace with the Gauḍiya doctrines. It is also stated that the Master suppressed thirteen out of sixteen names, and propagated only three, namely, Haré, Rāma and Krishṇa.[315]

But the old theory regarding the thirty-two Letters was not irretrievably lost. These Letters form the Nirākāra Mantra, as Achyutānanda informs us.[316] Buddha-Mātā kindly imparted (to Sudām) instructions on the Nirākāra Mantra of thirty-two Letters.[317] Said she to Sudām:—"Formless zone is this Rāsa-arena of Goloka. The worship of the Unformed Absolute prevaileth here and only such worship doth entitle the devotee to come to this place."

Saying this Buddha-Mātā repaired to the eternal Rāsa-arena.

7. The Theory of Pinda-Brahmanda

This theory has not been systematically dealt with. We have accepted only such statements, which are corroborated by more than one author.

The Identity of Pinda with Brahmanda.

According to this theory, the Universe (Brahmāṇḍa) may be identified with the Body (Piṇḍa). As Krishṇa says to Arjuna:—"All the universes may be located within the body. Piṇḍa and Brahmāṇḍa are the same and this fact I disclose before thee."[318]

315. Sunya Samhita, II. See also Gurubhakti Gita, Pt. III, 40.

316. "निराकार मन्त्र पहि द्वात्रिंश अक्षर"

Sunya Samhita, X.

317. "दया कले बुद्धमाता निराकार मन्त्र
द्वात्रिंश अक्षर उपदेश देले तत्व"

Sunya Samhita, X.

318. "ब्रह्मायड येते विधिमत पियडरे अछन्ति समस्त ॥
पियड ब्रह्मायड एकमत तो आगे कहि देलि तत्व ॥"

Virata Gita, IV. See also, Vedantasara Gupta Gita, I, and 36 Gupta Gita, XXIV.

Here we shall discuss some of the principles underlying the theory of Piṇḍa-Brahmāṇḍa.

Ashtanga Yoga.

For salvation, Ashṭāṅga-Yoga is necessary. "The basis of Ashṭāṅga-Yoga is the following:—Four phases of Sun and four of Moon."[319] "By practising Ashṭāṅga-Yoga, Air can be shut out from the body."[320]

Shat-Chakra.

There are fifty Airs in the body. Their abodes are the following, *viz.*, rectum, penis, navel, throat, eye and heart. These six limbs are known as six Chakras. Air from these limbs should be forced towards Sushumnā.[321]

Triveni.

Sushumnā along with the channels Iḍā and Piṅgalā form the Triveṇī, *i.e.* the Gaṅgā, Yamunā and Sarasvatī. "The eye-brows are the ghāts of Triveṇī."[322]

Iḍā=Iḍā represents the Ganges. Piṅgalā=Piṅgalā represents the Yamunā.[323] Sushumnā=Sushumnā stands for

319. "चारि कला चन्द्र चारि कला सूर्य्य अष्टाङ्गयोगर मूल"

36 Gupta Gita, XVI.

Compare—"इङ्गिला पिङ्गाला बुझिबा वाउ सन्धि
रवि शशि चलियाछे तारे कर वन्दि"

Goraksha Vijay, p. 147.

320. "योगे अष्टाङ्ग योग साधि रहिले पवन निरोधि"

Nirguna Mahatmya, I.

321. "पञ्चाश पवन पमन्त पार्थ षड़ चक्रे होन्ति आत यात"

Parache Gita, IV.

"षड़ चक्रु पवन तोलि एकाग्र करि शिशुमुना भरि"

Ibid, VIII.

For Shat-Chakra,—See also Gupta Gita, III; Amarakosha Gita, IV and 36 Gupta Gita, II.

Compare with this statement—

"शरीर संकेत बाउ कमल साधन।
षट चक्र भेद गुरु खेलाउक उजान॥"

Goraksha Vijay, p. 147,

322. "त्रिवेणी घाट ए भ्रलता"

Vedanta Sara Gupta Gita, V.

323. "इङ्गला भागिरथी नाम पिङ्गला यमुना उपाम"

Amarakosha Gita, II.

See also Brahmanda Bhugola, LXX and Parache Gita, X and VI

Siva Svarodaya, p. 5

the river Saraswati.[324] Iḍā is in the right nostril and Piṅgalā is in the left one. Sushumnā is in the inner cavity of mouth.

The Importance of Sushumna.

Sushumnā is the most important channel among the three, and lies between Iḍā and Piṅgalā. "Sushumnā is the gate of 'Trikūṭa'—the abode of Air."[325] "Mind and Air should be concentrated and fixed within Sushumnā."[326]

Importance of Trikuta.

Trikūṭa—We have already mentioned that Sushumnā is the gateway to Trikūṭa.[327] Trikūṭa is the junction of the three tubes and is situated within the two eyes.[328] "Air should be raised upwards and forced within Trikūṭa."[329]

Vaṅkunāla—Some writers locate it in the forehead (Kāumri Maṇḍala) and some identify it with the upper half of the nose. It is the seat of Brahma.[330] Kalpa Vaṭa—Kalpavaṭa is the palate or roof of the mouth.[331]

Haṁsa—It personifies Jīva-Brahma. It exists within Trikūṭa.[332]

324. "अधरे शिशुमुना स्थिति नदीर नाम सरस्वती"
Amarakosha Gita, II.
"मुखरे सरस्वती थाइ" *Ibid*, V.
"दन्त सन्धिरे शिशुमुना" Virata Gita, VI.

325. "पवनर घर त्रिकूट घटइ द्वार ता शिषुम्ना स्थान"
36 Gupta Gita, XXXIII.

326. "मन पवन एक होइ टेकिव शिशुधारे नेइ"
Brahmanda Bhugola, XVI.

327. See also Tulabhina, II. :—"त्रिवेणी त्रिकूटर घाट"
And Brahma Sankuli, III. :—"त्रिकूट दुआर । वहइ पादे शिशुमेरु ॥"

328. "वेनि चक्षुङ्क मध्ये स्थान त्रिकूट वोलि तार नाम"
Virata Gita, VI.

329. "उजाथि पवनकु नेइ त्रिकूट मध्ये भर तुहि"
Brahma-Sankuli.
See also 36 Gupta Gita, XXXIII.—"पवनर घर त्रिकूट घटइ"

330. "वंकुनाल परे ईश्वर परम नाम निराकार"—Gupta Gita, V.
"कपाल वंकुनाल होइ"—Virata Gita, VI.
The word "बेङ्कानाल" has been used in Goraksha Vijay, (p. 147) in connection with air-controlling.

331. "तालुकु कहि कल्पवट"—Virata Gita.

332. "त्रिकूट स्थानरे पुथि हंस खेलु थाइ"
Artha Koili. See also Sunya Samhita, IV.

Parama Haṁsa—He is the Absolute Being.[333]

Mana or Mānasa Sarovara—Air has been compared with water. Thus Trikūṭa, the abode of Air, has been taken to represent a tank—in which swims the bird Haṁsa.[334]

Brahmarandhra—"At the junction of two, (Iḍā and Piṅgalā) witness the way to Sushumnā. Trikūṭa is the peak of the Void. Over it, is the gateway to the seat of Brahma."[335] "Open the gate and see Alekh."[336]

Ardhamatra in the Body.

Ardhamātrā is to be located within the eye-brows.[337] Ardhamātrā is Mahāmāyā or Mahā-Durgā.[338] "Over Ardhamātrā is Vindu-Brahma. Ādi-Brahma manifests himself above Vindu-Brahma in the sky."[339] "If Ādi-Mātā can be propitiated, then you will be freed from worldly worries. Vindu (Brahma) will be perpetuated within the body and Air inside will be stationary."[340]

333. "परमहंस साक्षात निराकार पराए"

Sunya Samhita, X.

334. See Brahma Sankuli, VIII.

Compare :—"सरोवरे आछे पक्षी जानिह निश्चय"—Goraksha Vijay, p. 144.

335. "ए वेनि मध्यमे पुना सुषुमना वाट ।
शून्य मेरु वोलि ताकु वोलन्ति त्रिकूट ॥
तथि उपरे पुनारे ब्रह्मरन्ध्र द्वार"

Saptanga Yogasara Tika.

Compare this statement with :—

"गङ्गा यमुना दुइ धरए उजान ॥
इङ्गला पिङ्गला दुइ सुमेरुर जोरा ।
मेद्ध स्थाने आनिया वन्दी कर चोरा ॥"

Goraksha Vijay, p. 140.

336. "ब्रह्म कपाट फिटाइ अलेखकु देख"

Saptanga Yogasara Tika.

337. "भ्रूलता मध्ये अर्द्धमात्रा"—Virata Gita, VI.

338. "तहिं दुआरी महामायी घाट जगि छि वसि तहिं"

Brahma Sankuli, IV.

"सेहि द्वारे द्वारी दुर्गा महामायी"—36 Gupta Gita, XIII.

339. "अर्द्धमात्रा परे विन्दु ब्रह्म रूपे वसे ।
ब्रह्म परे आदि-ब्रह्म वसन्ति आकाशे ॥"

Chhatris Gupta Gita, VIII.

340. "प्रसन्न हेले आदि-माता कटिव भवभय चिन्ता ।
विन्दुटि पडिव अकटि पवने पडि यिव गणिठ ॥"

8. Demonstration of the Worship of the Void.

The process of Yoga is a complicated one. Mādhurī Dasa, a young Vaishṇava cenobite, practised Yoga. "He concentrated his mind within Triveṇī Trikūṭa. Internal Air was forced upwards. The mind got absorbed in the contemplation of Parama-Brahma."[341]

Practice of Yoga by Madhuri Dasa.

Achyutānanda gave a demonstration of "Śūnya Yantra" before king Pratāprudra, at the instance of the Brahmins. He explains the Śūnya Yantra, as follows :—

Sunya Yantra.

"I put the thirty-two Letters in the following manner. Under the Anāma (Anākshara) was Nāma (Ekākshara) placed. Then Kāmavīja (Klim) was written. The 5 Vargas (probably denoting 5 Pañchātmikas, *viz.* Jñyāna, Dhyāna, Jīva, Tatva and Parama) and 12 Mātrās (possibly signifying the distance of 12 Aṅgulas or Yojanas which is traversed by Haṁsa as a cow) were then sketched. I then drew the Yantra and placed it there." Having seen this the Brahmins were amazed and said, "Of a verity thou knowest the underlying import of spiritual matters." The king again said to Achyutānanda, "Hear me, O Dasa, thou hast drawn the Yantra. Now tell us the Mantra and the manner in which thou performest the worship with that Mantra."

Hearing the peremptory request of the king, Achyutānanda felt rather distressed in mind and said, "Hear then, O king, the Mantra of the worship of the formless Void. (Mantra nirākāra Śūnya-bhajana.) Āsana-Sudhi (purification of the seat) and Aṅga-nyāsa (the ceremonial touching of certain parts of the body) are not needed, nor have Sthānabhaṅga and Dik-bandhana to be observed. One has to sit in Śūnya and worship, to destroy

Sunya Mantra.

341. "माधुरी कुटीर करि योग आरम्भिला ।
त्रिवेणी त्रिकूट मध्ये चित्त स्थिर कला ॥
पवन उजाणि ये टेकिला उपरकु ।
हजिला परमहंस ध्याइला ब्रह्मकु ॥"

Sunya Samhita, XI.

death and to go to Goloka." The Brahmins became angry at his assertion and demanded a demonstration of the worship of the Void on the spot. Achyutānanda complied with their demand. Says he, "I placed the thirty-two Letters upon my heart and sitting straight up from the navel, became absorbed in meditation. Then with upturned face, I concentrated the mind and meditated of Nirākāra. Having thus lifted life up, I was soon sitting in the Void and lost in the contemplation of Parama Haṁsa." Witnessing this, the king was surprised and the Brahmins were speechless.[342] This incident leads N. N. Vasu to suppose that Achyutānanda was a follower of the esoteric Buddhism, though openly professing Vaishṇavism. We have already shown the fallacy of such a statement. Emphasis may be laid anew on the fact that the Medieval Vaishṇavism of Orissa freely absorbed religious ideas from Nāthism and Buddhism, but did not identify itself with either of them.

APPENDIX

The Table of Creation

	TULA BHINA Chap. I	GUPTA GITA I & VIII	36. G. GITA VIII	36. G. GITA X	VIRATA GITA I
1.	Mahāśunya	—	Ādi·Brahma	Mahāśunya	Mahāśunya
2.	Jyoti	—	—	Ādimūla	Sunya
3.	Sthūla	Sthūlaśunya	—	Sthūla	—
4.	Vindu	Vindu	Vindu	—	—
5.	Ardhamātrā	Ardhamātrā	Ardhamātrā	Ardhamātrā	Ardhamātrā
6.	Omkāra	Omkāra	Omkāra	Omkāra	Omkāra
7.	Trivīja	—	—	Trivīja	Trivīja
8.	Mahāmantra	—	—	—	Mahāmantra
9.	32 Letters	—	—	—	—

342. Sunya Samhita, Chap. IX. See also Chap XIII, for Sunya Yantra.

APPENDIX

The Influence of Buddhism on The Philosophy of Medieval Vaishnavism.

Buddhism undoubtedly influenced the philosophy of the Medieval Vaishṇavism.

The theory of "Piṇḍa-Brahmāṇḍa" was partly adapted from the "deha-vāda" of the Sahajiyā Buddhists. The Buddha-within-the-body was adored by the Sahajiyā Buddhists in place of external Buddha.[343] M. M. H. P. Sastri agrees with this hypothesis and remarks, "The Sahajiyās found the great world, *i.e.* the universe, within the human body."[344] Krishṇācharya and Lui were exponents of the Sahaja Vehicle.

Influence on the Theory of Pinda-Brahmanda.

N. N. Vasu has pointed out the Buddhist influence on the theory of Creation. According to the Mahāyānists, Ādi-Buddha or Svayambhu (*i.e.* The Self-existent) created in the beginning—the five Dhyānī Buddhas,—"for the duration of the present systems of the worlds." "This theory of creation," he opines, "is exactly what is to be found in Chaitanya Dasa's work Vishṇugarbha Purāṇa."[345]

Influence on the Theory of Creation.

Nevertheless, there is slight difference between the two conceptions. The five meditative Buddhas were of equal status. But Chaitanya Dasa states that Alekh or Aṇākāra Vishṇu assumed form and was named Nirākāra Vishṇu. Four subsidiary Nirākāra Vishṇu's were born out of original Nirākāra Vishṇu, who was thus *primus inter pares.*

343. "बोहि कि लाभइ एण वि देहे"-Dohakosh of Krishnacharya.
See the article of R. Basu. Bangiya Sahitya P. Patrika, 1334 B. S. No. 1

344. Introduction, Modern Buddhism in Orissa, p. 9.

345. Modern Buddhism in Orissa, p. 95.

Achyutānanda has referred to Nirvāṇa in Śūnya Saṁhitā. Krishṇa says to Uddhava that after the destruction of the world, he will keep Uddhava in the state of Nirvāṇa.[346] He says to Varuṇa that Nirākāra has made Varuṇa—the lord of the Nirvāṇa region.[347] Thus it is clear that the conception of Nirvāṇa was imperfectly understood.

Nirvana.

N. N. Vasu mentions that in Svayambhu Purāṇa of Nepal, Dharma has been represented as "Buddha-Mātā" or "Prajñyāpāramitā."[348] Achyutānanda refers to Buddha-Mātā in Śūnya Saṁhitā. Sudām repaired to the Rāsa Arena of eternal Rādhā-Krishṇa. As he approached the Arena, a Sakhī (female associate) came [349] and accosted him. She asked him the reason of his visit and introduced herself, as one of the eight Sakhīs of Mahāmāyā Mahā Durgā.[350] After imparting Nirākāra Mantra to Sudām, she returned to the Rāsa Arena.[351] Mundane Krishṇa told Sudām as follows:—

Buddha Mata.

"Verily hath Buddha-Mātā, the Sakhī of Ādi Śakti, said that I derive real devotion from the worship of the Formless."[352]

Professor A. B. Mohanty is of opinion that Buddha-Mātā is Mahāmāyā herself. She has been addressed as Sakhī—she being identical with Vrindā. We beg to differ with Professor Mohanty's opinion in the interpretation of the lines.

346. "अन्त काले आम्भे निर्वाण पदरे रखिवुटि तोते नेइ"

Sunya Samhita, XXV.

347. "निराकार निजे निर्वाण पुर अधिपति तोते कले निकर"

Ibid XXVI.

348. Modern Buddhism in Orissa, p. 110.

349. "एमन्त समये एक सखी तहुं आसि"—Sunya Samhita, X.

350. "महामाया महादुर्गा अष्ट सखी आम्भे" *Ibid.*

351. "गले बुद्धमाता नित्य रास मण्डपे" *Ibid.*

352. "बुद्धमाता आदि शक्ति सखी छन्ति कहि ।
निराकार भजने निर्मल भक्ति पाइ ॥

Sunya Samhita, XI.

Jagannāth was considered to be the Buddha incarnation of the Lord. In Dāru-Brahma Gitā of Jagannātha Dasa, Deulatolā of Krishṇa Dasa and in Śūnya Saṁhitā—the story of the manifestation of the Buddha incarnation is given. After the passing away of Krishṇa, the Lord appeared again as Jagannāth. Gautama-Buddha and later on Chaitanya appeared as the incarnations of Jagannāth. This matter will be discussed in detail in chapter ten.

The Conception of Jagannath as Buddha.

It is clear from Śūnya Saṁhitā that Buddhist philosophy (particularly of the Nāgārjuniya and Yogāchāra branches of the Mahāyāna school) was studied in Orissa, even by the Vaishṇavas. The philosophy certainly did not exist in its pristine form. So we find Krishṇa to be the expounder of the Buddhist philosophy. Nāgāntaka and Yogāntaka theories were grouped with Tāntric principles of expelling and killing. Achyutānanda had described the followers of the Nāgārjuniya school as 'hypocrites.' (Chhadma bhakta).

Study of Buddhist Philosophy by the Vaishnavas

But the doctrine of the Void, as expounded by Nāgārjuna, undoubtedly influenced the philosophy of Orissan Vaishṇavism. Nāgārjuna came to Orissa and preached Buddhism. In the 7th century A. D., Hiuen Tsiang found the Mahāyānists, "in all their glory and greatness," in Odra country. The Nāgārjuniya doctrine of the Void was but a reflection of the Great Brahmavāda, as inculcated in the Upanishads and the Gitā, and was thus acceptable to the Orissan Vaishṇavas.[353]

Influence on the Doctrine of the Void.

A word of caution is needed here. In spite of their references to Buddha, Buddha-Mātā and Nirvāṇa—Vaishṇavas like Chaitanya Dasa, Achyutānanda and others were not lacking in sincerity. Our opinion thus completely differs from that of N. N. Vasu who thinks that "though they outwardly professed the Vaishṇava faith

Criticism of the Opinion of N. N. Vasu.

353. Modern Buddhism in Orissa, pp. 2-3.

and propagated the Chaitanya cult, yet in their heart of hearts they were but sincere and staunch pioneers and champions of the long neglected and almost forgotten religion of the Mahāyāna School."[354]

Unfortunately he has wrongly interpreted some of the important lines of Śūnya Saṁhitā. He tries to trace a reference to the Buddhist Trinity by quoting this couplet :—

"बुद्ध माता आदिशक्ति संघ च्छन्ति कहि ।
निराकार भजने निर्म्मल भक्ति पाइ ॥"

The first line he translates as follows :—"I tell you, take refuge in Buddha —in mother Ādi Śakti or the first primordial energy (*i.e.* Dharma) and in the Saṅgha (congregation)."[355] We have consulted three different publications of Śūnya Saṁhitā, but we have not come across the word "Saṅgha."

We agree with Professor A. B. Mohanty who suggests :—

"बुद्ध माता आदि शक्ति सखी छन्ति कहि"[356]

Buddha-Mātā is the associate of the Primordial Energy.

N. N. Vasu has quoted the following lines from the same chapter of Śūnya Saṁhitā.

"बोइले अच्युत तुम्भे शुण आम्भ वाणी ।
कलियुगे बुद्धरूपे प्रकाशिलु पुणि ॥
कलियुगे बौद्धरूपे निजरूप गोप्य ।"

* * * * * *

The Lord said, "Listen, Achyuta, to what I say. In the Kaliyuga I have made Myself manifest again as Buddha. It is desirable, however, for you in the Kaliyuga to hide your Buddhistic frames of mind away from view."[357] This interpretation suits N. N. Vasu's conclusion, and so he further comments that Achyutānanda and his associates were "sincere Buddhists," but "they had to keep their Buddhistic frames of

354. Modern Buddhism in Orissa, p. 39.
355. Modern Buddhism in Orissa, p. 127.
356, Introduction, Anakara Samhita,
357. Modern Buddhism in Orissa, p. 126.

mind hidden under the guise of Vaishṇavism for fear of the persecution by the Brāhmaṇas and kings." It is for this that we find the following line in Achyutānanda's Śūnya Saṁhitā :—

"कलियुगे बौद्धरूपे निजरूप गोप्य"

"It is desirable in the Kali Yuga that the followers of Buddha should be disguised."

N. N. Vasu has omitted the next line as he could not understand.

That line is "एणु ये सकल मुनि जने देले शाप". We propose to translate the passage in the following way. "Hear me, O Achyuta. I shall reveal myself again in the Kali Yuga. I shall cover my (true) form in the Kali Yuga, appearing as Buddha. So did curse all the sages." The curse of the sages in question will be mentioned in chapter ten. The word 'Bauddha' also signifies Buddha.[358] Thus the influence of Buddhism on the Medieval Vaishṇavism was not so deep, as is supposed. Achyutānanda and his associates were pious and sincere Vaishṇavas. They exalted the worship of the Void no doubt, but they took it to be a feature of Vaishṇavism. Achyutānanda remarks, "The Hindus worship Alekh and the Turks (Muhammadans) worship Aleph. So discarding Aleph, the Hindus offer worship to Alekh."[359]

358. Cf. "बउद्ध रूपे महोदधि कूले। भोग विलसिबु तु सेतेवेळे ॥"
"बउद्ध रूपकु आगे धरिबे"
"श्रीहरि बउद्ध रूपे अवतरि केते भोग बिलसिबे"
Sunya Samhita.

359. "हिन्दु भजे अलेख तुरक अलेफ ये।
तेणु अलेफ तेजि अलेख हिन्दु भजे ॥"
Sunya Samhita, VI.

CHAPTER VIII

A. MATERIALS FOR THE HISTORY OF THE CHAITANYA AGE IN ORISSA.

Materials for the history of the Chaitanya Age in Orissa are not meagre. Texts written in Sanskrit, Bengali and Oriya, directly or incidentally allude to this period. Unfortunately few of these books are historically accredited accounts of the Chaitanya Age. All these texts are replete with legendary tales and ultra-human matters. Sectarian spirit has been prominent in most of these texts, and facts have been suppressed, ignored or exaggerated, according to the bias of the authors. Thus historical truths can be deduced, only by a comparative appraisal of the statements. Some of the texts in Sanskrit and Bengali, refer to the Chaitanya Age in Orissa, and they are mentioned below :—

SANSKRIT

1. Chaitanya Charitāmrita—It is popularly known as Murāri Gupta's Kaḍchā (Notes). Chaitanya Age in Orissa has been briefly treated in this book. According to the colophon, the book was completed in 1513 A. D.; but the Kaḍchā refers to the whole of the Master's life. Even his passing away has been mentioned. (I. 2. 12-14) It is generally considered that the last portion of the book has been interpolated later on. But Dr. B. B. Majumdar differs from this view.

2 & 3. Chaitanya Charitāmrita Kavya and Chaitanya Chandrodaya drama, by Paramānanda Sen Kavikarṇapūra. The

360. For further reference—Chaitanya and His Age, p. 61.
The Materials for the Biography of Chaitanya—Dr. B. B. Majumdar, pp. 69-77.
The Materials for the Biography of Chaitanya—Dr. S. K. De, Bangasri, Sravan 1340.

date of the Kavya is 1542 and that of the drama, 1572-73 A. D., as given in the colophons. The drama was written at the instance of Raja Pratāprudra – when stricken with grief after the Master's passing away. This very fact proves that the book was completed during the last years of the king or shortly after his death. Thus the date given in the colophon is wrong.

Dr. Biman Bihari Majumdar adduces other reasons to show that the book was written before 1541.[361] Kavikarṇapūra's books were written not long after the Master's passing away, and he was a courtier of Pratāprudra. Thus his writings give us the most reliable account of the Chaitanya Age in Orissa.

BENGALI

4. Chaitanya Mañgal by Lochan Das. This book does not claim the authority of a reliable book and is almost silent on the last days of the Master. The book was written between 1560 and 1566 A.D.[362] Dr. B. B. Majumdar is of opinion that Lochan's book is partly a free translation of Chaitanya Vilāsa in Oriya by Mādhava Dasa.

5. Chaitanya Mañgal by Jayānanda Das. Dr. D. C. Sen is quite enthusiastic in his admiration of the book. "We find many facts in this book" he writes "not mentioned in any other biographies. For instance, there is the important discovery made from this book that Chaitanya's ancestors belonged to Orissa. The manner in Chaitanya passed away from this world is a revelation, which we owe to this book alone."[363]

But Jayānanda was not a historian. Many of the incidents mentioned in his book are creations of his fancy, and these statements are generally accepted as historically true. Thus, his book has done more harm than good to the cause of history. The Master, in this book, gives

361. The Materials for the Biography of Chaitanya, pp. 88-94.

362. The Materials for the Biography, p. 254.

363. Chaitanya and His Age, p. 90.

political advice to the king. There is no reference to Rāmānanda's learned discourse with the Master.

On the other hand, he is rebuked by the Master for his indifference to Krishṇa-worship! The book was written in about 1560 A. D.

6. Chaitanya Bhāgavat by Vrindāvan Das. Vrindāvan wrote his book in about 1550 A. D. "The Master's relation with the Bengali devotees is the main theme of Chaitanya Bhāgavat."[364] Thus Vrindāvan Das has not described the Master's relation with the Oriya devotees, or his discourse with Rai Rāmānanda. Vrindāvan Das mentions the traditions regarding the Bhuvaneswar temples, and dwells on the sanctity of Jajpur. (Chaitanya Bhagavat, III. 2.)

7. Advaita Prakāś by Īśān Nāgar. Like Murāri and Kavikarṇapūra, Īśān also came into direct contact with the Master. The passing away of the Master has been described in this book. Dr. B. B. Majumdar doubts the genuineness of Advaita Prakāś.

8. Chaitanya Charitāmrita by Krishṇadās Kaviraj. The whole Vaishṇava theology has been summed up with a masterly precision in this book. "With the lay-Vaishṇavas however, the great attraction of the book lies in its delineation of Chaitanya's last days."[365] There is difference of opinion regarding the date of the book. The colophon of Charitāmrita bears a date (1537 Saka=1615 A. D.) which seems to be the correct one. But Nityānanda Das in his Prema-Vilās gives the date as 1581.[366]

Unlike Vrindāvan Das, Krishṇadās Kaviraj has referred to many Oriya Vaishṇavas in his book. But he has worked with

364. The Materials for the Biography of Chaitanya, p. 214

365. History of the Bengali Language and Literature, p. 483

366. For discussions on the date of the Book, see

1. Bharatvarsha, Magh, 1340 B. S.
2. Chaitanya and His Age, p. 95
3. Gaudiya, Vol. X, 39
4. The Materials, etc., pp. 350-60

the definite purpose of extolling Gauḍiya Vaishṇavism, and for that reason has excluded the non-Gauḍiya Oriya Vaishṇavas from his purview.

Krishṇadās Kaviraj has tried to mention the names of as many Oriya Vaishṇavas of the Gauḍiya School as possible. He is somewhat partial towards Rāmānanda Rai ; who was the foremost Oriya Vaishṇava of the Gauḍiya School, and a constant companion of the Master at Puri. Krishṇadās has followed the narration of Kavikarṇapūra, while describing Rāmānanda's discourse with the Master. Rāmānanda was made to repeat the conclusions of Bhakti-rasāmrita Sindhu (II. 8. 64-69) by Rūpa Goswamī, written in the last quarter of the 16th century. The conception of Rādhā's love has been adapted from Ujjal Nilamaṇi, written by the same Vaishṇava patriarch. (The Materials for the Biography of Chaitanya, p. 388) Rāmānanda recited Slokas (Ch. Charitamrita, II. 8. 40 & 44-45) which were composed almost after a century by Krishṇadās himself, and are to be found in his book, Govinda Lilāmrita. Rāmānanda also recited Slokas from Brahma-Saṁhitā (Slokas, II. 8. 29 & 30) when he met the Master, who was on his way to the south, though he had not seen a copy of that Text at that time. (The Materials for the Biography of Chaitanya, p. 368)

Ramananda's Character in Chaitanya Charitamrita

Krishṇadās has quoted Rāmānanda's poem, "Pahilahi rāga nayana bhaṅgé bhéla"—from Kavikarṇapūra's kavya (XIII. 46). But he omits the concluding lines, "Vardhana-rudra narādhipa māna Rāmānanda Rai Kavi bhāṇa" ; probably because an eulogy on the king was considered unbecoming for a devotee like him !

Prataprudra's Character in Chaitanya Charitamrita

Similarly, Pratāprudra's character has not been delineated accurately. The King of Orissa has been described as a devout Gauḍiya Vaishṇava, possibly because the Master lived for a long time and died in Orissa. There is no hint about the king's intimacy with the non-Gauḍiya Vaishṇavas of Orissa.

According to Kavikarṇapūra, the Master at first refused to see the king. Pratāprudra met him later on in the Guṇḍichā

Garden, where the Master lay in a trance of love. Krishṇadās Kaviraj has elaborated the subject-matter. The Master, no doubt, refused to see the king. But he allowed the devotees to introduce the king's son to him. On seeing the prince, the Master thought of Krishṇa, and lovingly did he embrace the prince. The Master was about to fall down, while dancing before the Car of Jagannāth, but the king held him up. The Master recovered composure and cried shame to himself, for having touched the king, a worldling. Kavikarṇapūra, Murāri Gupta or Vrindāvan Das have not mentioned these incidents. The king subsequently met the Master in the Guṇḍichā Garden. The Master revealed his Godhead to Pratāprudra. Murāri Gupta alone has referred to the Revelation, in his Kaḍchā. He writes that the Master showed his six-handed form to the king. (IV. 16. 20). Thus both the king and the prince were blessed by the Master.

Nevertheless, Chaitanya Charitāmrita is a *magnum opus* and is rightly considered to be the biography *par excellence* of the Master.

9. Bhakti Ratnākar by Narahari Chakravarti. This book was written in about 1725 A. D. The author incidentally alludes to the Master's life, though the main object of the book is to narrate the lives of Narottam, Śrīnivās and Śyāmānanda. He quotes the preceptorial table of the Gauḍiya Vaishṇavas, as prepared by Gopāla Guru, the disciple of Vakreśwar Pundit. The grief of the people of Puri—after the passing away of the Master—has been vividly described

Oriya

We shall now refer to the books written in Oriya.

10. Chaitanya Bhāgavata—Mention has already been made of this MS.
11. Chaitanya Vilāsa by Mādhava Dasa. He gives us no important new fact.
12. Chaitanya Adhivāsa by Govinda Śaraṇa Dasa. He was a mohunt of the Rādhakānta Math. This MS. has not yet been traced.

The following Oriya books and MSS. incidentally refer to the Master's life.

Incidental References

13. Śūnya Saṁhita—Achyutānanda Dasa.
14. Jagannātha Charitāmrita—Divākara Dasa.
15. Yaśovanta Dāsaṅka Chaurāśi Ājñya—Sudarśana Dasa.
16. Rāsa—Ananta Dasa.
17. Vedāntasāra Gupta Gitā—Balarāma Dasa.
18. Gurubhakti Gitā—By the disciples of Achyutānanda.
19. Avatāra Mālikā—Ascribed to Achyutānanda.
20. Chaitanya Gitā—This Oriya book, composed by Paramānanda Bhramaravara, narrates a dialogue between Rāmānanda Rai and the Master. This dialogue seems to be a creation of fancy. This book is lost, though its Bengali translation by Haribhakta Kaviraj survives.

Next, we come to the writings of Sadānanda Kavisūrya Brahmā. He was born in the village Saranakula in Nayāgaḍ State in a Brahmin family.[367] His patron was Raja Ghanaśyāma of Madhupur.[368] His real name was Sādhu Charan Dasa, and he was the sixth in preceptorial descent from Gadādhar Pundit. He flourished in the last quarter of the 18th century. Kavisūrya Brahmā was out and out a Vaishṇava of the Gauḍiya School. In the colophon of his Mohan Kalpa Latā MS., he writes that he composed a book on the early life of the Master in common language.[369] We could not trace the existence of this book. There is however another book, the authorship of which is ascribed to him, and which deals with the early years of Chaitanya's life. This MS., Viśwambhara Vihāra, is to be found in the library of Rasbehary Math, Cuttack.

Sadananda Kavisurya-Brahma.

In Chora Chintāmaṇi, he describes Krishṇa's dalliance with the milkmaids. In every chapter of the book he refers,

367. Prematarangini—Chap. XXIV. See also Chithau Chandrodaya MS.

368. Yugal Rasamrita Lahari, Chap. IX.

369. "चैतन्य जीवन बाल्य लीला विधिमते ।
"ब्रह्माण्ड-मङ्गल केवल पराकृते ॥"

Mohana Kalpalata.

367. Prematarangini—Chap. XXIV. See also Chithau Chandrodaya MS.
368. Yugal Rasamrita Lahari, Chap. IX.
369. "चैतन्य जीवन बाल्य लीला विधिमते।
"ब्रह्मायत-मङ्गल केवल पराकृते॥"

for comparison, to the doings of Chaitanya.[370] Some of the prominent Gauḍiya disciples of the Master have been mentioned along with him. In Nāma Chintamaṇi also, he has alluded to the Master and his Gauḍiya disciples. He also wrote Yugala Rasāmrita Sindhu, Prema Taranginị and Chiṭhāu Chandrodaya.

B. THE PRECEPTORIAL TABLES OF THE CHAITANYA MOVEMENT

The Vaishṇavas usually identify themselves with one of the four parental sects, whose exponents were Rāmānuja, Maddha, Nimbārka and Vishṇu Svāmi.

The Maddha Parentage of the Chaitanya Movement.

The Chaitanya Movement claims descent from the Māddha sect. But the Master never spoke of it. On the other hand, he criticised the Māddha Order, while at Uḍupi, for its attachment to rituals and knowledge.[371] So there is room for doubting the authenticity of the table of preceptorial descent.

Valadeva Vidyābhūsan, an erudite Oriya scholar of the Gauḍiya School, made the theory of Māddha origin popular by brilliant exposition in his Govinda-Bhāṣya Commentary of the Brahma Sūtras. The preceptorial list is not to be found in Chaitanya Bhāgavat or Charitāmrita. Bhaktiratnākar quotes a Sanskrit poem of Gopāla Guru Goswami enumerating the table of Apostolic succession. This list is also to be found in Gaura-gaṇoddeśa Dipikā of Kavikarṇapūra.

References in Oriya Literature.

The preceptorial table is to be found in the following Oriya books.

1. Bhakti Jñyāna Brahma Yoga by Achyutānanda Dasa
2. Īśwara Dasa's Chaitanya Bhāgavata
3. Jagannātha Charitāmrita by Divākara Dasa

370. "श्रीवास मन्दिरे आवेशे अवश गौराङ्ग धीरे धीरे चले" etc.
Chora Chintamani

371. Chaitanya Charitamrita, II. 9.

The reference in Achyutānanda's book shows that the Māddha parentage was accepted shortly after the passing away of the Master. It is evident that the Oriya writers could not follow it clearly. The tables of preceptorial descent are quoted below from different texts, for comparison.

THE PRECEPTORIAL TABLES

Gaudiya Account	Bhakti Jnyana Brahma Yoga	Iswara Dasa's Bhagavata, LXV	Divakara's Charitamrita, VII
1. Krishṇa	1. Bhagavāna	1. Nārāyaṇa	1. Vishṇu
2. Brahmā	2. Brahmā	—	3. Brahmā
3. Nārada	3. Nārada	2. Nārada	4. Nārada
4. Vyāsa	—		5. Vyāsa
5. Maddha	4. Maddha	3. Mādhavendra	—
6. Padmanābha	5. Padmanābha	- -	7. Padmanābha
14. Purushottama	..	4. Purushottama	..
15 Vyāsa Tirtha	-	5 Vāsava Tirtha	—
17. Mādhavendra	6. Mādhavendra	—	10. Mādhava Acharya
18. Īśwar Puri	7. Krishna (Keśava) Bhārati	6. Keśava Bhārati	11 Advaita
19. CHAITANYA	8. CHAITANYA	7. CHAITANYA	12. CHAITANYA
	9. Sāraṅga Ghosh	8. Vakreśwar	13. Gaurīdās
	10. Śyāma Ghosh	9. Hridayānanda	14. Hridayānanda
	11. Rāma-Krishṇa	10 Balarāma	15. Balarāma
	12. Nava-Kiśor	11. Jagannātha Dasa	16. Jagannātha Dasa
	13. Sanātana II		
	14. Achyutānanda		

Chaitanya was considered Krishṇa incarnate and his disciples passed for the cowherds and milkmaids of Braja. With the triumph of the Chaitanya Movement in Orissa, the Oriya Vaishṇavas of the Old School had to adjust their theories, so as to retain their influence.

The Gopalas of the Dvapara Age.

According to Gaura-gaṇoddeśa Dipikā by Kavikarṇapūra—Sundarānanda, Gaurīdās Pundit, Uddhāran Dutta, and Abhirām respectively were Sudām, Suval, Suvāhu and Śri-dām in the Dvāpara Age.

In Orissa, the róles of these Dvāpara Sakhās were appropriated by Achyutānanda and his companions.[372] So in Śūnya Saṁhitā, Nilkantheśvara Śiva consoles Krishṇa, (after the destruction of the Yādavas) as follows :—

"Thy companions Dāma, Sudām, Śrivatsa, Suval and Suvāhu, by name, shall be born again; when following the order of incarnations, Hari will manifest himself again. These five—Achyuta, Ananta, Yaśovanta, Balarāma and Jagannātha—will appear in the Kali Yuga and obey implicitly thy command."[373] It is further said, that Sudām shall bear the name Sundarānanda in the Kali Yuga. In his next birth his name will be Achyutānanda and he will be famous among the cowherd people.[374]

Sundarananda and Gauridas Pundit.

Sundarānanda was a disciple of the Master and Nityānanda. He was born at Maheshpur in the district of Jessore in about Saka year 1400.[375] Gauridās Pundit was considered to be the incarnation of Suval. He was a Brahmin, belonging to the district of Burdwan.[376] Hridayānanda Pundit was the disciple of Gauridās, and the preceptor of Balarāma.[377] In this way a link was effected between Balarāma and Gauridās. Balarāma, too, was considered to be the incarnation of Suval.

372. Iswara Dasa's Chaitanya Bhagavata, IVL
Gupta Gita, VII.
Guru Bhakti Gita, I, 32.

373. Sunya Samhita, XXVII.

374. Sunya Samhita, I.

375. Dvadas Gopal—Amulyadhan Roy, pp. 44-48.

376. Dvadas Gopal, pp. 59-62.

377. "श्रीमच्चैतन्य देवस्य गौरीदासाख्य पण्डितः
तस्य शिष्यस्तु गोस्वामी हृदयानन्द पण्डितः
तच्छिष्यो मत्त पूर्वस्तु बलराम इति स्मृतः
महानपि जगन्नाथ दासस्वत् परिचारकः"
Nitya Guptamani, XIX, Sl. 19.
See also Jagannatha Charitamrita, VII.

In Gurubhakti Gītā, further identifications follow. Thus:—

Sudām	=	Sundarānanda	=	Achyuta.
Suval	=	Gaurīdās	=	Balarāma.
Śrīdām	=	Abhirām	=	Ananta.
Suvāhu	=	Uddhāran Dutta	=	Yaśovanta.[378]

Jagannātha Dasa was not directly linked with the Gauḍiya Apostles. He was the disciple of Balarāma, and was Śrīvatsa in the Dvāpara Age.

We have already explained that the followers of the Old School of Vaishṇavism sought to identify themselves with the triumphant Chaitanya Movement. Orissan Vaishṇavism, on account of its eclecticism, was discredited as heterodox. So fictitious lists, claiming preceptorial descent from the Master, became necessary for the followers of the Old School. This attempt may be compared with Valadeva Vidyābhuṣan's exposition of the Māddha origin of the Gauḍiya Vaishṇavism. One wishes that the followers of Medieval School would have taken a bolder and more straightforward stand.

378. Gurubhakti Gita, Book I, 32. See also Foot-note 458.

CHAPTER IX

CHAITANYA AND HIS ORIYA FOLLOWERS.

"Orissa became such a stronghold of the Chaitanya faith that today the name of Gauranga is more commonly reverenced and worshipped among the masses in Orissa than in Bengal itself." *Kennedy—The Chaitanya Movement p. 75.*

For eighteen years the Master lived in Orissa. His route to the Jagannāth temple is even now known as 'Gaura-vāta' and his visit to Cuttack is commemorated every year by 'Bāli-Yātra' festival. Suryanarayan Das, a young research scholar of Orissa, feelingly speaks of the Master. "Śrī Chaitanya Dev's place in Orissa is unique. There is not a single village in Orissa in which he is not worshipped. Nearly seventy-five per cent of the Hindu population of Orissa are Vaishṇavas. * * * For nearly twenty years Orissa was Chaitanya and Chaitanya was Orissa. The king, the subjects, the high and the low—all were mad after him."[379]

In January, 1510 A.D. the Master was initiated into asceticism. Śachī Devi advised that he should stay in the holy place of Jagannāth, so that she might hear his news from the pilgrims visiting Puri.[380] From 1510 to 1516 the Master travelled extensively all over India with sojourns at Puri. "Thereafter at the age of 30, he settled at Puri and spent his remaining days in the constant adoration of Jagannāth."[381]

The Master had a large number of Oriya disciples. According to Śūnya Saṁhitā, the Master's followers numbered 12,000.

379. Vaitarani, Vol. XI, I.

380. Chaitanya Chandrodaya, VI, 9.
The Master came to Puri for the first time in Phalgun, Saka year 1431 and set off for the Deccan after two months.

381. Sir J. N. Sarkar—Chaitanya's Life and Teachings, p. 10.

His most famous Oriya disciple was Rāmānanda Pattanayak, better known as Rāmānanda Rai. "The nativity of our hero is alleged to be Bentpur in the district of Puri, where his kinsmen are still to be traced as Chowdhury Pattanaiks."[382] Rāmānanda was the son of Bhavānanda Pattanayak. He was appointed the governor of Rajmahendri. His bent towards religion made him unfit for the stern duties of a governor. No account was kept and public money was squandered.[383] Rāmānanda was the disciple of Rāghavendra Puri—whose Guru was Mādhavendra Puri.[384]

Ramananda Rai.

Krishṇadās Kavirāj has given a beautiful description of his first meeting with the Master. "Passionately did the Master embrace him and both tumbled down on the ground in excess of devotion, senseless with love, inert or perspiring, weeping, trembling with their hair standing on end, pale of hue and lisping Krishṇa! Krishṇa!"[385]

Ramananda and the Master.

He explained before the Master the graded means of gaining devotion. There is a ring of truth in Kennedy's remark in this connection. "The peculiar tenets of the Bengali Vaishnavas are here set forth with a theological relish and precision that suggests more of the systematic theologian than the eager dialogue between two devotees.[386]

At the Master's bidding, Rāmānanda resigned his post, and thereafter settled at Puri. There he, along with Svarūp Dāmodar, became the inseparable companions of the Master.

382. Rai Ramananda, by Bhakti Siddhanta Saraswati.

383. As the king says—"राजमहीन्द्रारे राजा कैनु रामराय।
ये खाइल ये वा दिल नाहि लेखा दाय॥"
Chaitanya Charitamrita, III. 9.

Vidyanagar is situated some twenty miles east of the modern Rajmahendri and on the south bank of the Godavari.

384. Vaishnava Itihas—Haralal Chatterji, p. 81.
Prataprudra Charit—Vaishnav Charan Das, p. 29.

385. Chaitanya Charitamrita, II. 8 (Sir J. N. Sarkar's Translation).

386. Chaitanya Movement, p. 37.

A few months after the Master's passing away, Śrinivās reached Puri. There he found Rāmānanda and Sārvabhauma talking of the Master, with tears streaming from their eyes.[387] Rāmānanda died before the grand festival of Kheturi, held in the Saka year 1504=1572 A. D.[388]

Ramananda—the Devotee.

According to Krishṇadas Kaviraj, "Rāmānanda was a great devotee and adorer of Vishṇu and his mind was proof against Krishṇa's illusion." He was reckoned as one of the three and a half "Pātras" of the world.[389]

He quoted a poem of his own in the Braja dialect which has been immortalized by the Master's appreciation. As the poem is a well-known one, the translation of only the last three lines is given below :—

6. "Now that Śyāma has forsaken me out of aversion and so, O Maiden, I am appointing you as the Messenger.

7. This is the way, a good looking man does love.

8. The poem has been composed in honour of king Vardhana-rudra by the poet Rāmānanda Rai." The maiden in question seems to be Madanikā or Paurṇamāsi who effected the union of Rādhā and Krishṇa in the Jagannāth Ballabha drama of Rāmānanda. The last line shows that the poem was composed before the poet met the Master.

The Master, in his last days, used to be overwhelmed by most distressing emotions, due to his love-madness for Krishṇa. Rāmānanda comforted him by reciting verses of Vidyāpati, Chaṇḍidās and Jayadeva. His poems are quoted in Padakalpataru by Vaishṇav Das, Kshaṇadā Gitachintāmaṇi (VIII. 6 and XXI. 6) of Viśwanāth Chakravarty, and in Padyāvali (Sloka No. 13) of Rūpa Goswami. We have found some poems in Bengali, which are attributed to Rāmānanda. But we cannot vouch for their authenticity.[390]

387. Bhakti Ratnakar, Chap. III.

388. *Ibid.* Chap. IX.

389. Chaitanya Charitamrita, II. 7.

390. See my article. Prabasi Aswin 1338 B. S.

Rāmānanda's predilection for the Gauḍiya School made him unpopular with the Medieval School of Orissa. Śūnya Saṁhitā does not mention his name, while Īśwara Dasa gives information which is meagre and often incorrect. Rāmānanda is stated to have died at Bārānasi or Biḍānasi near Cuttack, after imparting initiation to Kavir.[391]

Reference to Ramananda in Oriya Literature.

On the other hand, Īśwara Dasa is ten times more copius in his references to the five Associates, who are not mentioned at all in Chaitanya Charitāmrita.

Mādhavī Dasi was the sister of Śikhi Mohanty. Mādhavī was regarded as half a 'Pātra,' (the chosen follower) she being a woman. She was an old and anchoretic devout Vaishṇavī. She was a Karaṇa by caste and was appointed the 'Pānjia' (the temple chronicle-writer) by the king. By virtue of her scholastic attainments she was known as the 'brother' of Śikhi and Murāri Mohanty.[392] In the Dvāpara Yuga, her name was Kalākeli, who was a maid of Rādhā.[393] There is absolutely no reference to Mādhavī Dasi in the Medieval Vaishṇava literature of Orissa.

Madhavi Dasi.

Mādhavī may be styled the "Mirā Bai" of Bengali religious literature. Some of her poems in Bengali and Brajabuli are of surpassing beauty. Padas like "नीलाचल हइते शचीरे देखिते आइसे जगदानन्द" "(Jagadānanda comes from Nīlāchala to visit Śachī) are bound to appeal every reader. The agony of the aged mother—whose only surviving son (one, possessing all the virtues) had renounced the world—touched the heart of this old pious lady, though separated from Śachī by distance and language.

Madhavi as a Poetess

391. Chaitanya Bhagavata, LXV

392. "शुद्ध बुद्धिरथ माधवदेवी भ्रातरस्त इति तत्र समासन्"

Chaitanya Charitamrita of Kavikarnapur, Chap. XIII. 90.

393. Gauraganoddesa Dipika.

Junior Haridās, a young Bengali Vaishṇava, was once sent by Āchārya, to get a maund of rice from the house of Mādhavī Dasi. Somehow or other, he behaved indecorously and was consequently shunned by the Master.[394] Mādhavī had also to suffer due to the scandal caused by Junior Haridās ; and she gives vent to her feelings in one of her poems, "Everybody, who beholds the face of Gorā (Gaurāṅga), floats in the ocean of Love. But alas, Mādhavī is deprived of that bliss due to her own fault."[395]

Madhavī's misfortune.

Sikhi Mohanty—Śikhī Mohanty, the brother of Mādhavī, was the scribe of the Jagannāth temple.[396] At first he did not subscribe to the new movement. But one night he dreamt that Chaitanya was no other than Jagannāth himself. His brother Murāri was a devoted follower of the Master.

Janardana—He dressed the body of Jagannāth. Probably he was Janārdana Pati, the temple-servitor, who was a disciple of Jagannātha Dasa.[397]

Krishna Dasa—He held the golden rod of Jagannāth. According to Purushottam Chandrikā, it is the duty of the Parichhā, to hold the cane.

Gopala Guru—He founded the Rādhā-kānta Math at Puri, and was a disciple of Vakreśwar Pundit.

Mamu Thakur—He served in the temple of Gopīnāth at Puri.

Brahmin Vaishnavas—The following Vaishṇava worthies were Brahmins ;—Murāri, Vishṇudāsa, Śrīnātha Miśra, Rāmachandra, Paramānanda, Raghunātha and Oriya Haridāsa.[398]

394. Chaitanya Charitamrita, III, 2

395. "ये देखये गोरामुख सेइ प्रेमे भासे ।
माधवी बञ्चित हइल निज कर्म दोषे ॥"
Padakalpataru—edited by Satish Ch. Roy.

396. Chaitanya Chandrodaya, VIII. 6.
Charitamrita kavya of Kavikarnapura—XIII. 3.

397. Jagannatha Charitamrita, I, Sloka 89.

398. See Vaishnav Vandana books of Jiva Goswami, Devaki Nandan Das, and of Vrindavan Das II.

Svapneśwara bade the Master to dinner at Cuttack. (Chaitanya Charitamrita, II. 16).

Pradyumna Miśra—He was advised by the Master to take religious instruction from Rāmānanda Rai.

Introducing these Vaishṇavas to the Master, Sārvabhauma exclaimed ;—"These Vaishṇavas are ornaments of the holy city and all are devotedly intent on your feet."

Kasi Misra—He was in charge of the affairs of the Jagannāth temple.[399]

Because of the nearness of his house to the temple, it was selected as the residence of the Master.

"Gambhira"

The room alloted to the Master in Kāśi Misra's residence is known to the posterity as 'Gambhirā.' The word has no special significance, as generally supposed.[400]

Odra Krishnānanda and Śivananda—They are addressed as Odra, to distinguish them from their Bengali namesake.

Tulsi Parichha—He was a Pātra or officer of the king. He, along with king Pratāprudra and Kāśi Miśra, participated in the Nandotsava when the Master acted as Krishṇa.[401] According to Devakī Nandan, his surname was Miśra. He has also been mentioned in the Vaishṇav Vandanā books of Jiva Goswami and Vrindāvan Das II.

Jagannatha Mohanty—He dressed as Yaśodā, during the Nandotsava festival. Kānāi Khuntia had two sons, Jagannātha and Balarāma by name.[402] Jagannātha Mohanty seems to be a

399. Chaitanya Chandrodaya, VIII. 3.

400. "Gambhīrī" is the proper word, meaning a solitary cell. In Dinakrishna Dasa's book, Prastava Sindhu—Bhagavata, a bogus religious mendicant, advises a man to construct a small cell on a boat, fastening planks by iron nails. "से नाव भितरे एक गम्भीरी। पटा छाड़ु टुटा कपटा मारि॥" Then the man should enter within the cell. "गम्भीरी भितरे प्रवेश याइ" "In Gopi-Bhasha (Chap. X) Krishna took a Gopi to a small room for enjoyment. "गम्भीरी घररे सुरति कले"

401. Chaitanya Charitamrita, II. 15.

402. "कानाइ खुंटिया बन्द विश्वेर प्रचार।
जगन्नाथ बलराम दुइ पुत्र यार॥"
Vaishnav Vandana, of Devaki Nandan Das.

son of Kānāi Khuntiā. Khuntiā in Kānāi's case may be a designation of honour. Achyutānanda's father Dinavandhu Mohanty got the designation of Khuntiā from the king.[403]

An objection may be raised that no father and son would take up the *roles* of Nanda and Yasodā respectively. But the Master once dressed himself as Rādhā, while Advaita took up the *role* of Krishṇa—though he was a friend of Chaitanya's parents.[404]

Bhavananda and his Sons :—Bhavānanda Pattanayak was the father of Rāmānanda, Gopīnātha, Sudhānidhi, Kulanidhi and Vāṇinātha. All his sons were favoured by the Master.[405] Vāṇinātha served the Master for some time.

Rai Champati—Kavikarṇapūra and Krishṇadas Kavirāj do not refer to him. His poems are to be found in Kshaṇadā Gita Chintāmaṇi, (IX, 5) and in Padāmrita Samudra. Rādhāmohan Thakur, the compiler of the last-mentioned book, introduces him as an officer (Mahāpātra) of Pratāprudra. Rai Champati composed religious poems also in his mother tongue. "In his Harivilāsa Pravandha he glorified the king Purushottama Deva and his queen Annapūrṇā Paṭṭa-Mahādevi."[406]

Kanai Khuntia—The work of the Khuntiā is to supply garlands to Jagannāth.[407] Kānāi took the *role* of Nanda during the Nandotsava festival, (on Krishṇa's Nativity day) and the Master bowed before him.[408] He wrote a book of the name of Mahā-Prakāśa, which is not yet traced.

In Aprakāśita Padaratnāvali, a Bengali poem of Kānāi Khuntia has been quoted (No. 434). The ending couplet runs as follows :

"कानाइ खुँटिया कय मोर मन हेन लय
बाँशी हैल अवला वधिते"

403. Iswara Dasa's Chaitanya Bhagavata, XLVI.

404. Chaitanya Chandrodaya, III. 10.

405. Chaitanya Charitamrita, II. 10.

406. Introduction. Types of Ancient Oriya Prose & Poetry.

407. Appendix ; Types of Ancient Oriya Prose & Poetry. Also see footnotes, 254 & 255.

408. "पिता ज्ञाने नमस्कार कैल"
Chaitanya Charitamrita, II, 15.

"Says Kanai Khuntia : It seems to me that the flute is there only to kill the helpless women". One Kānhu Khuntiā was a disciple of Jagannātha Dasa.[409] He may be the Kānāi Khuntiā of the Gauḍiya texts.

Now we will refer to a few devotees whose names are not known to us. Sārvabhauma speaks of the 'highminded' Praharāja Mahāpātra. Praharāja was the surname and not the name. It is the business of the Praharāja to recite from the Vedas before Jagannāth. In one of his Jagannāth temple inscriptions, Kapilendra mentions one Mahāpātra Velaśvara Praharāja. Similarly, we are not told the names of two other Mahāpātra's, namely, Harichandan and Maṅgarāj. They were deputed by the king to attend the Master when he was returning to Bengal.[410]

The Gauḍiya texts refer to the following non-Brahmin Oriya Vaishṇavas ;—Vipra Dasa, Mādhava Patnaik, Kaśināth Mohanty, Baladeva Mohanty and Gopāla Guru. One Balarāma Dasa has been mentioned in the Vaishṇav Vandanā books of Devaki Nandan, Jiva Goswami, and Vrindāvan Das II. Probably Balarāma Mahapatra is meant by them.

Prataprudra.

King Pratāprudra is described by a writer of the Gauḍiya School, as the embodiment of Indradumnya.[411] He and his queens were devoted followers of Chaitanya.[412]

Prataprudra in the Gaudiya Books

The Gauḍiya books represent the king as a devout adherent of the Gauḍiya School, who neglected the affairs of the State towards the end of his life and passed his time in religious discussions with the Gauḍiya Vaishṇavas. Further-

409. Jagannatha Charitamrita, Chap, I, Sl. 16.
410. Chaitanya Charitamrita, II. 10
Chaitanya Bhagavat, III. 3.
411. Devaki Nandan Das — Vaishnav Vandana.
412 The following names of his queens are known—

Chandrakalā	—	Jayananda Das
Bhānumati	—	Iswara Dasa.
Padmāvati	—	Sarasvati Vilas.
Vidyukānti	—	Sudarsana Dasa
Gaurī	—	Divakara Dasa

more, Jayānanda states that the Master dissuaded the king from invading Bengal. According to Vrindāvan Das, the Master blessed the king as follows :—"Let thy mind be devoted to Krishṇa. Do nothing else but the work of Krishṇa. Chant always the name of Krishṇa."[413] Narahari Chakravarti has put the finishing touch to this portrayal of Pratāprudra. The king is stated to have handed over the kingdom to his son, in the life-time of the Master. (Prabhu Krishṇa Chaitanya Chandrer Vidyamāné) After the passing away of the Master, the king could no longer stay at Puri, and he left that place.[414]

N. N. Vasu writes in his Archæological Report of Mayurbhanj that Pratāprudra started for Vrindāvana ; but died on his way, at the village Rāmachandrapur in Mayurbhanj. The name of the village was changed in his memory to Pratāpapur. It is also said that he caused an image of Chaitanya to be carved out of Nimba wood. The image is still worshipped there.

Emphasis may be laid anew on the fact that the Gauḍiya version can not be fully relied upon. According to Jayānanda,

Criticism of the Gaudiya Version

the Master went to Cuttack to meet the king, by order of Jagannāth. He presented the garland of his neck to Chandrakalā, the chief queen of Pratāprudra.[415] The absurdity of such statements requires no further comments. We are inclined to believe that the Master's *role* as the political adviser, is a creation of Jayānanda's fancy.

Pratāprudra has been given a prominent place, only in one chapter of Chaitanya Bhāgavat. (III. 5) He meets the Master in the Guṇḍichā Garden and is blessed by him. But Murāri and Krishṇadās Kaviraj do not refer to this benediction. According to them, the Master revealed his Godhead to the king.

413. Chaitanya Bhagavat, III. 5.

414. Bhakti Ratnakar, III, p. 111.

415. "राजार शतेक स्त्री नाम चन्द्रकला।
गौर चन्द्र दिल तारे गलार दिव्यमाला"
Chaitanya Mangal, p. 103.

No other writer corroborates the account of Narahari Chakravarti. On the other hand, Kavikarṇapūra's description proves that the king faithfully performed his duty even after the passing away of the Master.[416]

Reference to Prataprudra in Oriya Literature

The Oriya texts refer to the king's devotion to the Master. The King's lament at the sight of the Master's passing away has been vividly described in Śūnya Saṁhitā (Chap. I) and in Jagannātha Charitāmrita (Chap. VII). The Master asked the king to provide lodging for the Bengali devotees.[417] The king joined the chanting party led by the Master.[418] Pratāprudra requested the Master to initiate him. The Master imparted the great Mantra into his ear.[419]

Prataprudra's Devotion to the Master.

The Oriya books tell us that the king also patronized the Vaishṇavas of the Medieval School, particularly the five Associates. At the complaint of the Brahmins, the king summoned Balarāma Dasa and asked him to expound the principles of the Vedānta.[420] Instead of doing so, Balarāma made an illiterate simpleton explain the Vedantic theory of Creation. Chaitanya had imparted the (great) Mantra to the king. Balarāma explained the 'Yantra' to him.[421] It is further stated that the king clasped Balarāma's feet and exclaimed :—"Chaitanya indeed is my preceptor. But

Prataprudra and Balarama Dasa

416. Chaitanya Chandrodaya, I. See also, Chaitanya and his Age, p. 235.
417. Iswara Dasa's Bhagavata—Chap. LXIII.
418. Iswara Dasa's Bhagavata—Chap. LXIV.
419. "शुणिण चैतन्य गोसाईं नृपति कर्ण दीक्षा कहि ॥
कर्णेण महामन्त्र देले समस्ते हरष होइले ॥"
Iswara Dasa's Bhagavata, Chap. XLIX.
420. Vedantasara Gupta Gita, I. Sunya Samhita, I.
421. 'Yantra' is necessary for the worship of the Formless One. As one Brahmin challenged Achyutananda "देखिबा दासङ्क शून्य भजन। किरूपे यन्त्रकु कले स्थापन॥" "Let us see the performance of the Void-worship by the Dasa, and how he sets up the Yantra."—(Sunya Samhita, X).

thou art a greater preceptor to me."[422] He presented money and dress to Balarāma. This statement, as it stands, cannot be believed. The evidence of Chaitanya Charitāmrita is sufficient to dispel the idea that Pratāprudra would give Balarāma Dasa a position more exalted than that of the Master himself. To us it appears to be as absurd as the alleged exposition of the Vedanta by an illiterate simpleton.

But there is no reason to disbelieve the fact that Balarāma Dasa was highly esteemed by the king.[423] In Yaśovanta's 84 Arts, (Chap. 42) Balarāma Dasa states that he had expounded the principles of the Vedanta before the king. He praises the devotion of the king in his books, Beḍā Parikramā and Amarakosha Gitā.

Little is known about Ananta Mohanty's relation with the king.

But materials are not lacking so far as Achyutānanda is concerned. Like Balarāma, he too was subjected to a trial

The King and Achyutananda.

of knowledge before the king. The Brahmins did not like the Void-worship, and they demanded that Achyutānanda must give a demonstration of the Void-worship before them. Achyutānanda agreed, and by controlling Air within the body he was at one with the Void. The Brahmins were put to shame. The king was highly pleased. He praised him unreservedly and gave away lands near the mouth of the Bāṅki river.

Jagannātha Dasa, like his companions, enjoyed the king's

422. "चैतन्य गुरु ये मोहर। परम गुरु ये तुम्भे मोर॥"

Vedantasara Gupta Gita, XXIV. This Chapter in the Union Press Publication is not to be found in the Utkal Sahitya Press Publication of Vedantasara Gupta Gita. Thus the chapter may be an interpolated one.

423. "महाराज प्रताप रुद्र पति। बलराम दासंकु गुरु चिन्ति॥
लभिले परम कारण।"

Vedantasara Gupta Gita—Chap. XVII, Union Press Publication; Chap. VII, Utkal Sahitya Press Publication.

patronage. According to Divākara Dasa, Gauri, the Paṭṭa-mahādevī, was a disciple of Jagannātha Dasa. There is a story in Jagannātha Charitāmrita, which shows the supernatural power of the Dasa, but it is lacking in good taste. Jagannātha proved before the king that he assumed female body for three days in every month. The king gave him a house to the south of the Mārkaṇḍeya shrine to dwell. This house formed the nucleus of the 'Oriya Math.'

The King and Jagannatha Dasa.

Yaśovanta Dasa did not lag behind his companions in the exhibition of occult powers. Thus when his fame was noised abroad, Pratāprudra sent for him. He astonished the king by causing leaves to grow on a dead Kadamba tree.[424]

The King and Yasovanta Dasa.

The Oriya texts clearly show that Pratāprudra patronized the five Associates and took keen interest in the Yoga principles which they expounded. Achyutānanda was a mere lad when the Master visited Puri. He gave the demonstration when he was a grown-up man. Thus Pratāprudra was interested in the principles of the Void-worship, even after he came into contact with the Master.

Eclectic Faith of Prataprudra.

In the beginning of Sarasvati-Vilāsa, Pratāprudra calls himself "श्रीदुर्गा वरपुत्र" (blessed by Durgā). He was supposed to be the favourite of Śiva.[425] When angry, he was looked upon by his enemies as Rudra the Dreadful.[426] Heramba has been supplicated for good fortune (Anantavaram inscription— dated about 1500 A. D.) and for protection. (Velicherla inscription dated 1510 A. D.) Durgā has been propitiated in the latter inscription by grant of land for meeting the expenses of her worship. He invoked the Boar for blessing in Anantavaram inscription. Thus the king was liberal in his religious views—though he persecuted the Buddhists as has been stated previously.

424. Yasovanta Dasa's 84 Arts, Chap. XXXIX.

425. "रुद्र अवतारे गजपति प्रतापरुद्र ये नृपति"
Vedantasara Gupta Gita, I.

426. "काल-रुद्र"—Anantavaram Inscription.

The king compiled a treatise on the Hindu Law, named Sarasvatī-Vilāsa. There is a poem in Bengali quoted in the 'Catalogue of old MSS.'[427] which bears the name of Pratāprudra in the *bhanitā.*

Prataprudra as a Scholar

Chaitanya and the Five Associates :

The Gauḍiya books are almost silent regarding the five Associates. On the other hand, several Oriya books affirm that the Associates were close followers of the Master, inspite of their non-allegiance to the Gauḍiya School.

So the first question will be this :—"what was Chaitanya's attitude towards the non-Gauḍiya faiths ?" Even from the Gauḍiya texts we find that the Master indiscriminately offered homage to the gods. He made no distinction in the propagation of the gospel of Love. "Jajpur was full of Śiva images. Lord Gaurāṅga bowed to each of them. Then with joyful heart, he went to behold Virajā Devi. In the bliss of gazing, love welled out and the Master prayed to Virajā for imparting devotion into his mind."[428] At the sight of the Śiva images, he used to be thrown into ecstasy. The exponents of Gauḍiya faith point out that Śiva is *par excellence* a Vaishṇava.[429] But Śiva has been made to admit the superior position of Krishṇa.[430] The Master was above all sectarian spirit of exclusiveness. He revered all other incarnations of Vishṇu including Rāma. But Sārvabhauma explained that Krishṇa's name is three times superior to that of Rāma.[431]

Chaitanya's Attitude towards non-Gaudiya Faiths.

427. Published by Bangiya Sahitya Parishad, Vol. III. The bhanita is "প্রতাপরুদ্রে কৃপা করহ আপনি"

428. Lochan Das's Chaitanya Mangal, Madhya Khanda. For the description of Chaitanya's devotion to Lingaraja of Bhuvaneswar, see Murari Gupta's Kadcha, Chap. VIII.

429. "বৈষ্ণবানাং যথা শম্ভু" Bhāgavata, XII. 13.6.

430. Chaitanya Bhagavat, II. 19 & III 2.
Chaitanya Charitamrita, I. 6 & I. 14.

431. Chaitanya Chandrodaya, VII. 27.

Chaitanya visited the shrine of Varāha at Jajpur and the temples of Nrisiṁha at Puri, Ahobal, Jiyaḍ and Pānā.

These references from the Gauḍiya texts show that the Master's devotion knew no barrier or distinction. His superhuman personality did not believe that salvation was restricted only to those, who believed in a particular form of Vishṇuite worship. He praised Anupam for his unflinching devotion to Rāma, and nobody was happier, when Murāri refused to abandon the worship of Rāma, the god of his vow.[432] Thus there is no reason to surmise that the Master was sectarian and exclusive in his religious opinion, and that he shunned those who professed tenets of the non-Gauḍiya Schools of Vaishṇavism. In this connection, the statement of Achyutānanda is interesting. "Chaitanya Prabhu is an erudite scholar in the Vedanta and Vedic studies. However learned a man is, he finds in Chaitanya his equal."[433]

In Śūnya Saṁhitā, Achyutānanda speaks enthusiastically of the Master's intimate relation with the five Associates. "The five Associates, Ananta, Achyuta along with Balarāma, Yaśovanta and Jagannātha, used to dance with Gaurāṅga Chandra".[434] In Chapter X, Śrī-Krishṇa informed Sudām that he is going to descend to the earth.

Chaitanya's Relation with the Five Associates.

"Thus ordered the Lord, 'goest thou Sudām. We shall meet again in the Kali Yuga. I shall reveal Myself in the form of Buddha.'

"Sundarānanda will be the name thou wilt bear. My manifestation (kalā) will appear at Navadvīpa, and will be named Chaitanya. Appearing in the world for the salvation

432. See Chaitanya Charitamrita, II. 15 & III. 4.

433. "महापण्डित श्री चैतन्य गोसाईं वेद वेदान्तरे सार
ये येमन्ते विद्या संखोला करन्ति पढ़न्ति सेहि प्रकार"

Sunya Samhita, I.

434. "अनन्त अच्युत घेनि यशोवन्त बलराम जगन्नाथ
ए पञ्च सखाहि नृत्य करि गले गौराङ्ग चन्द्र सङ्गत"

Sunya Samhita, I.

of the sinners, I shall preach the name of Hari from door to door. At that time thou shalt stay with us. Known by the name Achyuta, thou shalt save the cowherd class."

Rāsa, written by Ananta Dasa, is a rare MS., which contains a speech of the Master.

Thus said the Master :—"As he (Jagannātha) speaketh of the most secret knowledge, so I give him the epithet, "very great." Yaśovanta knoweth the facts, which are beyond the reach of other persons. Ananta knoweth the science of the Magical symbols. Achyutānanda speaketh of the past and present, whilst Balarāma explaineth the principles (of philosophy)."

The Demonstration of the five Associates.

In Yaśovanta Dasa's 84 Arts, we find Chaitanya seated in the Mukti Maṇḍapa along with the five Associates, the king and Sārvabhauma. The Master declared that the five Associates were the followers of Krishṇa, in every age. The Associates replied that they were but five branches of one tree. (Pañcha Śākhā). The Master called them[435] to his side and asked them to give a demonstration of their occult powers. He handed over the seed of a jack fruit to Jagannātha Dasa. The five Associates caused a tree, laden with fruits, to grow up from the seed.

Yaśovanta stated that the Lord was born and would be known as Chaitanya. By His order, the five Associates were born— to be his followers.[436]

Chaitanya is said to have explained the significance of sixteen names to Jagannātha Dasa, Śyāma Mantra of five letters to Yaśovanta, Tārak Brahma Mantra to Balarāma, the Mantra of

435. "कहन्ति चैतन्य गोसाईं पञ्च सखाङ्कु पाशें राइ ॥
बोइले जगन्नाथ दास मोर निकट वेगे आस ॥
पुणि राइले बलराम आस गो निकटे बहन ॥
यशोवन्त दास तु आस अच्युतानन्द शिशुदास ॥
प्रभुङ्क श्रीमुख वचन राइले गलु सन्निधान ॥"
Yasovanta Dasa's 84 Arts, Chap. XLII.

436. "जनम हेले भगवान चैतन्य प्रभु बोलि जाय ॥
ताङ्क आदारु पञ्च सखा जनम होइ संङ्गे लेखा ॥"
Yasovanta Dasa's 84 Arts, Chap. XLII.

one Letter to Ananta, and the Mantra of No Letters to Achyutānanda.[437]

References to Jagannatha Dasa in Gaudiya Literature.

Jagannātha Dasa is mentioned in Vaishṇav Vandanā books of Devakī Nandan, Jīva Goswamī and of Jaikrishṇa Das. Devakī Nandan speaks of him as a great singer, whose songs pleased Jagannāth.[438]

Jaikrishṇa Das states that Oriya Balarāma Dasa and Jagannātha Dasa are born in Orissa.[439] Most likely he means the two famous Oriya Vaishṇavas of those names. Krishṇadās Kaviraj refers to Jagannāth—Kāshṭhakāṭā, Tīrtha, Mohanty and Āchārya ; but is silent about Atibaḍa Jagannātha.

The Gauḍiya Vaishṇavas allege that Jagannātha started a heretical sub-sect of his own, known as 'Atibaḍi'. In Bengal also, there was one 'Atibaḍi' sub-sect of Rūpa Kaviraj,[440] and both had been tabooed by Totārām Babaji—a Vaishṇava divine of the Gauḍiya School.[441]

Chaitanya and Jagannatha Dasa.

Jagannātha's spiritual mentor was Balarāma Dasa.[442] Jagannātha begged the Master to initiate him into the name of Hari. "Hearing this, the Master was glad, and he ordered Balarāma to give initiation to Jagannātha, and to teach him the chanting of the name of Hari."[443] Balarāma faithfully obeyed the command of the Master.

437. Gurubhakti Gita, pt. III, Chap. XL.

438. "जगन्नाथ दास वन्दि सङ्गीत पण्डित ।
यार गान रसे जगन्नाथ विमोहित ॥"

Devaki-Nandan.

"वन्दे हि जगन्नाथ॰ यद्गानात् तरवोऽरुदन विवशा इव"

Jiva Goswami

439. "उत्कले जन्मिला उड्या वलराम दास ।
जगन्नाथ दास आर तथाइ प्रकाश ॥"

Vaishṇav Vandana—Jaikrishna Das

440. Rupa Kaviraj was excommunicated by Hemalata Thakurani (the daughter of Nityananda) whose disciple he was.

441. See the Gaudiya Magazine :—Vol. IX, 24

442. Nitya Guptamani, XIX, Sl. 19 ; Jagannatha Charitamrita, II ; Iswara Dasa's Bhagavata, LXV.

443. Jagannatha Charitamrita, II.

The translation of the Bhāgavata points out Jagannātha Dasa's devotion to Krishṇa. After describing the disappearance of Krishṇa from the Rāsa-Arena, the poet was beside himself with excess of emotion. He writes that his mind tried to pursue Krishṇa but failed. With great humility he attributes the failure to his own shortcomings.[444] Such expressions show what he really was—a sincere and devout Vaishṇava of the Medieval School.

The Story of 'Atibada' Designation.

According to Divākara Dasa, the Master bestowed upon Jagannātha Dasa the epithet of Atibaḍa—in recognition of his occult powers. Divākara's long statement has been abridged in the following lines.

One day the Master asked Jagannātha about his past births. With his characteristic humility the Dasa replied :—"Suffer me to recount the facts O Master, which are known to thee. Once, while I was meditating on Rādhā-Krishṇa, I forgot my mundane entity, in the bliss of imagination. Then I could realize that Rādhā and Krishṇa were gazing coyly at each other's face in Vaikunṭha. Krishṇa laughed and from that laugh wert thou born. Rādhā in response smiled prettily and I was born from her laugh. Thou wert commissioned to appear in the Kali Yuga for the salvation of the sinners."

The Master replied :—"Verily this is wonderful. Thou art then a partial manifestation of Śri Rādhā—the supreme object of Krishṇa's love ! Only the adepts are able to comprehend the mellowness of Rādhā's love. In sooth O Dasa, thou art a great person !" Then taking off his red-ochre coloured wrapper, he tied it round the head of Jagannātha Dasa and said, "Thou hast spoken great words. So wilt thou be known as Ati-baḍa."[445]

444. Jagannatha Dasa's Bhagavata, X, 30

445. "हरष होइले गोसाईं ॥

आपणा श्रीअङ्ग पाछोडि   कशा वसन अङ्गु काढि ॥

दासङ्क शिरे बान्धि देले   'अतिबड' बोलि बोइले ॥

अतिबड कथा कहिले   तेणु अतिबड होइले ॥"

Jagannatha Charitamrita, Chap. III.

Divākara Dasa did not stop with this. He had described with gusto, how Chaitanya's partiality for Jagannātha Dasa roused the jealousy of the Gauḍiya followers. They requested the Master to withdraw that designation of distinction. But the Master refused to accede to their request. They then asked him to set out on pilgrimage.

Jealousy of the Gaudiya Vaishnavas.

"Hearing this (suggestion) Chaitanya replied :—
"With all my desire and feelings I have taken shelter in Jagannāth. Whether I live or die, I can not leave Jagannāth."[446]

The Vaishṇavas tried their best to take away the Master from Puri. His partiality for Puri, they attributed to his long contact with the Oriya Vaishṇavas. But all their persuasions proved futile, as the Master turned a deaf ear to their words.

Angry at this flat refusal they now decided to abandon the Master. They said, "We, certainly, are not going to stay at Puri. What for shall we revere him ? Let us go to Vrindavāna, the early seat of the exploits of Govinda." They made their way to Vrindāvana. Occasionally they used to come to Puri to witness the Ratha-Yātrā festival ; but the dominating influence of Jagannātha Dasa hastened their departure.

This long description of Divākara Dasa is to be taken with a grain of salt. It is undoubtedly a highly embellished account, coming from the pen of a biassed and unscrupulous writer. Nevertheless, it seems to be based on truth. The probability is, that Chaitanya gave the epithet of "Ati-baḍa" to Jagannātha as a recognition of his merit and this made some of the Gauḍiya Vaishṇavas jealous. Beyond this we hesitate to believe.

446. "ए वाक्य शुणि श्रीचैतन्य प्रभावे कहिले वचन ॥
मोहर मन बुद्धि भावे शरण जगन्नाथ ठावे ॥
जीअई अवा मुँ मरइ जगन्नाथु मो अन्य नाहिं ॥"
Jagannatha Charitamrita Chap. III.

In Gauḍiya magazine (Vol. IX) we find a different account for the epithet of Ati-baḍa. It is stated that Jagannātha Dasa went to the Master's place to convince him about the excellence of his translation of the Bhāgavata. Chaitanya cut him short and declared "Hear me, O Sir. Thou hast indeed become a very great (Ati-baḍa) person. It is hardly befitting that relation should continue amongst us, now that thou art an exalted personage." The followers of Jagannātha Dasa took their cue from this conversation, and began to address him as "Ati-baḍa."

The Gaudiya Version for the Ati-Bada Epithet

The Gauḍiya anecdote is based on hearsay evidence. We have already seen that the Oriya Bhāgavata was Jagannātha's last composition. He died at the age of sixty and could not be more than forty-two years old at the time of the Master's passing away. Thus the book was composed certainly after 1534. This fact proves the absurdity of the Gauḍiya statement. According to Divākara Dasa, Jagannātha served the Master constantly for six years.[447] Inspite of his devotion to the Master, he was treated as a heretic. His sect is declared heretical by Totārām Babaji. We are at a loss to understand what authority the afore-said Vaishṇava worthy has, to declare so.

Absurdity of the Gaudiya Allegation.

This discussion in detail reveals a dark side of the Chaitanya Age in Orissa. It reveals that sectarian feelings prevailed among the followers of Chaitanya. Thus we find that Mādhavī Dasi has nowhere been mentioned in Oriya texts, while Krishṇadās and Vrindāvan Das are silent about the great Oriya Vaishṇavas, Ati-baḍa Jagannātha Dasa and his companions.

Sectarian Feelings in the Chaitanya Age.

Ati-baḍa Jagannātha Dasa is described as the partial self of Rādhā by Divākara Dasa. But Jagannātha Dasa himself is silent about Rādhā-idea. Only in Tulabhiṇā, he has spoken of eternal Rādhā. It is not unlikely his followers declared

447. "अष्टादश बपप ठारे श्री चैतन्य भेट हेले ।।
षठ वरष निरन्तर सेविले चैतन्य पयर ।।"

Jagannatha Charitamrita, XXIV.

him to be the manifestation of Rādhā, in imitation of Gadādhar Pundit's reputation as such,[448] and because of Jagannātha's birth on Rādhāshṭami day. Ati-baḍa Jagannātha has also been styled "the maid-servant of Jagannāth."[449] It is stated that the Master himself ordered him to dress as a woman[450] to initiate the chief queen of Pratāprudra.

Reference to Balarama Dasa in Gaudiya Literature.

In Chaitanya Bhāgavat there is reference to a Balarām Das, who was mad with the ecstasy of love.[451] But this Balarām Das seems to be a resident of the village Dogāchhi, near Krishnanagar. Jaykrishṇa Das speaks of Oriya Jagannātha and Balarāma Dasa. Devakī Nandan also refers to a Balarāma Dasa who is favoured by the deities Jagannāth and Balarām.[452] In all probability Balarāma Mahāpātra is meant by them.

Chaitanya and Balarama Mahapatra.

His first meeting with the Master has been described by Īśwara Dasa.[453] Balarāma's native place was Chandrapura. On his way to Puri, the Master halted at Chandrapura. Balarāma recognised him as the Lord, and anon he prostrated himself before the Master. With overflowing love, the Master raised him and embraced warmly. The Master addressed him Suvala and imparted Rāma and Tārak-Brahma Mantras into his ear.

'Matta' Balarama.

In the next chapter, Īśwara Dasa explains why Balarāma was known as 'Mad' (Matta). Once an elephant ran amuck and killed his keeper. There was a panic in the crowd. Balarāma Dasa chanted Hari's name before the mad elephant. The mad elephant now became docile like a lamb and bowed to the feet of Chaitanya.

448. Gauraganoddesa Dipika, Sls. 149 & 153.

449. Jagannatha Charitamrita, Chap. XI.

450 Nityaguptamani, Chap. XXII.

451. "प्रेमरसे महामत्त वलराम दास"

Chaitanya Bhagavat, III, 5

452. "वन्द उड़िया वलराम दास महाशय
जगन्नाथ वलराम यार वश हय"

Vaishnav Vandana

453. Iswara Dasa's Bhagavata, Chap. XLVI.

The Master embraced him and called him "Matta." Divākara also refers to this epithet.[454] In Yaśovanta's 84 Arts, Balarāma states that he was Suval in the Dvāpara Age. In the Kali, he was born as Sudra at Puri. The Lord informed him in dream that He was born at Navadvīpa, bearing the name Chaitanya. He along with his Associates were ordered to serve the Lord again.[455] Balarāma was devoted to Gaurīdās Pundit.[456] According to Kavikarṇapūra, Gaurīdās was Suval in the Dvāpara Age.[457]

Chaitanya and Yasovanta Mallika

Yaśovanta Dasa, when in his teens, was once watching over the corn-field to keep out deer and wild boars. The Lord appeared before him. Said He, "Chaitanya is my incarnation. Thou shalt serve at his feet. Being initiated by him, thou shalt save the sinners."[458] The Lord vanished and Yaśovanta set out in quest of the Master.

He beheld Gaurānga, the son of Śachī, who was the manifested self of Jagannāth. He prostrated himself at the feet of Chaitanya and on getting up kept the hands folded above the head. Chaitanya embraced Yaśovanta and addressed him Svarūpa Tīrtha. He initiated Yaśovanta into the name of Hari, and named him Suvāhu.[459]

Yaśovanta gave a demonstration of occult powers before the king and the Master. Sudarśana Dasa, the biographer and disciple of Yaśovanta was present there.[460]

454. "शुणि हरष प्रभु हेले मत्त वलरामे कहिले"
Jagannatha Charitamrita, II.

455. 84 Arts, Chap XLII.

456. "गउरी दास ये पण्डित मत्त वलराम सङ्गत"
Jagannatha Charitamrita, VII.

457. Gauragaṇoddeśa Dīpikā, Sl. 128.

458. Iswara Dasa's Bhagavata, Chap. XLVI.

459. "दर्शन कले शचीसुत गौराङ्ग आपे जगन्नाथ ॥
चैतन्य पादपद्मे पड़ि उठिण शिरे कर योड़ि ॥
यशोवन्तकु कोल कले स्वरूप तीर्थ नाम देले ॥
दीक्षा ये देले हरि नाम 'सुवाहु' नाम तो उपम ॥"
Iswara Dasa's Bhagavata, Chap. XLVI.

460. Yasovanta Dasa's 84 Arts, Chap. XLIII.

In the first chapter of Śūnya Saṁhitā, Achyutānanda narrates his early life. From his boyhood he was devoted to Krishṇa. His father took him to Puri to meet the Master.

Chaitanya and Achyutananda Khuntia.

"Worldly desires departed at the sight of the Master, and true knowledge dawned upon his mind. The son of Śachī ordered Sanātana Goswamī to give instructions to Achyutānanda."

Sanātana Goswami II (See the Preceptorial table) initiated him into the name of Hari. Achyutānanda then returned to Tripura, his native village. After ten years and ten months, a great change occurred in his life. It is said that Anādi-Brahma appeared before him,[461] and gave instruction on the Mantra of No Letters (Aṇa-Akshara). Achyuta's disciples were more prosaic and thus in Gurubhakti Gītā, the Guru was stated to be Chaitanya himself.

Whoever the Guru might be, his advent marked a turning point in Achyuta's life. He started for Puri, where he served the Master.

Achyutananda at Puri.

"Out of compassion, the Lord of Navadvīpa gave me cymbals and drums.**** * Kindly he taught me the tune, timing and sense of rhythm. He taught Mantras to me and put the cymbals into my hand."[462] Obeying the order of the Master, Achyuta set out on pilgrimage and returned after a long journey. Thereupon he met the Master.

"Gourāṅga Chandra, the ocean of mercy, was present on the main road. Words fail to describe the glory of the group of the Vaishṇavas thronged round him. Going in front of him, I cast myself at his feet and then stood up. The Moon of Navadvīpa was pleased at the sight of me. I received flowers which were offered to the deity. I passed a few days in that gathering of holy men. Then Ananta, Yaśovanta,

461. "आपथे अनादि अव्यक्त ब्रह्म श्री गुरु रूपेण भासि"
Anakara Samhita. See also Sunya Samhita, I.

462. Sunya Samhita, Chap. I.

Śrivatsa, *alias* Jagannātha and Balarāma joined me. Thus were all the five Associates present, and by order of Chaitanya, the chanting of the name of Hari from every house rent the air."[463]

Īśwara Dasa, as usual, has introduced a vision—so that the Lord might give the following message to Achyutānanda *alias* Sudām. "Thus said the Lord, 'My manifestation as Chaitanya is identical with Buddha."[464]

The Account of Iswara Dasa.

The Lord stated further:—"Thou shalt serve him and follow the path of devotion. Chaitanya is identical with me. Know the Parama-Haṁsa Mantra from him. Accept him as thy preceptor and propagate the name (of Hari)." The Divine message is repeated elsewhere in the same chapter.

"Listen, O Achyuta, to My advice. Take thy initiation from Chaitanya. Propagate the name (of Hari), O (embodiment of) Sudām, thou being a limb of Mine."[465]

Ananta Mohanty was an associate of Krishṇa in the Dvāpara Age. The Lord advised him to meet in the Kali Age Chaitanya, who will be His manifested self. ("Chaitanya mora nija dehī"). According to Īśwara Dasa, Balarām-Saṅkarshaṇa lived in the Vindu-Sarovara as the serpent Ananta, after the destruction of the Yādava clan. At the age of fifteen, Ananta Mohanty was told by a sage :—

Chaitanya and Ananta Mohanty.

463. "श्री गौराङ्ग चन्द्र करुणा सागर विजये वड़ दायडरे
वैष्णव मयडलि वेढ़ि शोभा तहिं कि उपमा देवि तारे ॥
श्रीह्यामुरे याइ शते दयडवत करिण उभा होइलि
देखिण आनन्द नवद्वीपचन्द्र प्रसाद फुल्ल पाइलि ॥
एमन्ते किछि दिन तहिं वञ्चिलि साधुङ्क मेलरे वसि
अनन्त ये यशोवन्त वलराम श्रीवत्स मिलिले आसि ॥
जगन्नाथ ,दास घेनि पञ्चसखा उदय होइले तहिं
घरे घरे हरि ध्वनि उछुलिला चइतन्य आज्ञा पाइ ॥"

Sunya Samhita, I.

464. Iswara Dasa's Bhagavata, Chap. XLVI

465. "शुण अच्युत मो बचन चैतन्य ठारु दीक्षा घेन ॥
से नाम प्रकाश तु कर सुदाम सखा अङ्ग मोर ॥"

Iswara Dasa's Bhagavata, Chap. XLVI.

"Hear me, O Ananta. Nityānanda, the embodiment of Saṅkarshaṇa, hath been born in Gauḍa Deśa. Chaitanya, the lord of the universe, will repair to Nilāchala, along with his companions. Thou wilt serve at his feet. Nityānanda is Saṅkarshaṇa and thou art his partial self. That is why, thou bearest the name "Ananta."[466] The sage further told him that he was Dāma in the Dvāpara Age. Chaitanya on his way to Puri visited Koṇārka. Ananta met him there and prostrated himself at his feet.

"Thus commanded Chaitanya, 'Listen, O Nityānanda. Initiate Ananta into the name of Hari, which is the best thing for instruction * * *' Hearing this message Nityānanda with joyful heart imparted the great Mantra into the ear of Ananta."[467]

Ananta is known among his followers as the incarnation of Balabhadra. Dayā Dasa who belongs to the sect founded by Ananta, reiterates this fact in his book, Ananta Sāgara Gitā (Chap. I).

Behind these tiresome tales of revelations, visions and miracles—there is undoubtedly a background of truth. It is not always easy to separate the kernel from the husk and much must therefore remain meaningless.

Concluding Remarks.

These references shed a new light on the history of the Chaitanya Age in Orissa. They reveal that the Vaishṇavas of the Medieval School also shared the affection of the Master. The Gauḍiya texts are almost silent about them. These Oriya books disclose the fact that all the followers of the Master did not

Importance of the Orlya Source.

466. Iswara Dasa's Bhāgavata, Chap. XLVI.

467. "चैतन्य प्रभु आज्ञा होइ शुण हो नित्यानन्द भाइ ॥
अनन्ते उपदेश कर हरिर नाम दीक्षा सार ॥
* * *
ए वाणी शुणि नित्यानन्द हृदये होइले आनन्द ॥
अनन्ते उपदेश कले कर्णे महामन्त्र कहिले ॥"

Iswara Dasa's Bhagavata, Chap. XLVI.

belong to the same camp. Subsequently we will find that the Oriya texts help us to locate the place of the passing away of the Master. The history of the Chaitanya Age will be one-sided, if it is solely based on the Gauḍiya source without consulting the Oriya texts.

APPENDIX

The Differences Between Gaudiya and Medieval Orissan Schools of Thought

Prima facie it seems strange that the exponents of the two Schools of Thought bearing allegiance to the same Master could not pull on well amongst themselves. Some of the salient points of difference between the two Schools may be discussed here.

The Medieval School of Orissa accepted the Rādhā-idea but maintained a novel conception, in conformity to their heterogeneous philosophy. Rādhā was considered as "Jiva", and Krishṇa as "Parama" Ātmā (soul).[468] The Lord entered within the womb of His own Śakti Yoga-maya, and was born as the twins Rādhā and Krishṇa.[469] The author of Gaṇeśa Bibhuti has gone to the absurd length of stating that Krishṇa and Rādhā are brother and sister.[470]

1. The Difference in the Radha-Idea.

According to the Gauḍiya theory, Krishṇa is the Absolute Being—the personal Godhead manifested in the transcendental

468. "जीवटि राधा अङ्ग होइ परम, कृष्ण अङ्ग सेहि"

Hetu Udaya Bhagavata, Chap. I.

"जीवात्मा अटइ राधा परमात्मा हरि"

Sunya Samhita, III.

469. "से योगमाया आसनरे ताहाङ्क वेनि कुच परे
श्री राधा कृष्ण विहरि या नाम मोक्ष अधिकारी,"

Premabhakti Brahma Gita, Chap. II.

470. See the theory of the Causation of Rama, in Chapter VII.

plane. Rādhā is the plenary cognitive power of the soul. Though she is the serving counter-part of Krishṇa, she must not be identified with the conditioned soul, (Jīvātmā) who belongs to a lower plane.

2. The Eternal Abode

"Nityasthali" or the eternal Ābode has been described in Padma Purāṇa.[471] Arjuna goes there in the form of a woman, with the aid of Tripurā.

This conception has been utilised by the writers of the Medieval School. Since its restoration by the Master, Vrindāvana steadily eclipsed the sanctity of Puri. The Medieval School exalted the eternal Vrindāvana at the expense of the mundane one. Thus Krishṇa of Dvārakā failed to show the eternal Ābode to his eight queens (Śūnya Saṁhitā); or to Rukmiṇī (Rahasya Mañjarī). Mundane Krishṇa ("Mānava Vishṇu") was cursed by the formless Krishṇa of the eternal region, for trespassing into the eternal Arena, (Nāmaratna Gītā). The eternal Arena in Goloka is the zone of the Void.[472] Achyutānanda addresses eternal Krishṇa as the personified Void.

The very idea of formlessness is repugnant to the Gauḍiya doctrine. As the Master said to Sārvabhauma,

"The Supreme Being is full of all powers and yet you describe Him as formless. The Shrutis that speak of Him as Abstract exclude the natural and set up the unnatural."[473]

3. The Theory of Pinda-Brahmanda.

The theory of "Piṇḍa-Brahmāṇḍa" or "Universe within the Body" is not entertained by the Gauḍiya School of Vaishṇavism. But in Virāṭa Gītā, Krishṇa says to Arjuna that all the Brahmāṇḍas are within the body (Piṇḍa) and thus these two are identical. In Gupta Gītā, he says to the same patient listener that Mathurā stands

471. "नित्यं बृन्दावनं नाम नित्यरास महोत्सवम्"
Padma Puranā, Patala Khanda, LXIII.

472. "निराकार मण्डल ए गोलोक राहास" Sunya Samhita, X.

473. Chaitanya Charitamrita, II, 6. (Sir J. N. Sarkar's translation).

for the head.[474] Mathurā is also identical with the Void.[475] There are fourteen Universes in the human Body, including two in the mouth.[476]

The Old School of Thought exalted the sanctity of Puri. Nilāchala was taken to be the replica of the eternal Abode of Krishṇa.[477] As Yaśovanta Dasa says :—

4. The Superior Sanctity of Purushottam Kshetra.

"Behold Nilāchala, which is eternal and greater than all other holy places. Gokula, Mathurā, Vrindāvana, Dvārakā, etc., all these holy places including Kāśi, are present here. Thus a crore of holy places are to be found in this place, whose sanctity baffles description."[478] Jagannāth has been identified with 'Aṇākara Vishṇu.'[479] Baladeva and Subhadrā have been described as Rādhā's self by Balarāma Dasa.[480] But Divākara Dasa, as usual, is more outspoken. Says he :—

"What is known as Goloka, the eternal Abode, is identical with Nilāchala. Even in a crore of ages, its sanctity will not diminish. All the sixteen phases are present in Jagannāth, whose one phase is the son of Nanda. One phase expanded into sixteen, and Krishṇa was born at the abode of the Gopas."[481] According to Jagannātha Dasa's Dāru Brahma Gitā, the body of Krishṇa, after he had passed away, was brought to Purushottam Kshetra for cremation. Professor A. B. Mohanty adds to the list of the books.

474. Gupta Gita, VII.
475. Tula Bhina, IX.
476. Virata Gita, VI.
477. Vedantasara Gupta Gita, VII (Union Pr.) See also XXI.
478. Premabhakti Brahma Gita, V.
479. "से अनन्त पुरुषोत्तम से अणाकार विष्णु जाण"
Vedantasara Gupta Gita. (Union Pr.) IV. (U. S. Press.)
480. राधाङ्ग बलदेवङ्कर राधाङ्ग सुभद्रा देवीङ्कर"
Vedantasāra Gupta Gita, XXI (Union Press.)
481. "येहुँ गोलोक नित्यस्थल सेहुटि गिरि नीलाचल ॥
कोटिए युग येवे याइ एथिर लीला न सरइ ॥
श्री जगन्नाथ षोल कला एथु कलाए नन्द बला ॥
कलाके षोल कला होइ येनि जन्मिले गोपे याइ ॥"
Jagannatha Charitamrita, XVIII.

"Purushottam Kshetra is the embodiment of all holy places. This fact has been established by Balarāma Dasa in Vedāntasāra Gupta Gitā, Achyutānanda Dasa in Gurubhakti Gitā and in his poems, by Divākara Dasa in Jagannātha Charitāmrita. Dinakrishṇa Dasa has explained the same fact in Nāmaratna Gitā and Rasavinoda. He has similarly hinted at this in his Rasakallola. Bhupati Pundita has reiterated this in his Prema-Pañchāmrita."[482]

Needless to say, the Gauḍiya Vaishṇavas never extol Nilāchala, at the expense of Vrindāvana.

5. The Worship in Female Dress to Imbibe Sakhi-Bhava.

Totārām Babaji, a theologian, has declared the Sakhi-bheki sect (*i. e.* those who imitate the dress of a female Associate of Krishṇa) heretical. Jagannātha Dasa used to wear the dress of a female, to imbibe her feelings. In Premabhakti Brahma Gitā, Krishṇa explains "devotion through love" (Prema Bhakti) to Arjuna.

Fortunate is he, who serves the band of milkmaids and who assumes (mentally) the body of one of the chief eight milkmaids ; imitating her while dressing himself as a female. He would worship the feet of Śri-Krishṇa with sole attention and would speak as follows :—

"O Lord of the Universe, the consort and the beloved of the Gopis ; I am but the servant of the milkmaids. Have O Lord, mercy upon me."[483]

Though Gadādhar Das and Narahari Sarkar used to dress as a 'Sakhi,' to imbibe her feelings, such a mode of worship is not popular among the Gauḍiya Vaishṇavas.[484]

482. See the Preface of Prema-Panchamrita.

483. Premabhakti Brahma Gita, III. See also Vedantasara Gupta Gita, IV, (Union Press edition)

484. But see the biography of Radharaman deva, for justification of Sakhi-idea. Vol. V, p. 276.

In Kali Santaraṇopanishada, Brahmā is said to have informed Nārada that without the chanting of the "Mahā-Mantra," salvation is impossible in the Kali Age. This great Mantra is commonly known as "Harê-Krishṇa Mantra." Rūpa Goswamī in his Stavamālā (Ist hymn, Sl. 5) refers to the chanting of the Mantra by the Master.

6. The Principle of Sixteen Names and Thirty-Two Letters.

Valadeva Vidyabhusan, the great Oriya Vaishṇava of the Gauḍiya School, explains this Śloka in his Stava-mālā Bibhūshaṇa commentary on Rūpa Goswamī's text, and refers to the Master as one "whose tongue used always to dance because of muttering of Harê-krishṇa Mantra, consisting of sixteen Names and thirty-two Letters.[485] In Medieval Oriya literature, the sixteen Names stand for the sixteen Gopīs of the eternal Arena. The Master, it is stated, found the Mantra consisting of thirty-two Letters, unsuitable for the masses. So he suppressed thirteen Names and maintained only three—"Harê, Rāma and Krishṇa." These three Names he expanded into sixteen Names.[486] According to Achyutānanda, the thirty-two Letters represent the abode of the Void.[487] While demonstrating the Void-worship before the king, he called back to his mind the thirty-two Letters. The Gauḍiya doctrines, on the other hand, are bitterly opposed to any such interpretation.

Valadeva's Comment.

The Medieval Vaishṇava texts generally place the words

485. "षोड़श नामात्मना द्वात्रिंशदक्षरेण मन्त्रेणोच्चैरुच्चारितेन
स्फुरिता कृतनित्या रसना जिह्वा यस्य सः"

Stava-mala Bibhushaṇa Commentary,

486. "बत्रिश अक्षर नाम निरन्तर घोष
थाउ येते मन्त्रमान एथिरु प्रकाश ॥
ए नाम गुपत करि तिनि नाम कले
हरे राम कृष्ण बोलि प्रभु आज्ञा देले ॥
हरे हरे अष्टनाम कृष्ण नाम चारि
राम नाम चारि गोटि षोल नाम सरि ॥"

Sunya Samhita, II.
See also Gurubhakti Gita, III. 40.

in the following order—Harè, Rāma, and Krishṇa. But the Gauḍiya order is Harè, Krishṇa and then Rāma.

7 The Natha and Buddhist Influences.

The Medieval School of Vaishṇavism was influenced by the Philosophy of Nāthism and Buddhism. Thus "Ghaṭa (haṭa) yoga" has been described in Aṇākāra Saṁhitā. A pious Vaishṇava like Yaśovanta wrote the account of Rājā Govinda Chandra. Jagannāth was conceived as Ādi-Buddha. Gautama Buddha and Chaitanya were considered to be his incarnations. Vira Siṁha, a Buddhist leader of Nāgārjuniya School, was regarded as an ardent devotee of Krishṇa. Buddha-Mātā is the name of a female associate of Tripurā, while Balarāma Dasa refers to Dharma-mātrā. Chaitanya Dasa's six Vishṇus are but the imitations of six meditating Buddhas.

Thus, inspite of its indebtedness to Nāthism and Buddhism—the Medieval Vaishṇavism of Orissa was essentially Vishṇuite in its features. It was not Buddhist-Vaishṇavism, *i. e.*, Buddhism in the disguise of Vaishṇavism.

Unfortunately, by Vaishṇavism, N. N. Vasu has meant the uncompromising orthodox type of the Vishṇuite cult. So he has depicted Achyutānanda and his associates as insincere hypocrites. Achyutānanda enjoins on his disciples not to divulge the 'knowledge of Brahma' (Brahmavidyā) before the egoists, atheists or the hypocrites.[488] It is a pity, that he himself has been called an atheist and a hypocrite.

487. "द्वात्रिंश अक्षर वायु निराकार घर" — Sunya Samhita, X.

"निराकार घर पछि द्वात्रिंश अक्षर'' — Ibid.

488. Sunya Samhita, II.

CHAPTER X

CHAITANYA—AS THE INCARNATION OF BUDDHA-JAGANNATH. THE PASSING AWAY OF CHAITANYA

In several texts of the Medieval Orissan School, Chaitanya has been conceived as an incarnation of Buddha. *Prima facie* it seems to be a paradox, as the Master himself had denounced the Buddhists.

Chaitanya's Criticism Against the Buddhists.

Chaitanya declared before Sārvabhauma Bhattacharya that:—"He is a wretch who denies form to God; touch not, behold not that slave of Death. The Buddhists are atheists from not respecting the Vedas."[489] But in the Medieval Vaishṇava Philosophy of Orissa, Chaitanya was supposed to be the living embodiment of Jagannāth—who was Ādi-Buddha.

Achyutananda explains this curious conception in Śūnya Saṁhitā. Krishṇa was disconsolate at the thought of destruction of his clan. He gave vent to his feelings before Varuṇa, the lord of the sea.

"Out of indignation, the sage Ashṭāvakra had cursed my clan to destruction," he lamented.[490] "My son had forsooth committed a little fault. For this the sage had done injustice. In addition to that, he had spared me not. I shall have to destroy my own clan! Listen, O Varuṇa, to my words. Bringest anon, the disc of destruction, from Maṇipura. Verily will I destroy my clan. The sages will then be satisfied and let this (story of vengeance) be known in all the ages." Varuṇa sent for Nilkanṭheśvara Śiva of Puri, who hastened to console the grief-stricken Krishṇa. Seeing Śiva, Hari

489. Chaitanya Charitamrita, II, 6.
(Sir J. N. Sarkar's translation)

490. "अभिशाप देइ मो वंश नाशि । क्रोध वहि अष्ट वक्र तपस्वी ॥"
Sunya Samhita, XXVII.

became restless. Out of indignation, tears trickled down his cheeks.

"Hear me, Sadāśiva," he exclaimed. "I have destroyed my city without compunction. I was so long enjoying luxury, befitting a king,—which the sages could not tolerate. My child happened to be spoilt due to excess of affection. Did Ashṭāvakra know it not, that he cursed him ?" Nilakanṭheśvara consoled Krishṇa with soothing words. "O Hari," he replied. "Why art thou overcome with grief ? We knew it beforehand that thou wouldst destroy the Yādava clan. * * * After the destruction (of the Yādava clan) thou wouldst repair to thy abode. Then as Buddha on the sea coast, thou wouldst enjoy majestic splendour. * * * At first, thou wouldst be worshipped as the Sacred Log, (Dāru Brahma) on the sea-coast. Thither thy family would serve thee.

Krishṇa was thus consoled. The fatal arrow of Jarā the Śavara struck his foot and he passed away. Jagannātha Dasa continues the legend in his Dāru Brahma Gitā. The Pāṇḍavas brought the body to Purushottama Kshetra for cremation.

Krishna's Passing Away.

"At first not even a hair was burnt and this caused anxiety to the Pāṇḍavas. On the sixth day (of burning) hands and legs were consumed. To assume the form of Buddha, the Lord gave up His hands and legs."[491]

The Divine oracle was then heard :—

"Cast the Body of the Lord unto the sea. In the Kali-Yuga He would be worshipped as the Sacred Log."[492] Thus Vishṇu

491. "षष्ठ दिवस अन्तरेण पाद ये पाणि हेला क्षीण ॥
बउद्ध रूप हेवा पाइँ पाद पाणि छाडिले तहिँ ॥"

Daru Brahma Gita.

492. "समुद्रे मेलिण दिअ प्रभु देवराजा
कलियुगे पाइबे से दारु ब्रह्म पूजा"

(Jagannath) Deulatola. See also Daru Brahma Gita.

in his Buddha incarnation came to be known as Jagannāth.[493] Krishṇa manifested himself in the Kali Age as Buddha-Jagannāth.[494] In Gitā (IV. 7-8) Krishṇa declares that he would appear in every Age to save the righteous and destroy the sinners. The Buddha-Jagannāth incarnation had the same mission. But the sinners grew up again like weeds. Thus further incarnations of Buddha-Jagannāth became necessary to destroy them.

Gautama-Buddha—the Incarnation of Jagannath.

Gautāma-Buddha was one such incarnation. In comparison to Ādi-Buddha Jagannāth's age, he was considered to be a child. Gautama-Buddha did not live even for a century. So further incarnations followed. Chaitanya was another incarnation of Jagannātha-Buddha, and Krishna's associates were born as his followers.

Even after Chaitanya, we hear of the advent of Buddha incarnations. At the fag end of the 17th century flourished Rāmānanda Ghosh, who claimed to be the incarnation of Buddha, for salvation of mankind.[495]

Krishna's Message to Sudam.

Before his passing away Krishṇa informed Sudām *alias* Achyuta that he will appear in the Kali Yuga again, as Buddha, because of the curse of the sages. (Śūnya Saṁhita, XXVII.)

The same message is repeated in another chapter of the book. The Lord (Krishṇa) told Sudām that He would appear in His Buddha incarnation in the Kali Yuga. He also said, "My partial manifestation will appear at Navadvipa, and shall

493. "ठाकुरे बोइले राजा होइलु कि वाइ
कलियुगे वसिवु बउद्धरूप होइ ॥" (Jagannath) Deulatola.
"संसार जनंकु सेहु तारिवा निमन्ते
बउद्ध रूपरे विजे अछि जगन्नाथे ॥"
Sarala Mbh. Sabha Parva.

494. "निज वंश घेनि बउद्ध रूपरे नीलाचले अछि रहि"
Sunya Samhita, XXX.
"श्रीहरि वउद्ध रूपे अवतरि केते भोग विलसिवे"
Sunya Samhita, XXX.

495. "Buddhavatara Ramananda"—Haraprasad Commemoration Book, Vol. I.

be known as Chaitanya."[496] Thus Jagannāth is the full and Chaitanya the partial manifestation of Krishṇa.

Chaitanya has been described as the partial manifestation of Jagannāth, the Ādi-Buddha.[497] Even in Gauḍiya literature, the Master was regarded as the living embodiment of Jagannāth.[498] But the Gauḍiya theory stopped at this point, while according to the Orissan conception :—

(1) Chaitanya was the incarnation of Buddha-Jagannāth.
(2) He absorbed himself into the image of Jagannāth.

Buddhavatara Chaitanya.

In Chaitanya Bhāgavata of Īśwara Dasa, Chaitanya has been described as the incarnation of Buddha, at the end of every chapter. The Lord says to Devakī :—

"Mankind will be steeped in the abyss of ignorance (Acheta). So I shall assume the name Chaitanya. I shall impart words of wisdom as a scholar, and will be known as the incarnation of Buddha."[499]

The Lord similarly informs Achyutānanda that Chaitanya is the embodiment of Buddha. So Achyuta should follow the path of devotion by serving at his feet.[500]

496. "आम्भ कला पुणि याइ नदीया द्वीपरे
चैतन्य रूपरे प्रकाश होइबु ये थरे ॥"

Sunya Samhita, Chap. X.

In this connection see p. 112

497. Jhumar Samhita, by Nirakara Dasa. Chap. XXII.
Gurubhakti Gita, III. 2.

498. "आइला सचल .जगन्नाथ नीलाचले"

Chaitanya Bhagavat, III. 5. 126.

"सचल अचल जगन्नाथ एक ठाँइ" Bhakti Ratnakar, p. 100.
For similar idea, see Kavikarnapur's Chaitnanya Chandrodaya,
VI. 44 & VIII. 7.

499. Iswara Dasa's Bhagavata, Chap. III

500. "बोलन्ति प्रभु भगवान   बउधा रूप मो चैतन्य ॥
ताङ्क चरणे सेवा कर   भक्तिर पथकु आवर ॥"

Iswara Dasa's Bhagavata, XLVI

THE PASSING AWAY OF THE MASTER

The conception of Chaitanya as the incarnation of Buddha, gathered round him after his demise. The passing away of the Master has been described in the following Oriya books :—

(1) Śūnya Saṁhitā, (2) Jagannātha Charitamrita, (3) Īśwara Dasa's Bhāgavata and (4) Prema Taraṅgiṇī.

The Statement of Achyutananda.

Achyutānanda's description of the passing away of the Master is quoted below :—

"King Pratāprudra was (on that day) present near *Kalārāe'ta*.[501] At this time Gaurāṅga Chandra, after going round the exterior wall, entered into the temple (carrying the staff and waterpot) with his followers. The great Raja was present there along with his councillors and ministers. While devotedly they were gazing at the image, the temple resounded with the name of Hari."

"Lord Chaitanya, the great dancer, chanted the name of Hari and like a flash of lightning immersed himself within the sacred body of Jagannāth."[502] "The formless Brahma revealed himself from the Void into the world to show his exploits. Destroying ignorance (*i. e.* darkness) and imparting the knowledge of Truth, he got absorbed into the full manifestation of the attributes (*i. e.*, in Jagannāth, who is the embodiment of the sixteen *kalā*). Just as fire in swallowing up fire knows no check—similarly, (Chaitanya,) the embodiment of celestial attributes absorbed himself within a similar entity, before one could clearly visualize. Witnessing this (disappearance) the king broke into loud wailing and there was a general lamentation. Gradually the followers went back to their destinations. After the Lord's (Jagannāth's) supper, the servitors finished the service of

501. Kalaraeta—A place near Jagmohana Mandapa.

502. "चैतन्य ठाकुर महा नृत्यकार राधा राधा ध्वनि कले
जगन्नाथ महाप्रभु श्री अङ्गे विद्युंप्राय मिशि गले"

Sunya Samhita, I.

the deity. Arranging the bed they bolted the door of the room. The Lord of the world thus retired with Lakshmī for sleep. At day-break, the Lord of the Universe was dressed in festive dress. From Mādhava Full Moon day, the king conducted a grand festival. (माधव शुक्लपूर्णमी दिन ढारु महोत्सव राजा कले) After the termination of the festival, held for a month, everybody retired to his respective place."

"Mādhava" is a vague word which signifies both the spring season and the month of Vaiśākh. The Master was born on the Full Moon day in the month of Phālguna. It is not likely that his birth-day was celebrated with a long festival, shortly after his passing away. The mention of Lakshmī and the festive dress of Jagannāth indicate a festival at the time of Chaitanya's passing away. Thus Achyutānanda seems to have referred to the Chandan-Yātrā festival which commences from the third day of the Full Moon, in the month of Vaiśākh. The Oriya Pānji generally quotes the following couplet, in connection with the Full Moon day in the month of Vaiśākh :—

The Month of Madhava.

"माधवे शमनुप्राप्ते राकापति विराजिते ।
वर्षे वर्षे प्रकुर्व्वीत पुष्पदोला महोत्सव. ।।"

The Statement of Divakara Dasa.

Divākara Dasa mentions Chaitanya's passing away in his book as follows :—

Thinking thus, (that he should return to his own abode) he absorbed himself within the image of Jagannāth. Thus he vanished into Jagannāth's body, (which is identical with his own) unperceived by all. The king was mad with consuming grief. "O Master," he bewailed, "why have you disappeared ?"[503]

In the last chapter of Chaitanya Bhāgavata of Īśwara Dasa[504]

503. Jagannatha Charitamrita, VII.

504. "इति श्री चैतन्यभागवते बौधावतारे श्रीचैतन्यचन्द्र स्वर्गारोहणे सबैशुचि नाम पञ्चशठि अध्याय"
Iswara Dasa's Bhagavata.

the Master's passing away has been described more than once.

The Statement of Iswara Dasa.

Vāsudeva Tīrtha, a prominent Sannyāsi of Puri, could not believe that Chaitanya had disappeared into the body of Jagannāth. Thus said the monk :—

"Listen to me, O Īśwara. I hear you have written a 'Śāstra' on Chaitanya's life. Whence have you secured the information that Chaitanya got absorbed within Jagannāth ? Briefly explain this to me, because any person will doubt (the veracity of your statement)."

After a few lines, the passing away has been described.

"Thus passed several days and again befell the Chandan-Yātrā festival. On the third day of the Full Moon in the month of Vaiśākh, Chaitanya dressed himself (as befitting the occasion). He joined the procession of the chanters on the main road. The king accompanied him as did many Brāhmaṇas. * * * * Thus went the embodiment of Krishṇa, (Chaitanya) to the temple. Getting near the golden throne (of Jagannāth) he beheld the god, on the throne. Chaitanya besmeared the sacred body (of Jagannāth) with sandal paste, and gazed at the Lord, who illuminates the world. The king was by his side, and he also beheld Jagannāth-Krishṇa, the holder of the conch-shell. Chaitanya himself is the embodiment of Krishṇa—the illuminator of the world and the deliverer of mankind. The king personally witnessed the absorption of Chaitanya within the image of Jagannāth. His indignation (!) knew no bounds and despair filled his heart. Getting composed, all (the devotees) consoled Nityānanda. With the help of the devotees, the king performed the Chandan-Yātrā festival. Whilst Nityānanda Dasa was alive, the Master repaired to Vaikunṭha."

The last few lines of this statement are repeated elsewhere in this chapter :—

"Chaitanya departed for Vaikunṭha. The king, after performing the (Chandan) Yātrā festival, celebrated another festival in memory of Chaitanya. Then Nityānanda returned (to Bengal)."[505] Thus he supports Achyutānanda's statement.

We find that these three statements agree about the facts:—
(1) Chaitanya passed within the temple-precincts of Jagannāth.
(2) The king witnessed the scene.

Iśwara Dasa categorically affirms that the Master's disappearance took place on Akshaya-Tritiyā, which falls on the third day of the Full Moon in the month of Vaiśākh.

Even if we tentatively accept his date, we may inquire about the disposal of the body. The king of Sampurninagar made similar inquiry.

"Hearing of the disappearance of Chaitanya into sacred image, from the lips of the venerable sage Agastya, the king bowed at his feet. With great humility he declared, 'A strange fact hast thou related, O sage."

Then he put forward his query :—"(Thou sayest that) Chaitanya, while besmearing sandal paste, vanished into the sacred image. Thus, Chaitanya merged his identity into Jagannāth's body. * * * * But whither goeth the body of Chaitanya ? I entertain doubt as to this. Briefly explain this to me and thus drive out misgiving from my mind."[506]

Agastya complied with the royal request. First of all he explained that the Lord appeared from the Void in material form to display illusion (Māyā) and was known by the name Chaitanya. Fulfilling His mission, He vanished into Jagannāth.

"Chaitanya got absorbed within the god of the blue mountain. The form and spirit of Jagannāth and Chaitanya were of identical nature. It was witnessed by all but nobody noticed what befell to the *illusory body* (Cf. Jayānanda's Chaitanya Maṅgal—"Māyā śarir tathā rahila paḍiyā"—His illusory body lay there behind). Jagannāth, the fascinator of the three worlds,

505. "चैतन्य वैकुण्ठ गमन याक्षा सारिया नृपराया ।
चैतन्य महोच्छा करइ विजे नित्यानन्द गोसाईं ॥"
Iswara Dasa's Bhagavata, LXV.

506. Iswara Dasa's Bhagavata, LXV.

saw the material body of Chaitanya. He ordered *Kṣhetra-pāla.*[507]—'Anon shalt thou carry away this material body in air and place it on the Ganges water'. At Jagannāth's bidding Kṣhetrapāla carried the *body* (śava) in air and placed it on the Ganges water. Thus the Lord revealed Himself in the form of Chaitanya (for some time); and at length got immersed in the Ganges water."[508] The river Prāchī in the district of Puri is a sacred river. It is said that Mother Ganges bathes in the Prāchī river at Gomatī Tīrtha, on the third day of the waxing moon in the month of Vaiśākh. The sinners, while bathing in the Ganges, leave their sins in the water. So she bathes (in the Prāchī) in the form of a black cow and emerges out of water as a white cow. She gets rid of all sins (due to the contact with the sinners) by beholding Amareśvara Śiva.[509]

Thus according to Īśwara Dasa, Chaitanya passed away in the temple of Jagannāth on Akshaya-Tritīyā day. His body was immersed in the Prāchī water at Gomatī Tīrtha. On that day the Ganges appears in the Prāchī every year. This Tirtha is situated at a distance of thirty to forty miles from Puri, and is popularly known as Lalitā-Tīrtha.

507. An attendant—deity of Jagannath.

Cf. "क्षेत्रपालं.नमस्कृत्यं नरसिंह तथा द्विजाः"

Purushottam Mahatmya", Chap. VII, in Niladri Mahodaya.

Niladri Mahodaya. The Mahayanists also worship Kshetrapala. (See A. Avalon's The Principles of Tantra, p. 37.)

508. "सेहि स्वरूपे श्री चैतन्य लीन ये नीलाद्रि लोचन ॥
श्री जगन्नाथ कलेवर येकात्मा येकाङ्ग शरीर ॥
समस्ते येमन्त देखन्ति माया शरीर न जाणन्ति ॥
चैतन्य-पिण्ड, सिंहासन देखन्ति त्रैलोक्य मोहन ॥
क्षेत्रपालंकु आज्ञा देइ ये पिण्ड निअ वेग करइ ॥
अन्तर्द्धे नेइ गङ्गा जल मेलिण दिअ क्षेत्रपाल ॥
श्री जगन्नाथ आज्ञा पाइ अन्तर्द्धे नेले शव वहि ॥
गङ्गारे मेलि देले शव से सब होइलाक सर्व (?) ॥
चैतन्य रूप प्रकाशिले गङ्गारे लीन होइ गले ॥"

Iswara Dasa's Bhagavata, LXV.

509. Prachi Mahatmya, Chap. XII.

The Bengali versions should be quoted here, for the sake of comparison. Jayānanda's statement is as follows :—

The Statement of Jayananda.

"While dancing at the Vijayā of the Car festival in the month of Asharh his left toe was suddenly pierced by a brick (lying on the road). * * * On the sixth day of the moon, the pain in his toe grew severer, and he was forced to take his bed in the garden. (Ṭoṭā) Here he told the Pundit Goswāmi that he would leave the earth next night at 10 o'clock. Celestial garlands of many coloured flowers were thrown on him from the unseen. Celestial singers began to dance on the high way. The gods began to cry out, 'Bring the heavenly chariot'. The Master mounted into Vishṇu's car with the figure of Garuḍa on the spire. His material body lay behind on the earth, while he went to Vaikuntha."[510] Here by the word Ṭoṭā, Jayānanda most likely indicates the Ṭoṭā of Kāśī Misra, as the last resting place of the Master. In many places of his book he uses the word Ṭoṭā, to indicate that garden.[511] Thus according to Jayānanda, the Master, while sick, was treated at Kāśī Misra's Ṭoṭā and passed away on the seventh day of the full moon at 10 P. M.

Next, we shall refer to the description of Lochan Das in the third part of his book. This description is omitted in the Gauḍiya Math edition of this book.

The Statement of Lochan Das.

"Getting up reverently to behold Jagannāth, the Master (wended his way and) gradually reached the Lion Gate. Along with the followers accompanying him, he quickly entered the temple precinct. The Master looked all around but could not see (Jagannāth). Then he contemplated. The door itself got closed from within. He with a heavy heart quitted that place. On the seventh day of the full moon in the month of Āshārh, the Master supplicated (Jagannāth) with a sigh. * * * * On Sunday noon in the third 'Prahara' the Master absorbed

510. Jayananda's Chaitanya Mangal, p. 150.

511. Chaitanya Mangal, pp. 100, 105, 109.

himself in the image of Jagannāth. The Parichhā Brahmin (of Guṇḍichā house) forthwith rushed outside, bewailing, "Alas, what shall I say" ! Seeing the Brahmin, the devotees pleaded, "Listen, O Parichhā. Open the gate, please, as we are eager to meet the Master." Seeing the distress of the devotees, the Parichhā exclaimed, "The Master hath disappeared within the Guṇḍichā-house ! ("Guṇḍichā bāḍir madhye Prabhur haila adarśan") I have personally witnessed the communion of Lord Gaura (and Jagannāth) and affirm that what you hear (from my lips) is absolutely true. * * * When Raja Pratāprudra heard the news (of the Master's passing away) he and his family members lost consciousness."

Lochan Das's statement suffers from vagueness. The course of event, in all probability, was as follows :—Chaitanya repaired to the main temple, in an ecstatic mood. He could not find the image, as Jagannāth had been taken to the Guṇḍichā house. So thither he went alone by a side-door, while his followers were waiting before the closed main gate of the Jagannāth temple. While they were waiting in vain, the Parichhā (temple-Superintendent) came and informed them that the Master had passed away in the Guṇḍichā house. This passage admits of other interpretations.

A third version comes from the pen of Īśān Nāgar. His book Advaita Prakāś refers to the Master's passing away. Īśān was the Master's contemporary and had had the fortune of serving him personally.[512] His description is short and vague.

The Statement of Isan Nagar.

"One day, Gaurāṅga after visiting Jagannāth, entered the Jagannāth temple, mumbling, "(Where art thou) O Lord". As he stepped within the door got closed by itself. There was a great apprehension in the mind of the followers. After some time, the door opened itself. (Not finding the Master) Everyone guessed that Gaurāṅga had passed away."[513]

512. Advaita Prakas, XVIII.

513 "एक दिन गोरा जगन्नाथे निरखिया ।
श्री मन्दिरे प्रवेशिल हा नाथ बलिया ॥

References in the Authoritative Gaudiya Texts.

The authoritative Gauḍiya texts are almost silent on the Master's last days. According to the Gauḍiya canon, the Master was the joint manifestation of Rādhā and Krishṇa, and thus any question of death was *a priori* absurd. As a Vaishṇava scholar explains, "Sri-Chaitanya was not a human being although He lived amongst us in human form. He was no other than the supreme Lord Himself, who reveals His transcendental form in the world from time to time."[514]

Vrindāvan Das in his Chaitanya Bhāgavat is completely silent about the passing away. Krishṇadās Kavirāj simply states that the Master disappeared in the Śaka year 1455.[515] Kavikarṇapūr at the end of his Chaitanya Charitāmrita likewise informs that the Master returned to his celestial abode, after exhibiting his exploits for forty-seven years. Thus the Charitāmrita texts do not give us any idea about the exact time and place of the event.

The Statement of Narahari Chakravarti.

Narahari Chakravarti wrote his book, Bhaktiratnākar, in the first quarter of the 18th century. In the third chapter (Taraṅga), Śrinivās's journey to Puri is described. Śrinivās started from Bengal on the fifth day of the waxing moon in the month of Māgh, with the blissful expectation of meeting the Master. On his way to Puri he heard of the Master's disappearance.[516] It took usually a month to reach Puri. Raghunāth Das, on his first visit to Puri from Saptagrām, covered the distance on foot in

प्रवेश मात्रेते द्वार स्वयं रुद्ध हैल ।
भक्तगण मने वहु आशंका जन्मिल ॥
किछु काल परे स्वयं कपाट खुलिल ।
गौराङ्ग अप्रकट सभे अनुमान कैल ॥"

Advaita Prakas, XXI

514. "Philosophy of Srikrishna Chaitanya"
Tridandiswami B. P. Tirtha. Harmonist—June. 12. 1935.

515. "चौद्दशत पञ्चान्ने हइल अन्तर्द्धान"

Chaitanya Charitamrita, 1, 13.

516. Bhaktiratnakar, Chap. III

12 days.[517] But Narahari does not state whether Śrinivās covered the distance within the usual time or not.

But he locates the place of disappearance. In the 8th Taraṅga, Māmu Ṭhākur, showing the place to Narottam Das, says :—

"Behold Narottam, here Gaurahari told something to the (Gadādhar) Pundit. * * * * (Suddenly) he entered into this temple of Gopināth. He vanished and never came out (of the temple) again.[518] This statement is echoed in Prema Taraṅgiṇi of Sadānanda Kavisūrya Brahmā.[519]

Here we propose to weigh and appraise the statements made by the writers.

The Location of the event.

(1) Chaitanya passed away within the temple of Jagannāth.
—Stated by Īśwara Dasa, Divākara Dasa, Achyutānanda and by Īśān Nāgar.

(2) He passed away in Guṇḍichā House.
—Stated by Lochan Das.

(3) He passed away in the Toṭā of Kāśi Misra.
—Stated by Jayānanda

(4) He passed away in the temple of Gopīnāth.
—Stated by Narahari and Sadānanda

Accepting the verdict of the majority, we are of opinion that Chaitanya passed away, out of exuberant ecstatic emotion, *near* the image of Jagannāth. Thus we reject the third and fourth versions.

The Time of the Passing Away.

It is difficult to fix up the exact time of the Master's passing away.

517. Chaitanya Charitamrita, III. 6

518. "ओहे नरोत्तम एइ खाने गौरहरि ।
ना जानि पण्डिते कि कहिल धीरि धीरि ॥

* * * *

प्रवेशिला एइ गोपीनाथेर मन्दिरे ।
हैला अदर्शन पुनः ना आइला वाहिरे ॥"

Bhaktiratnakar, VIII.

519. "अष्ट चालिश बरषे अन्तर्द्धान तोटा गोपीनाथ स्थाने"

Prema Tarangini. Chap. XXXVI

(1) According to Jayānanda and Lochan Das, the Master passed away on Sunday the 7th day of the waxing moon, in the month of Āshārh. Sir J. N. Sarkar, who accepts Jayānanda's statement writes as follows :—

"At last on the 14th June 1533, his physical frame broke down under such prolonged mental convulsions and self-inflicted torments, and he passed away under circumstances over which the piety of his biographers has drawn the veil of mystery."[520]

(2) According to Īśwara Dasa, the Master passed away on the third day of the waxing moon, in the month of Vaiśākh. Achyutānanda also seems to have referred to this date.

(3) Narahari Chakravarti does not refer to an exact date. Śrīnivās starting from Bengal in the month of Māgh, is ordinarily expected to have heard the dismal news in Māgh or Phālgun. But Śrīnivās might have been detained somewhere. Thus the statement is a vague one and does not serve our purpose.

From this brief conspectus of details we come to the conclusion that the Master passed away *near* the image of

Conclusion.

Jagannāth—either on the 7th day of the full moon in the month of Āshārh at the Guṇḍichā house, or that sad event took place on the third day of the full moon in the month of Vaiśākh, at the Jagannāth temple.

For greater certainty we must be content to wait. Further researches may mend the matter one day. It is to be noticed that the two contemporary writers—Achyutānanda and Īśān Nāgar—locate the event in the Jagannāth temple. But Jayānanda and Lochan Das definitely agree on a particular date. The concurrent testimony of the two Chaitanya Maṅgal books, should be brushed aside, only if further researches strengthen the evidence of Īśwara Dasa's Bhāgavata.

520. Chaitanya. Introduction, p. 11

But Babu Phani Bhusan Dutta calculates the date to be the 29th June, 1533 Śri Chaitanya Jataka, p. 18

The Master's passing away before the image of Jagannāth, helped the theory of Buddha incarnation. It was believed by the Vaishṇavas of the Medieval School that after fulfilling his mission in the world, the partial self of Buddha absorbed himself in the full manifestation of Buddha, *i. e.*, Jagannāth.

The Reason for the Theory of Absorption in Gopinath.

Possibly to counteract this propaganda, Narahari spread the information that the Master absorbed himself within the image of Gopīnāth. The Master was supposed to be the embodiment of Rādhā, who manifested herself to taste the emotion of separation from Krishṇa. Mentally he acted as Rādhā, when in his last days he constantly pined for Krishṇa. Thus, a fitting end would be an absorption—not within Buddha-Jagannāth ; but within the image of the Lord of the Gopis, Rādhā being Gopī par excellence.

It is to be noticed that the books of Īśān Nāgar and Jayānanda are tabooed by the Gauḍiya Vaishṇavas for their references to the passing away of the Master. This offending portion in Lochan's book is usually deleted. But Narahari's book is in the approved list of the Gauḍiya texts, though he too is guilty of similar misconduct. The conclusion is obvious. Though the Gauḍiya Vaishṇavas were at first reticent about the Master's passing away, they had to circulate an approved version at least from the 18th century, to counteract the notion of absorption within Jagannāth. It gave rise to a rhyme too :—

"What shall I say ; whither shall I go ? Words are failing me (to describe the grief). I have lost Gorā-chānd in the house of Gopīnāth !"[521]

One wishes that the veil that had been drawn over the incident would be penetrated, one day. The last resting place of a superman, adored by millions, is lying somewhere in obscurity. No sign is visible there, to save the place from profanation—to allow the devout to offer their fervent homage !

521. "कि करिव कोथा याव वाक्य नाहि सरे ।
गोराचाँदके हाराइलाम गोपीनाथेर घरे ॥"

After the passing away of the Master, Puri gradually lost its popularity. Vrindāvana under the six great Goswāmi's became the chief centre of Neo-Vaishṇavism. It thus ousted Puri—now bereft of the halo of the Master.—From its eminent position. Raghunāth Das Goswami left Puri for Vrindāvana. Raghunāth Bhatta also left Puri and settled there during the lifetime of the Master. The political unrest, which led to the loss of Orissa's independence in 1568, made Puri too hot for peaceful religious contemplation. Even the two great Oriya Vaishṇavas, Śyāmānanda and Valadeva Vidyābhusan, lived at Vrindāvana and not in their own country.

Puri—After the Passing Away of The Master.

Symananda.

Śyāmānanda was the disciple of Hridaychaitanya and Jiva Goswami. He and his disciple Rasikānanda propagated the Gauḍiya doctrine all over Orissa.

Valadeva Vidyabhusan.

Valadeva Vidyābhuṣaṇ was the disciple of Viśwanāth Chakravarti. He silenced the opponents of the Gauḍiya School in 1628 at Galtā near Jaipur, by proving that the Gauḍiya School is an offshoot of the Māddha School and thus, not of obscure origin. His celebrated Govinda Bhāṣya commentary on the Brahma-Sūtras won for him the title of Vidyābhuṣaṇ, from the Gauḍiya patriarchs of Vrindāvana.

The Modern Vaishnavism in Orissa.

The Medieval Vaishṇavism of Orissa was declared heterodox by the triumphant Neo-Vaishṇavism, and gradually died away. Even the followers of Achyutānanda or Ati-baḍa Jagannātha Dasa will not now talk of Buddha-Māta, Tantra Mantra Yantra or of Buddha incarnation.

The Vaishṇavas of Orissa now adore Chaitanya and Nityānanda. They love to sing Bengali devotional songs. As I write, a Sankirtana party, mostly consisting of villagers with hardly any knowledge of Bengali, passes by the road. I come to the door to hear the song. The song is in Bengali though sung with Oriya intonation.

"प्रेम विलाते नगर पथे निताइ गौर एलोरे ।
निताइ गौर एलोरे भाइ गौर निताइ एलोरे ॥"

Nityānanda and Chaitanya are now deified. No Oriya pauses to think that Nityānanda was a Bengali, and Chaitanya was born and brought up in Bengal. With them have penetrated the Bengali influence, even to the obscure interior of Orissa, in the field of religious thought. The triumph of Chaitanya Movement is now complete. But this spiritual victory has been achieved at the cost of much, which was distinctly Orissa's own in the domain of thought and philosophy.

Ask an Oriya Vaishṇava and he will tell you a good deal about the Gauḍiya Divines. But he has only a nodding acquaintance with the history of the five great Oriya Apostles. He certainly knows of the Chaitanya Bhāgavat in Bengali, but has not heard the name of the Chaitanya Bhāgavata in Oriya.

We pause here and ask, how far the rejection of the Medieval in favour of the Modern Vaishṇavism is a change for the better.

CHAPTER XI

HOW FAR THE CHAITANYA MOVEMENT WAS RESPONSIBLE FOR THE FALL OF THE EMPIRE OF ORISSA

Pet theories in history are difficult to eliminate. It is generally believed that Chaitanya and his Neo-Vaishṇavite movement are responsible for the fall of the Orissan empire.

R D Banerjee's Criticism Against the Chaitanya Movement.

The same view has been held by R. D. Banerjee, in his History of Orissa, Vol. I.

"Suddenly, from the beginning of the 16th century" he writes "a decline set in the power and prestige of Orissa with a corresponding decline in the military spirit of the people. This decline is intimately connected with the long residence of the Bengali Vaishṇava Saint Chaitanya in the country."

"We must admit that Chaitanya was one of the principal causes of the political decline of the empire and the people of Orissa. Not only that ; *The acceptance of Vaishnavism or rather Neo-Vaishnavism, was the Real Cause* of the Musalman Conquest of Orissa twenty-eight years after the death of Pratāprudra.*** A wave of religious fervour passed over the country, and during the Reformation, Orissa lost not only her empire but also her political prestige."

"In Orissa, on account of its acceptance by the royalty, Neo-Vaishṇavism became fashionable and powerful officers of Pratāparudra like Rāmānanda Rāya, the governor of Rājmahendri before its final loss, and Gopinātha Barajenā, that of the Muljyāṭhā Daṇḍapāṭ or Medinipur were the most notable converts after the king himself."[522]

522. History of Orissa Vol. I, p. 329-331.

Unfortunately, R. D. Banerjee has exaggerated the evil effects of Neo-Vaishṇavism upon the political history of Orissa. He represents that the decline in the power, prestige and military spirit of the people was suddenly manifest after 1510, and the Chaitanya Movement caused this decline. It seems as if an eclipse suddenly darkened the midday sun.

Political Condition of Orissa Under Purushottama.

But the decline was gradual in process and it can be detected even before the 16th century. "Purushottama lost more than one-half of his ancestral dominion within five or six years of his accession." The Bahmani Sultans annexed the Godāvari-Kistnā Doab. Sāluva Narasiṁha of Vijayanagar was a constant source of trouble and anxiety to the Gajapati kings. Purushottama recuperated due to the smile of fortune.

The murder of the great Muslim general and statesman Mahmud Gawan in 1481 caused a complete paralysis of the Muslim activities in the Deccan for twenty-five years.[523] "The last real Sultan" Muhammad Shah III died in 1482, and Purushottama could easily reconquer the Doab from the hands of Mahmud Shah (1482-1518)—the worthless successor of Muhammad Shah. The disruption of the Bahmani kingdom relieved the Gajapati King from any strong and concentrated pressure, from the south-western direction.

In Vijayanagar, the weak successors of Narasiṁha Sāluva somehow maintained their power upto 1505, when the kingdom of Vijayanagar passed into the hands of a new dynasty, founded by the Tuluva minister Vira Narasiṁha Nāyaka.

In Bengal, similar chaotic condition prevailed. The influence of the Abyssinian palace guards was supreme in the reigns of the last few weaklings of the Ilias Shahi dynasty, and this was followed by a short spell of Habsi rule in Bengal. In 1493, the nobles elected Sayyid Hussain Shah as the Sultan and the Habsi regime in Bengal thus ended.

The political horizon of Orissa was not yet overcast with

523. History of Orissa, Vol. I, p. 314.

cloud, when Pratāprudra ascended the throne in 1497. Prataprudra ought to have utilized the chaotic condition, that prevailed in Vijayanagar and Bahmani kingdoms. Hussain Shah's hold upon the throne of Gauḍ was not then firm. But Pratāprudra's inactivity helped the enemies to gather strength.

Lack of Foresight in Prataprudra.

In 1510 the great Krishṇadeva Rāya ascended the throne of Vijayanagar. Minor hostilities immediately began and the Gajapati had to move to the south to protect the southern boundaries of his empire which extended upto Udayagiri in the Nellore district. Thus at the time of the Master's first advent into Orissa in 1510, the king was not present.[524]

The Attack of Krishnadeva.

Krishnadeva's campaign against the Orissan empire began in 1513. In 1514 he captured Udayagiri and in 1515 Koṇḍaviḍu in the Guntur district. He imprisoned prince Virabhadra and in 1516, advanced as far as Siṁhāchalam.[525] The Gajapati had no other alternative and had to sign a humiliating treaty. Probably he had to cede territory south of the Godāvari and to give his daughter Jaganmohini in marriage to Krishṇadeva.

Hussain Shah was not slow in taking advantage of the forced absence of the Gajapati from the north.[526] In 1509 he invaded Orissa and destroyed innumerable images.[527]

The Attack of Hussain Shah.

"Amara Surathān (Amir Sultan) disfigured the images within the Jagannāth temple precincts. The Gajapati got this piece of information at his camp in the south. He started for Puri. At his approach the Sultan retreated."[528]

The Kāvāli copper plate of Pratāprudra of the Śaka year 1432 (1510-11 A. D.) refers to this war with the Sultan. We

524. Chaitanya Bhagavat, III, 3
525. "Historical Inscriptions of South India"— Sewel & Aiyangar, p. 240.
526. Chaitanya Chandrodaya Drama, VI-14.
527. Chaitanya Bhagavat, III. 2 & 4
528. Madla Panji

learn from the inscription that the Sultan was defeated and whole of the Orissan territory overrun by him was recovered.

According to the version of the Mādla Pānji, Govinda Vidyādhar Bhoi, the minister of the Gajapati, betrayed him and sided with the Sultan. Pratāprudra lost heart and concluded peace with Hussain Shah. He handed over the administration to Govinda Vidyādhar,[529] and henceforth reigned only in name.

The Alleged Coup-d'etat by Govinda-Vidyadhar

We do not accept this statement as substantially correct. Govinda's treachery might have compelled the king to forgo the advantage which he might have gained as the result of his victory over the Sultan. But the last portion of the statement has little inherent plausibility. Not to speak of the Gauḍiya texts, even the writings of the contemporary Oriya Vaishṇavas do not refer to this *de facto* ruler of Orissa.

Ferishta states that Quli Qutb Shah of Golconda conquered the area between Koṇḍaviḍu and Siṁhāchalam. Banerjee tentatively places the incident between the years 1519-22, with misgivings about the veracity of Ferishta's statement.

The Victory of Quli Qutb Shah

Thus Dame Fortune who smiled on his father, deserted him. Pinned on three sides by formidable enemies, Pratāprudra put up a gallant defence. The military strength of the kingdom had been sapped by the wars of aggression, waged by Purushottama and Kapilendra. The exhaustion was noticeable at this time. The people rolled in luxury, with the wealth plundered from Kāñchi to Triveṇi. The conclusion of such a state of affairs could be easily foreseen. "Vijayanagar inscriptions prove that Pratāprudra had descended to the level of employing Musalman mercenaries in his campaign against Krishṇadeva Rāya."[530] The Chaitanya Movement can be hardly blamed for this sad decline in military

Causes of the decline.

529. "ताहाङ्क मूले राजा राज्यभार देले"

Madla Panji

530. History of Orissa : By R. D. Banerjee, Vol. I, p. 325.

spirit of the people. Chaitanya came to Puri for the first time in February 1510, but he did not settle down before 1512. He met the king in 1512 or 1513. It is difficult to believe that the fall of Udayagiri and Koṇḍaviḍu was the result of this meeting.

Criticism against the Officers of the State.

According to R. D. Banerjee, "powerful officers of Pratāprudra" became "converts" to Neo-Vaishṇavism, consequently neglecting the state affairs.

His statement is only partially true. According to Nunez, all the chiefs of the states were gathered at the siege of Koṇḍapalle. Had they been zealous converts to Neo-Vaishṇavism, we should have seen them at Puri. Officials of the type of Gopīnāth Baḍajenā paid only lip-homage to Neo-Vaishṇavism.

Criticism against Ramananda Rai.

R. D. Banerjee has severely criticised the conduct of Rāmānanda Rai. He "betrayed his trust to his own people by retiring from his position on the weakest frontier of the country, and one may ascribe the fall of Koṇḍaviḍu, Koṇḍapalle and Rājmahendri, to their being left in charge of young and inexperienced officers like the Prince Virabhadra on the retirement of Rāmānanda."[531]

This statement implies that Rāmānanda was a competent officer, whose premature retirement was calamitous for the country's cause. We have already made it clear that Rāmānanda proved to be a failure as an administrator. He was a learned theologian, devoted to the contemplation of heavenly things. That was not exactly the business of one, who was expected to govern.

A man of Rāmānanda's type was singularly unfit to hold the reins of government in war time. Thus we find that the Gajapati was served by incompetent officers like Rāmānanda, and Vīrabhadra, unscrupulous ones like Gopīnāth Baḍajenā, and by knaves like Govinda Vidyādhara.

531. History of Orissa, I, p 332.

Be it said to the credit of Pratāprudra that he maintained the independence of the state though attacked from all sides.

Criticism Against Prataprudra

But R. D. Banerjee has not spared him. He quotes Jayānanda's statement that "Pratāprudra has consulted Chaitanya about invading Bengal but the saint had dissuaded him, pointing out that the war would have a disastrous effect on his own country." The great historian is a trifle melodramatic when he concludes on the authority of Jayānanda that, "The advice of Chaitanya was sufficient to cause this cowardly and religiously-minded king to desist from a proper defence of his own territories."

Jayānanda's statement is contradicted by the words of the Master himself. Sārvabhauma said to the Master :—"Here is Pratāprudra Ray, eager to meet you." The Master clapped his hands to his ears, murmured an appeal to God, and replied, "Why such an improper speech, Sārvabhauma ? I am a hermit withdrawn from the world. For me to meet a king or a woman is fatal like a draught of poison"[532] "He professed anger in order to warn his followers against consorting with worldly-minded men."[533] It is difficult to believe that the Master, inspite of such assertion, took up the *role* of adviser in political affairs.

Pratāprudra met the Master for the first time in 1512 or 1513. Up to 1517 he was engaged in active hostility with the Raja of Vijayanagar. The Godāvarī remained the southern boundary of the Orissan empire in 1540.[534] Towards the north, the frontier reached Pichhaldā on the Rupnārāyaṇ.[535] The empire stretching from the Godāvarī to the Rupnārāyaṇ was maintained without further dismemberment by armed resistance to the enemies.

532. Chaitanaya Charitamrita, II. 11.

533 *Ibid* II, 13.

534. History of Orissa, I, p. 326. "Krishnadeva's achievement (in his Campaign against Prataprudra) was meagre." Dr. K. S. Aiyangar, Cambridge History of India, Vol. III, p. 497.

535. Chaitanya Charitamrita, II, 16.

In a previous chapter we have shown that the king did not altogether abandon his attachment for the Medieval School of Vaishṇavism that flourished in Orissa. He extended his patronage to Jagannātha Dasa and his companions, though they were regarded as heterodox by the Gauḍiya Vaishṇavas. It is clear that inspite of his predilection for the Gauḍiya Vaishṇavism the king of Orissa did not neglect his kingly duties. He patronized the Oriya scholars, took a keen interest in their exposition of religious philosophy, and fought against his enemies. His great rival Krishṇadeva Rāya too, was a Vaishṇava. But his religious scruples did not deter him from waging aggressive wars.

The True Character of the Gajapati.

Thus it will be far from historical truth to suggest that king Pratāprudra was out and out a Gauḍiya Vaishṇava and that he, in his old days, was a victim of religiosity.

It would be futile to pretend that Neo-Vaishṇavism had absolutely no baneful effect on the political history of Orissa. In the capital at least, a large section of the people engaged themselves in chanting the name of Hari, quite oblivious of the dangers which threatened the state.

The Baneful effect of Neo-Vaishnavism.

It is difficult to exonerate the action of the followers of the Master in an embezzlement case. Gopināth Baḍajenā, a brother of Rāmānanda, went scot-free due to their intervention, and it certainly had unwholesome effect on the morale of administration.[536]

The triumph of the Chaitanya Movement was not complete in the life-time of the Master. Jagannāth was still the state-deity of Orissa and symbolized the Mediæval School of Vaishṇavism. He was the Buddha incarnation of Vishṇu. He was Ādi-Buddha.

The Final Triumph of the Chaitanya Movement.

536. "गोपीनाथ पट्टनायक रामानन्द भ्राता।
राजा मारितेछिल प्रभु हैल त्राता॥"
Chaitanya Charitamrita II, 2

In 1568 Orissa lost her independence, and Jagannāth his status. His image was thrown to fire, his shrine was desecrated. Defeated, disgraced and despondent—the nation of Kapilendra and Pratāprudra now found time to attend to the Sermons of Love and Pacifism.

Real Cause of the Fall of the Empire of Orissa.

The *real cause* of the fall of the empire was not the "acceptance of Neo-Vaishṇavism," but the weakness of the successors.

It is a law of Nature, that no family can produce an uninterrupted line of geniuses. The tottering empire, surrounded by powerful foes, was like the "bow of Ulysses" which only a strong man could handle.

Pratāprudra died in 1540 A. D., and within twenty-eight years no less than seven kings belonging to three different dynasties occupied the throne.[537]

Weakness of the Royal Authority.

Taking advantage of the weakness of the centripetal force, the Sāmanta chiefs, specially the Bhañjas grew turbulent. Thus, in a country where the administration is autocratic, the succession of the ill-conditioned kinglings spelt disaster.

Assassination, rebellion and struggle for power brought about internal anarchy, Govinda Vidyādhar Bhoi murdered the sons of his master. His grandson Narasiṁha had to atone for his sin. Mukundadeva Harichandan, the commander-in-chief, murdered him to pave his own way to the throne.

537. The Later Kings of Orissa.

Pratāprudra (1497-1540)

Kāluā Deva (1540-41) Kakhāruā Deva (1541-42)

Govinda Vidyādhara (1542-53)

|

Chakrapratāp (1553-57)

|

Narasiṁha Jenā (1557-59) Raghurāma Jenā (1559-60)

Mukunda Deva Harichandan (1560-68)

Along with these traitors, there were others who were ready to sell their mother country. Govinda Vidyādhar's nephew Raghu Bhañja Chhotarāya twice invaded Orissa, with the help of Muhammad Khan Sur. Ramachandra Bhañja, the commander of Sarangarh betrayed the cause of Mukundadeva, at the darkest hour of the country's history.

The Traitorous Officers.

It is difficult to link this sickening tale of moral turpitude with the Chaitanya Movement, which taught mankind to be faithful and honest.

The Conclusion.

Similarly, centuries ago, senility crept into the spirit of the inhabitants of Navadwipa, long before Chaitanya was born there. The story of Bengal's submission to Ikhtyaruddin Khalji is a disgraceful one ; and no devotion to a religious movement serves as an extenuating cause in that case.

Thus, Vaishṇavism or no Vaishṇavism—the succession of weaklings, the moral degeneration of high officials of the state and the decline in the military strength of the nation—would have brought about the downfall, sooner or later.

At this fateful hour of stupor, there appeared Kalāpāhāḍ, the "Black Ogre," as the messenger of Nemesis. The treachery of the titled blackguards made any effective resistance impossible and Kalāpāhāḍ encountered no stiff opposition in his task of the conquest of Orissa.

In 1568 A.D., the last Hindu empire in India was wiped out of existence. The Chaitanya Movement was one of the many causes that precipitated the catastrophe, but it was not the real cause—nor even an important one !

SUPPLEMENTARY NOTES TO CHAPTER ONE

P. 8. HALA'S FLORUIT :—The statement regarding Hāla is wrong. He was the seventeenth king of the Sātavāhana dynasty. (The dynasties of the Kali Age, by F. E. Pargiter pp. 36 and 71). As Pulumayi, the 23rd king of this dynasty lived in the Second Century A. D., Hāla's Floruit must be earlier at least by a century. But then he has described Rādhā simply as a Gopi. (मुह मारुएग तं कद्र गोरश्रं राहिआएँ अवणेन्तो—Gāthā Saptasati—1.89).

P. 19. THE CAR FESTIVALS :—Kauṭilya has referred to the construction of 'Devaratha' (chariot of the gods) in his book, Artha-Śāstra. (Syama Sastri, p. 175. Edition of 1915). In Pariśishṭa Nirvāṇa of Hemachandra Suri, (edited by Jacobi, p. 68) Car-festivals in honour of two Jaina Saints have been mentioned. But Car-festivals were more popular in Buddhism.

SUPPLEMENTARY NOTES TO CHAPTER TWO

P. 25. THE CONQUEST OF UTKALA BY CHODAGANGA :—Choḍagaṅga's conquest has been mentioned in the following texts :

(1) The Mādlā Pāñji : It states that Choḍagaṅga defeated Suvarṇa Keśari and conquered Orissa.

(2) Gaṅgavamśānucharitam, a Sanskrit Kāvya by Vāsudeva Rath: Chuḍaṅga or Gauḍa Gaṅga vanquished the king of Utkala and occupied his throne.

(3) Lāṅguleśvara Itihāsa (Local Records, Vol. 37 : Oriental MSS. in Madras Museum) : A Pāṇḍya Brahmin called Sāyantana was a devotee of the image Lāṅguleśvara Svami, in the city of Kolāhala in Kaliṅga. He had two sons named Vāsudeva and Choḍagaṅga. Choḍagaṅga reduced the Barabāti fort of Nrisiṁha Keśari, and became the king of Utkala. Choḍagaṅga states in his Korni Grant, (second series) that one of his ancestors named Kolāhala built the city of Kolāhalapura in the Gaṅgavādi Vishaya. Eighty-two kings of his lineage is stated to have ruled at Kolāhalapura.

(4) Jagannāth Kaifiyat: (Madras Local Records, No. 14-6-28) Vāsudeva Vāhinipati, the commander of the Keśari king of Orissa, proved false to him and invited Chuḍaṅga Deo from Karṇāṭa country. Chuḍaṅga Deo expelled the Gajapati ruler from Cuttack, the capital of Orissa, and usurped the throne.

P. 25. CHODAGANGA'S SUZERAINTY OVER THE KINGS OF UTKALA AND VENGI :—Choḍagaṅga refers to the "propping up," of the failing fortunes of the Utkala and Veṇgi kings *for the first time* in the Korṇi Copper-plates of Śaka 1034=1112 A. D.

P. 25. THE DATE OF THE CONQUEST OF UTKALA :—"When it is remembered that in his Śri-Kūrmam inscription dated 1135 A. D., he refers to his newly-made conquests in the three-quarters including Utkala, it will be believed that not till that year, his sovereignty was fully established over that country."

("History of the Eastern Gangas of Kalinga" R. Subba Rao, J. A. H. R. S. VII. pt. i).

P. 26. CHODAGANGA'S DEVOTION TO SAIVISM :—Many stone inscriptions, belonging to the reign of Chodagaṅga, are found in Nīlkanṭheśvara temple at Nārāyaṇapuram. These inscriptions record grants made by private persons to the temple. In 1081 A. D., the king granted a village to Rājarājeśvara Siva. (Vizagapatam Copper-plates, first set). In 1084 A. D., Choḍagaṅga, "the devout worshipper of Maheśvara," gave away the village Sellada, in modern Tekkali Taluq, for worship and services of the goddess Bhagavatī. (Annual Report of South Indian Epigraphy, No. 6 of 1918-19). In the Korṇi Grant of 1081 A. D., the king has been styled "Parama Māheśvara." In 1128 A. D., Choḍagaṅga and his wives visited the temple of Bhīmeśvara at Drākshārāma in the Godāvari district, and made several gifts. (South Indian Inscriptions, Vol. IV.) In 1141 the king presented five lamps to Champakeśvara Śiva temple in the Ganjam district, wishing to be blessed with a son.

P. 26. CHODAGANGA'S PREDILECTION FOR VAISHNAVISM :—In the Second Korṇi Copper-plates of Śaka 1034=1112 A. D., the king is styled both "Parama Māheśvāra" and "Parama Vaishṇava." This land-grant contains an invocation to Lakshmi in the beginning, and the genealogy is traced from Vishṇu. (Ananta). Both these features are absent in the first set of the Korṇi Plates. In the second Vizagapatam Grant of Śaka 1040=1118 A. D.—the donees are Vaishṇavas and the king is called "Parama-Vaishṇava" only.

P. 30. KAMARNAVA VII (1147-1156 A. D.) AND RAGHAVA :—(1156-1170 A. D.) Mr. R. Subba Rao has referred to seven inscriptions of the time of Kāmārṇava, and to five inscriptions, belonging to the reign of Rāghava. ("The History of the Eastern Gangas," J. A. H. R. S., Vol. VIII, pt. 3.) They were especially devoted to Kūrmeśvara.

P. 31. MADA :—Prof. A. B. Mohanty writes that Māḍa is equivalent to about half a tolā. (Introduction, Ancient Oriya Prose and Poetry) We relied on his statement which seems to be wrong. "We know from an inscription of Narahari Tirtha that the Coin Māḍa is a Telegu form of the Sanskrit word Nishka" (J. A. H. R. S. VIII, pt. I.) Its value and weight can not be precisely determined. But we can form an idea by referring to two Nrisiṁha temple inscriptions of the time of Narasiṁha IV. No. 812 (S. I. Inscriptions, Vol. VI), dated Śaka 1312, records the gift of a Mango-garden purchased for 60 Māḍas to the god. It was also ordained that the annual rent of 4 Māḍas due from the garden should be utilised for providing offering to the deity. The king's wife Uttamādevi endowed 53 Māḍas to the treasury of the deity, thus providing for oil to burn a lamp in perpetuity in the temple.

P. 34. SUN-WORSHIP IN KALINGA :—The Nilkantheśvara temple at Nārāyaṇapura contains an Oriya inscription which records the setting up of an Āditya image in that temple in the reign of Rājarāja I. (Annual Report, South Indian Epigraphy, 1926-27) In the grants of Choḍagaṅga dated Śaka 1006 and 1040, Sun is depicted on the seals.

P. 36. THE ABANDONMENT OF THE SUN TEMPLE :—The temple of Koṇārka was abandoned before 1627. According to the

Mādlā Pānji, Narasiṁha instead of Mukunda Deva II was the Raja of Khurdā at that time. He ordered for the measurement of the abandoned temple in 1627.

P. 38. PURUSHOTTAMA OF THE GANGA DYNASTY :—Mr. R. Subba Rao has tried to prove that Purushottama was but another name of Bhānu Deva II. (J. A. H. R. S., Vol. VIII). But he has not refuted all the points raised by R. D. Banerjee, who argues that Purushottama of the Gaṅga dynasty was an usurper. The Puri plates refer to the 7th Aṅka or regnal year of Purushottama. A Siṁhāchalam inscription, dated Śaka 1236=1314 A. D., belongs to the 9th Aṅka of Purushottama.

P. 38. THE LAST YEAR OF NARASIMHA IV'S REIGN :—R. D. Banerjee alludes to a Śri-Kūrmam inscription of Narasiṁha IV of the year 1435 A. D. But the latest Śrī-Kūrmam inscription of Narasiṁha IV (as quoted in "South Indian Inscriptions," Vol V) is dated A. D. 1402-3. His latest Nrisiṁha temple inscription is dated A. D. 1414. (South Indian Ins., Vol. VI)

SUPPLEMENTARY NOTES TO CHAPTER THREE

P. 41. THE ACCESSION OF KAPILENDRA :—It is stated in Gaṅgavaṁśānucharita that Kajjala Bhānu was the 18th and the last king of the Gaṅga dynasty. Returning after a conquering expedition, he found (like Richard II of England) that Kapilendra, a minister, had seized the throne in his absence. Kajjala Bhānu retired to the south and occupied by force the principality of Gudari-kaṭaka in the Ganjam district. Raja of Tekkali refers to a tradition prevailing in the south, concerning the accession of Kapilendra. Kapila Sāmantarāya, according to this tradition, was the minister and brother-in-law of the last Gaṅga King Sāna Narasiṁha. Taking advantage of the weakness of the Gaṅga king, he captured the throne. Jajñeśvara was his father, and his mother's name was Belamā. He granted lands in the Godāvari-Kistnā Doab to the Brahmins in memory of his parents in Śaka 1370=1448 A. D.

("A new Copper-plate Grant of Kapilendra"—Raja of Tekkali—Sahakara, XX, No. 9).

P 44. THE KANCHI EPISODE :—We get the following informations from the inscriptions.

Bhubaneswar inscription of Śaka 1359 :—Kapilendra called himself the master of ninety millions of people of Karṇāṭa. (History of Orissa, Vol. I, p. 302). Two other inscriptions refer to this title.

Sl. 8 of the Anantavaram Ins. of Pratāprudra :—Prince Hambira or Hamira conquered Southern India at Kapilendra's command.

S. I. Ins. dated 1455 (Quoted in The Historical Inscriptions of Southern India by Sewel and Aiyangar) :—Kapilendra was in occupation of the Kistnā district.

The Oruganti Ins. dated 1459 A. D. :—Hambira Deva Kumāra-Mahāpātra records his victory over the Bahmani Sultan.

Sl. 13 of the Anantavaram Ins :—King Nrisiṁha Deva of Karṇāṭa was made a prisoner by Purushottama. He made peace with Purushottama by ceding Udayagiri (in the Nellore district) and its adjoining areas.

Munnur Ins. of 1464 A. D. (Quoted in The Hist. Ins. of Southern India) :—Kumara Mahāpatra Kapileśvara, the son of Hambira Mahapatra, was the Viceroy of Koṇḍaviḍu.

S. I. Ins. of 1466 A. D. (Quoted in The Hist. Ins. of S. India) :—Sāluva Narasiṁha regained his possessions lost to the Sūryavaṁśi Kings.

S. I. Ins. of 1469 A. D. (Quoted in The Hist. Ins. of S. India) :—Purushottama marched southward as far as Conjevaram (Kāñchi). But it may refer to a southward raid in 1464 A. D.

S. I. Ins. dated 1515 A. D. (Quoted in The Hist. Ins. of S. India) :—Narahari Pātra, a son of Kumāra Hambira Mahapātra, served under Prince Vīrabhadra, and was taken prisoner when the fort of Koṇḍavinu capitulated.

These records show that Hambira was, in all probability, the son of Kapilendra. His sons, Kapileśvara Kumāra Mahāpatra and Narahari Pātra served under Purushottama and his son. Purushottama defeated Śāluva Narasiṁha, and plundered Kāñchi. This place is near Chandragiri, which was the capital of S. Narasiṁha. Sāluva Narasiṁha seems to be the Kāñchi king of the tradition. The Anantavaram inscription mentions him as the King of Karṇāta. Prataprudra's mother, Rupāmbikā, was the princess of Karṇāṭa. (Introduction, Sarasvatī Vilāsa). She might be the daughter of Sāluva Narasiṁha, who ruled over a principality within the Vijayanagar empire. "The Karṇāṭa kingdom was known to the foreign writers—as the kingdom of Vijayanagar, from the name of its capital. But in the country itself it has always been called the Karṇāṭa rājya or the kingdom of Karṇāṭa. ("Krishṇadeva"—J. A. H. R. S., Vol. II, pts. 3 & 4). Purushottama sacked Kāñchi and Vidyānagar or Vijayanagar, and the two incidents were confused in the tradition.

SUPPLEMENTARY NOTES TO CHAPTER FOUR

P. 48. VASUDEVA RATH, THE AUTHOR OF GANGA VAMSANUCHARITA :—Vāsudeva was the court poet of Purushottama, who belonged to the Gudarikaṭaka line of the later Gaṅga kings. Vāsudeva lived in the beginning of the 19th century.

P. 41. THE SRI-KURMAM AND NRISIMHA TEMPLES :—The Kūrmeśvara temple at Śri-Kūrmam and the Nrisiṁha temple at Siṁhāchalam were the most famous centres of Vaishṇavism in South Orissa. These temples are full of inscriptions, incised on stone slabs, recording gifts to the temples. It was believed that the burning of a lamp in perpetuity would increase the donor's merit. Gifts were made in cash or in kind. Some of the purposes of the gifts are mentioned below :—

Attainment of heaven by the deceased relatives ; welfare of the kingdom, or prosperity of the king ; provision of Tāmbulam (betel-offering) or Amritamaṇi (milk-offering) for the deity ; supply of ghee, sugar, pudding, castor oil, camphor or sandal-wood for the deity's use ; maintenance of the services, and lastly for the sake of singing verse in praise of the deity by the dancing girls. Besides the Devadāsī girls, there were the temple-maids (Guḍisāni) for fanning the gods.

Auspicious occasions like Nijasvarūpam, (exposure of the true form) Akshaya Tritīyā, Solar eclipse and the Sankrānti days were duly observed in the Siṁhāchalam temple, and gifts were presented to Nrisiṁha. Gifts were made especially on the day of Śrī-Jayanti (Janmāshṭami) to the Śrī-Kūrmam temple.

Śrī-Kurmam Inscriptions—

Choḍagaṅga visited the Kūrma temple in 1135 A. D. and gave rich presents to the deity. (South Indian Inscriptions, Vol. V) The numbers of inscriptions relating to the reigns of his successors are noted below.

Kāmārṇava VII—4, Rāghava—5, Rājaraja II—2
Anaṅgabhima II—2, Rājarāja III—2, Anaṅgabhima III—5
Narasiṁha I—16, Bhānu Deva I—5, Narasiṁha II—17
Bhānu Deva II—4, Narasiṁha III—14, Bhānu Deva III—7 and Narasiṁha IV—5

Simhachalam Inscriptions—

Nrisiṁha temple became famous after the advent of Narahari Tīrtha. The numbers of the inscriptions belonging to the reigns of Anaṅgabhīma III and his successors are noted below.

Anaṅgabhīma III—2
Narasiṁha I—2, Bhānu Deva I—5, Narasiṁha II—22
Bhānu Deva II—5, Narasiṁha III—4, Bhānu Deva III—12 and Narasiṁha IV—89.

These inscriptions are published in the Volumes V and VI of the 'South Indian Inscriptions.'

P. 48 The Maddha Teachers :—Narahari Tīrtha, the disciple of Maddhāchārya, took a leading part in the introduction of the Māddha cult in Kaliṅga. From the inscriptions, it appears that he reached South Orissa in the reign of Anaṅgabhīma III. (1211-1238 A. D.) Narahari was the Māṇḍalika or governor of Kaliṅga in the reign of Narasiṁha II. He conferred various gifts on Kūrmeśvara and Nrisiṁha.

An inscription, dated Śaka 1215=1293 A. D., states that Narahari set up images of "Rāmanātha, Sītā Parameśvarī and Lakshmaṇa Devatā" at Śrī-Kūrmam.

"To the end of the Gaṅga lines," writes Mr. R. Subba Rao, "we get a Nrisiṁha followed by a Bhānu, and both are names of Vishṇu. This change is known to have taken place on account of the advent of Narahari Tīrtha from 1230 A. D." ("History of the Eastern Gaṅgas of Kaliṅga" J. A. H. R. S. Vol. VIII, pt. I) His work was carried on by his disciple Jagannātha Tīrtha. The other important Māddha teachers, who lived in the 14th century, were Narasiṁha Bhārati, Vāsudeva Bhārati and Rāghava. They are known to us from the inscriptions in the Śrī-Kūrmam and Siṁhāchalam temples.

P. 51. SAIVISM UNDER THE SUCCESSORS OF CHODAGANGA :—

Choḍagaṅga's successor did not altogether neglect Śaivism. A queen of Kāmārṇava, made a gift of land to the temple of Aniyaṅka Bhīmeśvara Śiva at Mukhaliṅgam in the Parlakimedi Taluq. Two inscriptions, relating to the reign of Rājarāja II, record gifts made by private persons to the temple of Madhukeśvara Śiva at Mukhaliṅgam. Anaṅgabhīma III gave away a flower-garden to the temple of Bhīmeśvara Śiva at Drākshārām.

After his reign the Śiva temples of South Orissa gradually lost the royal patronage.

SELECT BIBLIOGRAPHY

Epigraphical

The Hathigumpha Ins.—J. B. O. R. S. Vol. III. pt. 3 & 4.

The Ananta-gumpha Sculpture—Cambridge History of India, I, p. 640.

Ins. of Mathara Chief Pravanjana—Utkala Sahitya, Vaisakh 1338.

Copper-plate records of Sailodbhava Kings—J. B. O. R. S., Vol. IV. pt. 2.
The Prachi. Vol. III. pt. 3.

Ins. of the Early Kara Kings—Epigraphica Indica, Vols. XIV. & XV. J. A. H. R. S., Vol. VI. pt. 3 & 4.

The Grant of Tribhuvana Mahadevi—J. B. O. R. S. Vol. VI. pt. 4

The Grant of Dandi Mahadevi—J. B. O. R. S., Vol. V. pt. 4.

Ins. of the Somavamsi Kings—History of Orissa, and Orissa in the Making.

Ins. of the Bhanja Kings—J. B. O. R. S., Vol. II. pt. 2.

Ins. of the Eastern Ganga Kings—J. A. S. B. 1903.

"Uriya Ins. of the 15th and 16th Century A. D."—J. A. S. B. 1893.

The Ins. of Narasimha IV.—J. A. S. B. 1895.

Ins. of Bhavadeva Bhatta—Epigraphica Indica, Vol. VI.

Inscriptions of Kalinga and South India—South Indian Inscriptions, Vols. IV, V, VI.

The Historical Inscriptions of Southern India—Sewel and Aiyangar

Annual Reports of the Assistant Superintendent of Epigraphy, Southern Circle, 1919-1930.

The Korni Copper Plates—J. A. H. R. S. Vol, I. pt. I and Vol. III. pt. I.

The Vizagapatam Grant of 1118 A. D.—Indian Antiquary, Vol. XVIII.

The Anantavaram Grant of Prataprudra—Utkala Sahitya, 1337.

The Velicherla Grant of Prataprudra—J. A. H. R. S., Vol.XI pts. I. & II.

Literary Sources

Sanskrit

The Utkal Khanda of Skanda Purana—Bangabasi Edition

Brihat Samhita—Varaha Mihira—Bombay Edition

Prapannamrita—Anantacharya

The Bhagavata Purana—Published by Ramnarayan Vidyaratna

Chaitanya Chandrodaya — Kavikarnapura — Published by Ramnarayan Vidyaratna

Chaitanya Charitamrita — Kavikarnapura — Published by Ramnarayan Vidyaratna.

Gauraganoddesa Dipikā—Kavikarnapura

Nityaguptamani—Divakara Dasa

Parsuram Vijaya—Published in the Prachi Magazine

Abhinava Venisamharanam — Published in the Prachi Magazine

Saraswati Vilasa—Prataprudra

Chaitanya Charitamrita — Murari Gupta — Published by M. K. Ghose.

Gangavamsanucharita—Vasudeva Rath.

South Indian

The Telugu Sources of Krishnadeva Raya's reign—J. A. H. R. S. Vol. IV. pt. 384.

The Gangavamsavali of Parlakimedi—J. A. H. R. S., Vol. II. pts. 3, & 4

Sources of Vijayanagar History—Dr. Krishnaswamy Aiyangar.

Bengali

Vaishnav Vandana of Jiva Goswami & of Vrindavan Das II —Quoted in the Materials for the Biography of Chaitanya.

Narada Samvada—Krishnadas Misra
Purushottam Chandrika—Bhavani Banerjee
Goraksha Vijay—Edited by Munshi Abdul Karim.
Chaitanya Charitamrita—Published by the Gauḍiya Math, Calcutta
Chaitanya Bhagavat—Published by the Gaudiya Math, Calcutta
Bhakti Ratnakar—Narahari Chakravarti—Published by R. N. Vidyaratna.
Chaitanya Mangal—Lochan Das.
Chaitanya Mangal—Jayananda—Published by N. N. Vasu.
Advaita Prakas—Isan Nagar.
Vaishnav Vandana—Devaki Nandan Das.

Oriya

Vedantasara Gupta Gita—Balarama Dasa—Union Press and U. S. Press
Brahmanda Bhugola—Balarama Dasa—Radhanath Press
Chhatris Gupta Gita—Balarama Dasa—Mukura Press
Saptanga Yoga Sara—Balarama Dasa—Dutta Press
Jagannatha Charitamrita—Divakara Dasa—Union Press
Harivamsa—Achyutananda Dasa—Utkala Sahitya Press
Sunya Samhita—We have consulted three different publications, published by Arunodaya Press, Dutta Press, and by Cuttack Printing Company, for a correct reading.

(The Prachi Society Publications)

The Madla Panji—Quoted in Types of Ancient Oriya Prose and Poetry
Anakara Samhita—Achyutananda Dasa
Brahma Sankuli—Achyutananda Dasa
Gurubhakti Gita—The followers of Achyutananda
Vishnugarbha Purana—Chaitanya Dasa
Nirguna Mahatmya—Chaitanya Dasa
Parache Gita—Dvaraka Dasa
Siva-Svarodaya—Yasovanta Dasa
Rahasya-Manjari—Devadurlabha Dasa

Prema-Panchamrita—Bhupati Pundita
Rasa-Kallola—Dinakrishna Dasa
Gopi-Bhasha—Janardana Dasa
Vata-Avakasa—Balarama Dasa
Prema Bhakti Brahma Gita—Yasovanta Dasa
Mathura Mangala—Bhakta Charana Dasa
Avatara Malika—Ascribed to Achyutananda
(Cuttack Printing Company Publications)
The Mahabharata—Sarala Dasa
Vilanka Ramayana—Sarala Dasa
Jagamohana Ramayana—Balarama Dasa
Amarakosha Gita—Balarama Dasa
Beḍa Parikrama—Balarama Dasa
Namaratna Gita—Dinakrishna Dasa
Govinda Gita—Dvaraka Dasa
Prema Tarangini—Sadananda Kavisurya Brahma
Tulabhina—Jagannatha Dasa
Arthakoili—Jagannatha Dasa
Daru Brahma Gita—Jagannatha Dasa
Ganesa Bibhuti Tika—Bhupati Bhanja
Gupta Gita—Balarama Dasa
Virata Gita—Balarama Dasa

Oriya MSS.

Chandi Purana—Sarala Dasa
Chaitanya Bhagavata—Iswara Dasa
Rasa—Ananta Dasa
Yasovanta Dasanka Chaurasi Ajnya—Sudarsana Dasa
Virasimha Chautisa
Bhakti Jnyana Brahma Yoga—Achyutananda Dasa

Journals

We have consulted the following Journals of Orissa :—
In English—The Prachi (now defunct)
Vaitarani
The Journal of Orissa Academy

In Oriya—Sahakara
Naba-bharata
Utkala Sahitya

The Gauḍiya Math, Calcutta, publishes the Gauḍiya (in Bengali) and the Harmonist (in English). These are the leading journals, representing the opinion of the Gauḍiya Vaishṇava community.

Other Journals are mentioned in proper places.

MODERN WORKS

English

History of Orissa—R. D. Banerjee
Orissa—Hunter
Orissa—Sterling (Balasore Edition)
Orissa in the Making—B. C. Majumdar
Orissa and Her Remains—M. M. Ganguly
Chaitanya's Life & Teachings—Sir Jadunath Sarkar
Early History of the Vaishnava Sect (2nd edition)—Dr. H. C. Raychaudhury
The Outlines of the Religious Literature of India—Dr. J. N. Farquhar
The Modern Buddhism and its Followers in Orissa—N. N. Vasu
The Chaitanya Movement—Kennedy
History of Bengali Language and Literature—Dr. D. C. Sen
Chaitanya and His Age—Dr. D. C. Sen
The Erotic Principle and Unalloyed Devotion—N. K. Sanyal
"The Eastern Ganga Kings of Orissa"—M. M. Chakravarti. J. A. S. B., 1903
"The History of the Eastern Gangas of Kalinga"—R. Subba Rao. J. A. H. R. S. Vols. VII & VIII
"The Legend of Raja Gopichand"—Proceedings, Sixth Oriental Conference
"The Language and Literature of Orissa"—M. M. Chakravarti. J. A. S. B., 1898
Creation—as explained in the Tantras—Sir J. G. Woodroffe
"The Date of the Jagannath Temple"—M. M. Chakravarti. J. A. S. B. 1898

Oriya

The Types of Ancient Oriya Prose & Poetry—Prof. A. B. Mohanty

The Typical Selections from Oriya Literature—B. C. Majumdar

History of Oriya Literature—Vinayak Misra

History of Oriya Literature—Tarini Rath

Sarala Charita—Mrintunjaya Rath

Atibada Jagannatha Dasa—M. M. Sadasiva Misra

"Life of Jagannatha Dasa"—Sahakara, Kartika 1343

"Matta Balarama Dasa"—Sahakara, Vol. IX.

Prachina Utkala—Jagavandhu Dasa

"Saivism in Orissa"—K. N. Mahapatra—Nababharata, 1341 Oriya Year

"History of Buddhism in Orissa"—S. N. Rajaguru—Utkala Sahitya, Vaisakh, 1338 Oriya Year

"South Orissa"—S. N. Rajaguru—Pous, 1337, Utkala Sahitya

"The Inscription of Chandrika Devi"—Sahakara, Vol. XV

"An Inscription of Kapilendra Deva"—Raja of Tekkali—Sahakara, Vol. XX.

Bengali

Chaitanya Chariter Upadan—Dr. B. B. Majumdar

Mandirer Katha—Gurudas Sarkar

The Races & Castes of Bengal, Vol. II—N. N. Vasu

Konaraker Bibaran—Nirmal Basu

Prataprudra Charita—Vaishnav Charan Das

Gopinath Charitamrita—Binod Chaitanya Das

Vaishnav Itihas—Haralal Chatterjee

Gambhirai Sri Gauranga—Rasik Vidyabhusan

Jagannath Temple—M. M. Sadasiv Misra

"Kshirachora Gopinath"—B. K. Chatterji, Bharatvarsha, 1330 B. S.

"The Historical Sanctity of Jagannath"—B. N. Roy, Bichitra, 1341 B. S.

"Atibadi Jagannatha Dasa"—Gaudiya, Vol. II, 33 & Vol. IX, 24

INDEX

* indicates an image
The names of the books are printed in italics